MICHIGAN'S COUNTY COURTHOUSES

Michigan Supreme Court Rotunda

MICHIGAN'S COUNTY COURTHOUSES

John Fedynsky

WITH A FOREWORD BY
Justice Stephen Markman, Michigan Supreme Court

THE UNIVERSITY OF MICHIGAN PRESS | *Ann Arbor*

Published in the United States of America by
The University of Michigan Press
Manufactured in the United States of America
⊗ Printed on acid-free paper

2014   2013   2012   2011   5   4   3   2

A CIP catalog record for this book is available from the British Library.

Library of Congress Cataloging-in-Publication Data

Fedynsky, John.
    Michigan's county courthouses / John Fedynsky ; with a foreword
by Stephen Markman.
        p.   cm.
    ISBN 978-0-472-11728-4 (cloth : alk. paper)
    1. Courthouses—Michigan. 2. Historic buildings—Michigan.
3. Public buildings—Michigan. 4. Michigan—History, Local.
5. Counties—Michigan—History. 6. Architecture—Michigan—History.
I.   Title.
F567.F43 2010
977.4—dc22   2010004472

ISBN 978-0-472-03493-2 (pbk. : alk. paper)
ISBN 978-0-472-02748-4 (e-book)

DEDICATED TO *the people who conceived, built, maintain, and vivify the county courthouses of Michigan*

FOREWORD

Justice Stephen Markman, Michigan Supreme Court

There is perhaps no institution more indispensable to a free society than that of the rule of law. This book is about the venues within which this institution is most clearly on display in Michigan, its eighty-three county courthouses. While the rule of law is a magisterial institution, not each of these courthouses can be similarly described. Some courthouses are plain, some are antiquated and not always charmingly so, and some are little more than functional. Yet, what these courthouses have in common is that each stands at the center of its community, each has been the source of strength and continuity in these communities, and each has played a considerable part in the history and progress of each of these communities for over 170 years.

We often take for granted the rule of law that is in evidence every day within our county courthouses—the rules of procedure that apply equally to all, the impartiality of the judge, the jury of peers, the openness to the press and public, the application of a statutory and common law that have been given meaning over the decades and centuries, the requirements that innocence be presumed and guilt be determined beyond a reasonable doubt, the guarantees of a written constitution, and even the work of the court reporter to ensure that meaningful appellate review can be obtained of what has occurred at trial. Yet, the rule of law is an institution absent throughout most of the world, and absent throughout most of history. For most people and for most times, it has been the exception, not the norm. What occurs with little ceremony every day in Harrisville, Hastings, and Hart reflects an institution that has contributed to unprecedented levels of individual freedom, economic prosperity, and governmental stability in our country. Within the four corners of the courthouses meticulously pictured and described in this book, Michigan has pursued, and mostly has succeeded in securing, the ideals of "Freedom, Equality, Truth, and Justice," inscribed upon the stone of our state's Hall of Justice in our capital city.

While this book is predominantly a history of the county courthouses of Michigan, it is also incidentally a history of the small towns in which these courthouses are mostly located. In other words, it is a history of Michigan. Thoroughly researched, it tells the stories of the architectural, social, and political centerpieces of these towns. There are the political quarrels, the competitions and tensions among communities, the fires and explosions, the heroes and the embezzlers, and the prominent, the eccentric, and the obscure. There are the figures of Michigan history—Schoolcraft, Cass, Mason, Blair, Cooley, and Bishop Baraga—and the figures of national prominence—Jackson, Van Buren, Bryan, McKinley, and Roosevelt.

And, of course, there are the criminal trials in which those whom the people have appointed to carry out the first responsibility of government, the "establish[ment] of justice" and the "insur[ance] of domestic tranquility," are engaged on the frontlines in this task of upholding our first civil right, the right to be free from criminals and violent predators. Here, we learn about the matter of the poisoned cake, the Meredith sharpshooter, the stagecoach robberies, the Kentucky Raid, the Battle of Sherman, the Mormon Migration, the horse and the pig thieves, the axe murderer who himself became the victim of a homicide, the war on the railroads, the murder of Nega, the lynching on the courthouse lawn, the Cadillac militia, and law and order in Copper Country. In between its descriptions of the memorable, this book takes care never to lose sight of the courthouse, foremost, as the venue of the routine trial, the day-to-day dispensation of justice, the quotidian obligations of law enforcement, and the array of measures by which our nation upholds the rights, and the entitlement to equal treatment, of Americans.

Also, while taking note of the occasional departures from the norm, John Fedynsky makes clear that Michigan, as with other Upper Midwestern states, has been blessed with an honest and responsible judiciary from its very earliest days. As William J. Cox observed in his *Primer of Mich-*

igan History, even the earliest settlers of Michigan "took an active interest in the wise and honest government of their adopted state," and this is clearly reflected in the history of our judicial branch. "We the people" of Michigan have been well served by our judiciary. With few exceptions, our judges been honest and competent arbiters and have avoided confusing the majesty of the law with their own personal standing.

This book will certainly become the definitive work on an overlooked part of Michigan history, surpassing Maurice Cole's excellent and long out-of-print book *Michigan's Courthouses.* It is a wonderful compilation of facts and anecdotes, recounting the historical and architectural details, while celebrating the gargoyles and cannons. It is both a reference and a book to be read.

I envy John Fedynsky the opportunity in preparing this work to have traveled the roads, and backroads, of Michigan, and to have visited so many of its small towns. There are no more engaging and evocative towns than those of Michigan—New England not excepted. To spend time in these communities is to experience a not-yet-disappeared America of traditional values and pleasures. Former governor John Engler once made a commitment—and to the best of my recollection he lived up to it—to visit each of Michigan's eighty-three counties every year during his three terms in office. Yet, I cannot imagine that he enjoyed the same luxuries of time as has John Fedynsky over the past several years in immersing himself in these communities—communities in which there is a "special richness of life that brings back warm memories and a smile," to quote Manny Crisostomo's portrait of small-town Michigan, *Main Street.* One will gather at least some of that sense from this book.

As one who at an early age has worked and distinguished himself in both the state and federal judicial systems, and now as an assistant attorney general, John Fedynsky is unusually well situated to undertake a book of this sort. And he succeeds magnificently, in my judgment.

CONTENTS

INTRODUCTION

COURTHOUSES ARE SYMBOLS. Physically they stand, but figuratively they speak. They embody the purposes for which they were created: law, order, justice, the American way, and the promise of a better tomorrow. Whatever their shape, station, or locale, the ideals are the same. Each is, in its own unique way, a gem of the people.

This writer had an inchoate sense of these truths before embarking on visiting each circuit courthouse of Michigan's eighty-three counties. Experience affirms the hypothesis. As any Michigan traveler should know, rarely is it difficult to find the county courthouse. Get a map, drive to the county seat, and surely there she stands on a hill or on a primary thoroughfare, which is often called Main, State, Division, Huron, Ottawa, or Saginaw Street. Once found, however, the building is less readily known.

Sifting through the written record reveals that the story of each building is intertwined with stories of, usually, the building's successor, always, the organization of a sizeable tract of frontier land, and, inevitably, people. Public buildings, like persons, belong to family trees. For Michigan the typical evolution begins in the cabin, tavern, or hotel of a prominent local settler and progresses through incarnations of simple log or wooden clapboard and then opulent stone or brick before arriving in modern and utilitarian form. There are myriad exceptions to this rule, and they add variously to the diverse set of Michigan county courthouses.

The counties themselves fall into separate categories. There are the many which waged costly and sometimes violent political and legal battles over the location of the county seat. Fortune and sacred honor rode on the outcome. There are the first-settled and more populous counties that gave way to future organization of smaller counties: Wayne, Kalamazoo, Saginaw, Oakland, Macomb, Kent, and Mackinac, to name a few. There are the coastal counties, deriving great benefit from Lakes Erie, Huron, Michigan, and Superior. The landlocked counties have their charms too, from the western Upper Peninsula's Iron and last-

organized Dickinson to the dual band of southern counties along the ancient Native American trails that interstate highways now track. The name origins range from native tongues to French and Irish to individual commemoration, including military figures, presidents, governors, and, notably, the Cabinet Counties of the Andrew Jackson administration. It is no secret that Michigan entered the Union when spoils for the victors were as expected as they were unabashed. Its borders contain a vast and varied land, second in area only to Georgia among states east of the Mississippi River. Separately, this writer observes that a disproportionate number of Michigan counties begin with the letters C, M, or O.

At bottom, there are the people. The human element of the inanimate objects described herein cannot be denied. Verifiable facts and local lore blend to weave dramatic tales of outrageous crime, courtroom intrigue, backroom dealing, jury determination, and judicial prerogative. Unsurprisingly, human frailty and failing are apparent in the known cases of corruption and mob rule. But noteworthy counterbalance abounds: released jail inmates assisting with evacuating and extinguishing a courthouse fire, residents during a natural disaster seeking and finding physical refuge behind the sure walls of the courthouse, and vigilant legions of homebound defenders arrayed in wartime throughout the courthouse towers scanning the skies for signs of foreign invaders. Then there are the homey touches that emphasize the "house" half of Michigan's courthouses: local folk dropping off plants in the courthouse atrium for use as a winter greenhouse, cows grazing on the public square, county fairs in or near the courthouse, and locally made artwork hanging in public hallways. The courthouses thus bear within their walls a richness of soul endowed by the good people who make each one special.

A sampling of stories could never fully account for the goodwill imbued within and emanating from Michigan's courthouses. The narrative is necessarily demonstrative, not exhaustive. Similarly, this writer must fall short in any attempt to thank the individuals who assisted in the fruition of the ambitious writing project he conceived as a law student. He thanks the many devoted local historians, community archivists, maintenance workers, judges, attorneys, county clerks, civil servants, and fellow citizens who, like the invisible hands of innumerable small breezes, breathed infinite kinetic energy into the endeavor. In particular, the author wishes to thank Stephen Markman, Robert Precht, David H. Sawyer, William B. Murphy, Mike Murphy, and Mark Hoffman for their kind support. He is further indebted to the late Maurice F. Cole for an earlier helpful gathering of information and photographs in *Michigan Courthouses Old and New*. Finally, Michigan's fine network of libraries and historical societies was indispensable.

Like all creative efforts, the work is never completed, only abandoned. Each profile bound within this compendium is a snapshot of the county as it was sometime between 2004 and 2009. The author is keenly aware of, to a point, the instant obsolescence of a book written about county courthouses, for myriad intervening events both catastrophic and constructive can alter the landscape of what he seeks to capture. But there is comfort in knowing that the subject he selected is, as far as he can see, alive, well, and, happily, a work in progress.

ALCONA COUNTY

HARRISVILLE—Alcona County prides itself as first among Michigan's eighty-three counties, at least alphabetically. "First of '83'" appears prominently in its county symbol, which adorns its county buildings in the form of large wooden signs.

Alcona means "fine and excellent plain" or "favored land." Henry Rowe Schoolcraft, an influential state official who named many northern counties, is said to have coined the name by juxtaposing three syllables never before combined. "Al" is Arabic for "the." "Co" is the root of a word meaning plain or prairie. "Na," when it ends a word, means excellence or "fine or excellent place." The name replaced the original 1840 name of the county, which was Negwegon in honor of a Native American chief and an ally of America during the War of 1812. His name means "Wing" or "Little Wing."

The Legislature organized the county in 1868, and Harrisville was designated the county seat. Earlier, the town was called Davison's Mill for an early settler. Benjamin Harris and his sons bought the pine lands and water privileges, renaming the locale for their surname, which was given a post office named Harrisville on September 16, 1857. It was incorporated as a village in 1887 and as a city in 1905.

At various times the county was previously attached to Cheboygan, Alpena, and Iosco Counties. It wasted little time once it was organized in its own right. Its board of supervisors first met on May 8, 1869, and voted for $3,000 in bonds for a courthouse, which voters approved in August. An additional $3,000 was approved in April 1870, the year that construction was completed.

Joseph Van Buskirk directed the initial construction of the courthouse, which was completed in the same year. Later construction added more room, such as a basement, to the building, which served until 1953. It was a modest yet elegant two-story brick building. It was deeper than it was wide, with rows of rectangular windows along its sides. The front entrance had a few arched windows. High above the entrance was a distinctive tower, which cast forth an unmistakable silhouette.

Friday the thirteenth of November 1953 will not soon pass from the memory of Alcona. On this day the courthouse burned to the ground. The fire originated in

Artwork inside Alcona County's courthouse depicts its 1870 predecessor.

the basement and engulfed the building despite everyone's best efforts. Most county records were saved. Everything was moved to temporary facilities around town, including a veterans' club. Insurance proceeds and money from the county's general fund paid for the newer brick courthouse, which is modern in design with a flat roof. Lettering along one of its sides proclaims itself not just a courthouse but the Alcona County Building.

The building was dedicated on June 9, 1956. Ralph S. Gerganoff of Ypsilanti, who designed a number of other Michigan courthouses, was the architect. The Davison-Rose Company was the builder.

Inside the lobby of the building is an antique fire engine built in Cincinnati. Alcona purchased it at the turn of the twentieth century from Chelsea. It sits on four wheels and has a hundred-gallon tank. The purchase price was $450, with one-third up front and the remainder with interest over the following years. It was taken out of service in 1925. For many years it occupied a street corner. A former Harrisville mayor and his wife worked to restore it, which led to indoor displaying.

Elsewhere, the interior of the building is more functional and, as some might observe, spartan. The courtroom is modest and has high windows and a paneled ceiling with hanging fans above the tile floor. The walls are cinder block and painted a lighter shade above eye level. There is a simple wooden bench and jury box, plus unadorned benches for the public. Blue fabric cushions do provide jurors and spectators with some comfort. The rear of the courtroom features portraits of past circuit judges who have served Alcona.

One of them likely presided over the case of the pacing defendant. A former county official recalled with some humor the man who inventively tried to beat the rap for some unremembered charge in the 1960s. As the jury deliberated, he pensively walked up and down the sidewalk below the window of the jury room. His intent reportedly was to exhibit his great concern and to sway the jury in favor of acquittal. He must have walked for miles, because the verdict was not announced until about 11:00 p.m. The jury found him guilty as charged.

His walk on the favored land of Alcona along the shore of Lake Huron in northeast Michigan is but one small chapter in the larger story that the courthouse in Harrisville stands ready to witness, record, and tell. Its story is the first of eighty-three.

ALGER COUNTY

MUNISING—Alger County is home to some of North America's oldest place-names. Some derive from the native Ojibwa, whereas others are literal French and English translations of the original Ojibwa name. Munising, the county seat, comes from Minis-sing, which means "place of the island." Across the bay from Munising in Lake Superior is Grand Island. Some of the French names still in existence, such as Au Train, appeared in French maps in the sixteenth and seventeenth centuries.

But the name of the county is relatively new, for its namesake lived to see the creation of the county. Russell A. Alger was a prominent figure of public power and private wealth. He was a lumber baron estimated to hold over 100,000 acres of land. He served as governor of Michigan, secretary of war for President William McKinley, and U.S. senator.

Before the arrival of permanent European settlers, Alger County had a stream of visitors. Etienne Brule and his companion Grenoble went by about 1619. Two fur traders—Pierre Esprit Radisson and his brother-in-law Medand Chouart, Sieur de Groseilliers—came in 1658. Jesuit missionaries Rene Menard, Claude Allouez, and Jacques Marquette visited in 1660, 1665, and 1669, respectively.

The Northwest Fur Company sent the first European settler to the area to establish British interests in 1763, the year that French rule ended after the French and Indian War. Several years later, America gained jurisdiction, and in 1820 territorial governor Lewis Cass led an expedition to Upper Michigan, stopping at Grand Marais and Grand Island.

From 1843 to 1885, Alger was part of Schoolcraft County, which depended first on Chippewa and then on Marquette County until 1871 for local government. Schoolcraft would govern the territory of Alger only for a short while because the Legislature saw fit to establish Alger County on March 17, 1885.

From May to October, much debate and maneuvering surrounded choosing the county seat. Munising, Au Train, Grand Marais, and Wetmore were all vying for the designation. Au Train won by sweetening the deal. It enhanced its bid by offering "a suitable building" free for a year, an offer that no competitor could match. At the time, Au Train only had one building to offer, Charlie Schaffer's Au Train Hotel, the sole building in town. The county used it free of charge for two years.

A new courthouse was completed in October 1887 for $5,300 on land that Schaffer donated. It was a green-framed two-story structure topped with a cupola. Its iron-fenced courtyard had a small Native American cemetery with house-covered graves. Due to the trouble of transporting prisoners to and from the jail in Marquette, Alger County had its own jail by 1890.

By the turn of the century there was a strong push to move the county seat to Munising, which had grown much larger in population. Other points in its favor were its central location, the poor travel routes to Au Train, a need for a larger jail, and a lack of accommodations in Au Train. It was reported that witnesses and others involved in proceedings at Au Train often had to sleep on the floor of the courthouse.

The 1902 courthouse in Munising as it appears in a photograph on display in the current courthouse

Voters approved the move in 1901, and there was a new courthouse in Munising by 1902. It featured an ornate design mainly of salmon-colored stone. Atop it was a large statue of Lady Justice holding scales. At one point during the 1960s, some imp painted a pink bikini on her, causing a local stir that drew national media coverage. Earlier, some of the bronze statuary had been donated to the World War II effort.

On November 16, 1978, the lady and the courthouse above which she presided met an untimely end. Fire gutted the whole building. The sheriff noticed it at 5:40 a.m., and it was under control by 8:00 a.m., but the structure was beyond repair. The records, though, were in fire-resistant vaults that the fire department watered down in order to prevent any paper from igniting. There was some water damage, and many of the records had to be spread out across the street from a gas station to dry. The fire department saved an adjoining school and church.

Before a modern replacement could be erected on the site of the old courthouse, Alger County went through a transition period in which county offices and records were scattered about temporary office space all over the city.

Though lacking the grandeur of its predecessor, the current Alger County courthouse carries the mantle with a keen awareness of its lineage. A painting of the old building hangs above the jury box in the circuit courtroom, while a photograph is in the hallway. A local artist designed a large wooden tableau with the county seal and the words "Alger County Complex" to hang on the north exterior wall facing the Lake Superior shore where centuries ago visitors and settlers first landed.

ALLEGAN COUNTY

ALLEGAN—Henry Rowe Schoolcraft, Michigan's expert on Native Americans, gave Allegan its name. Some claim it is a compound of parts of different indigenous words, but it has no real meaning of its own. Another interpretation is that it denotes the name of a tribe in the Allegheny Mountains. It was meant for a northern county, but the territorial Legislature assigned it to the land between Grand Rapids and Kalamazoo when it defined the boundaries in 1831.

At first, the townships making up the eastern third of the county were attached to St. Joseph and then Kalamazoo County for civil purposes. The other two-thirds fell under the jurisdiction of Cass County. They were united in 1835, and circuit court was first held in November 1836 in whatever structures had large rooms.

The itinerant court convened in such varied places as a schoolhouse, a Methodist chapel, a basement, and the jailer's building. The court and county offices endured a scattered arrangement until 1889. The building that first welcomed the court now houses an attorney's office and was moved to stand across the street from the current courthouse.

The first jail was built in 1840 for $1,567.98. For $528.50 the county in 1847 completed a twenty-by-forty-foot brick structure with a tin roof to house records and some county offices. The clerk was directed to fix up the room in the jailhouse for court. It served until the spring of 1854, at which time the county purchased a two-story Baptist church and refinished the upper room for a courtroom.

It was architecturally eclectic—a Greek temple with a bell tower atop an English basement. In 1853 the first county fair was held in the basement. The small frame building had an attached jail made of lean-to logs. The jail was described as damp and unhealthy. Prisoners reportedly claimed that they did not dare turn over in bed for fear of rolling out of the jail.

After the Civil War there was a push for new courthouse, but voters rejected the bond proposal. The issue was revisited in 1869 when the court was in danger of caving in. Voters approved $6,000, which paid for a two-story brick building with a stone foundation measuring about forty by fifty feet. It was designed in the Italianate style and was first occupied in 1872. There was still no special space for court, however, and the earlier building continued to serve until it was condemned in 1887.

Court moved about town again. In the meanwhile, voters approved a compromise measure allowing the county to spread a $45,000 bond over three tax rolls beginning in 1889. The cornerstone was laid on August 29, 1889, and the large Romanesque stone court on a hill was completed in June 1890 at a cost of $43,854.88. The city and county in 1903 split the $1,200 cost of installing a clock in the tower.

Town boys vied for the honor of winding the clock, whose four faces were notoriously difficult to synchronize. Residents joked that sometimes the clock was right only twice a day.

In 1933 the court presided over perhaps its most sensational misdemeanor trial. Fred L. Ring was tried for indecent exposure in the wake of the Labor Day raid of his nudist colony with twenty or thirty followers in the Allegan woods. He theorized that exposure to air and sunlight was healthy and that the practice was moral because children who grow up with nudists lose their sexual curiosity. The skeptical sheriff was not persuaded. He considered nudists sexualists and had Ring prosecuted. Local officials wanted to root out the nudist foothold in their midst. They even offered to drop the charges if Ring admitted violating the law and promised to never again practice nudism in Allegan. He refused to sign the agreement.

The jury convicted Ring, and he was ordered to pay $356 in fines and costs and to spend sixty days in the county jail. At sentencing, Judge Fred T. Miles castigated Ring for playing up his crime "in the public press and on the degenerate stage." Miles chastised Ring for deceiving himself into believing that he was "a martyr to pure air and sunshine."

The same judge is remembered for chiding a stentorian attorney to lower his voice. The attorney's voice is said to have rattled the basement all the way from the courtroom on the second floor. The attorney would calmly apologize and then slowly get worked up again before long.

Rays of light and shafts of wind no doubt invaded the court when it was razed in 1961. Alleged overcrowding and a fire marshal's safety concerns motivated the action. Some residents to this day decry the decision, stating that county supervisors misled the public regarding the necessity of the measure. They find solace in the fact that the stone walls of the purportedly unstable building took three days to demolish and that several elected officials were not sent back to office after subsequent elections.

The stone monolith stood overlooking its L-shaped successor's construction. This way, records and offices could be directly moved into the new building, designed by Ralph S. Gerganoff. Named for a county commissioner, the county building is called the Ralph B. Sytsma Memorial Center. An addition was built in 1994. Meanwhile, the county built several of its service facilities other than courts and a jail on a 220-acre complex just north of the county seat.

The bell and 1889 cornerstone of the courthouse were preserved and stand before the local county museum, which is the old brick jail across the street from the new modern facility. A judge's bench, jurors' chairs, a docket book, and

other items are on display in the basement. The disassembled clock is kept there too, in the hopes that someday a new tower will be built for it.

Apart from these items and the original courthouse across the street, there is another small symbol of continuity near the court: a Civil War memorial. It was moved during construction and afterward placed near where it originally stood. The figurine holds a sword and the American flag, which is unusual because most memorials from that era depicted rifle-bearing soldiers. A local association of women raised money for its pedestal. The county paid $600 for the statue. The memorial was dedicated on May 30, 1904.

For about thirty years beginning around 1970 the figurine stood unarmed, perhaps due to natural strain from the weight of the sword or maybe because of vandalism. The county does not know, but recently a metal shop teacher at the local high school created a replacement made of stainless steel. A close observer can see that the sword shines more than the rest of the pot metal figurine, which was rededicated October 21, 2000. It looks over the Kalamazoo River, standing guard over the land Schoolcraft unwittingly named.

ALPENA COUNTY

ALPENA—The art deco courthouse of Alpena County is a milestone of a monolith. It was constructed in such a way that it is quite literally one piece of concrete. Its emergence in the dead of winter proved to the world that such construction could happen in a cold-weather climate.

The county and its seat share a name, which according to a number of formulations means "partridge." Early settlers no doubt took advantage of hunting the native partridge or ruffed grouse. Earlier, the town was called Fremont in honor of John C. Fremont, the Republican candidate for president in 1856. The county had a previous name too: Anamickee, for an Ojibwa chief whose name means "Thunder." The region is known to this day as Thunder Bay, and for about five weeks in 1859 the post office in the town of Alpena had the same name.

In the summer of that year, according to one account, the first "law business" transpired. Leonard Jewell arrived by sailboat and illegally sold liquor. He was detained, along with the rudder to keep his anchored craft from leaving. He was brought to justice and fined. Officials who allowed him back onto his boat to get the fine money were shocked and befuddled to see him make his escape, navigating with an oar. Much to their chagrin, they had no boat to give chase. There was solace in the fact that he never did return.

Beginning February 7, 1857, Alpena County was organized. It was previously attached to Mackinac and Cheboygan Counties. The act of organization designated the county seat at the mouth of the Thunder Bay River, provided that land for county use was donated. George N. Fletcher donated a parcel, but it would not welcome a court for twenty-five years.

Court convened from 1858 to 1863 in the upper floor of a building that later was widely known as a grocery store and a garage. The site was variously called the P. M. Miller, Myers, and Johnson Blocks. From 1863 to 1870 the Hitchcock Courthouse, named for a local deacon, was the county court. A fence and dense forest surrounded it, giving it the look of a stockade, according to an early observer. It burned down on December 12, 1870, taking with it many county records. The fire happened a half hour after a neighborhood church hosted an oyster supper. The cause was probably a stove placed in the probate judge's chambers to stew oysters and make coffee.

Until the early 1880s the court moved from place to place, including the Union School and the rooms above the Potters Brothers' hardware store. In 1881 construction began on a more durable brick courthouse. Great debate surrounded whether to locate the building downtown or, as the county eventually decided by popular vote, on the land given by Fletcher that would revert back to private ownership if not used. Today, the site is hardly away from downtown as the city has grown considerably. The contract went to Samuel Boggs and W. H. Phelps. Circuit court moved in on February 13, 1883.

The courthouse was mainly brick, with lighter stone for the first few feet above the foundation. It was two stories high with an arched entryway and sloping roofs angling up toward a tower. Wood fences and a turnstile surrounding the building kept cattle off the courthouse lawn. The building met its end in a fire on November 22, 1932.

Court moved for a while to the upper floor of the city hall, and county offices relocated to the Fletcher Building across the street from that building. The county met rigorous standards to apply for and receive a $70,000 loan and a $40,000 grant under the Public Works Act, which took some time. Difficulty in obtaining materials created more delay until work finally began in August 1934 with the laying of the cornerstone. The architect was William H. Kuni of Detroit, who also designed Alpena's twin courthouse in Caro, the seat of Tuscola County. The general contractor was the Henry C. Weber Construction Company of Bay City.

About 81,500 labor-hours, or one person working eight-hour days for about thirty-four years, went into the art deco courthouse, which was dedicated on October 21, 1935. It was the first monolithic structure in the Midwest. The foundation, walls, roof, columns, and floors were made of concrete joined by reinforcing steel bars holding together the separately poured slabs such that the whole mass is a single stone. Construction happened during sub-zero weather (which some had thought impossible), thanks to a vertical steam boiler running around the clock and connected through a belt-line system of steam pipes running near the concrete slabs.

The 240,000-cubic-foot building measures about ninety-six feet long by sixty-seven feet deep and about thirty-seven feet tall. Were its concrete instead poured to pave a road, it would stretch five-eighths of a mile. The total cost of the building was about $130,000, or fifty-four cents per square foot.

The floor of the lobby is terrazzo, with brass liners separating the various colors. Terrazzo is cement in which various colored marble chips are placed before the cement sets. Once it does, the surface is ground to a smooth surface, revealing the colored marble.

American walnut and birch trim stained to match finish the courtroom, judge's chamber, and the first-story hall. Cork lines the wall of the courtroom, a relic of a time before air conditioning when there was a need to muffle noise that entered through open windows. The geometric lines characteristic of the art deco style appear throughout the building, particularly in the public benches of the courtroom and the faux columns outside. Molded into the front facade of the building are scales above the word "justice" and tablets with roman numerals above the word "law."

The decorative finishes between the columns raised some controversy when they were repainted in 1999. An effort was made to restore them to their original color. Original tin metalwork turned green, which probably prompted the county to paint it burgundy at some point. It was being repainted a brighter shade of red when some objected to it as gaudy and others as historically inaccurate. The painters scraped the paint and found that silver and gray were the first colors, which is the color that was restored. Earlier, the interior of the building had been restored in the 1980s to its original design.

In 1975 the courthouse annex, which houses district and probate court, opened across the street in a building that once served a local youth club. Circuit court is sometimes held there, particularly when access for the disabled is an issue. The 1935 building as a historic structure is not required to comply with the Americans with Disabilities Act.

Long before that legislation went into effect, Hon. Arthur J. Tuttle spoke at the building's dedication. He drew inspiration from the inscription about the capitol of California, which reads, "Give me men to match my mountains." For the Alpena County Courthouse, he said, "Give me men to match my pine." The call is apt, given the dignity of the cement monolith atop its terracelike hill.

ANTRIM COUNTY

BELLAIRE—The vacating of an old courthouse usually marks the end of a county ever holding court there. The building will eventually either meet the wrecking ball or get converted for some other purpose, often as a historical museum.

Antrim County's restored courthouse stands as a prominent example bucking the trend. A cadre of individuals with a sense of history and a determined will put the court back in the house that stood empty for twelve years between 1978 and 1990.

Originally named Meguzee ("Eagle") in 1840 for the chief who ceded lands to America, Antrim County was renamed along with several other Michigan counties for a county in Ireland. Though some say that Irish settlers were reminded of Irish terrain, historians question the theory based on the fact that few Irish settled in Antrim. Some attribute the naming of several Michigan counties after Irish territory to the work of a nameless bureaucrat or a quiet legislator in Lansing. Antrim reportedly means "solitary farm."

The area was decidedly solitary in its early history. The census in 1860 recorded only 148 settlers, with all of them located on the coast of Lake Michigan in the western edge of the county. Elk Rapids, the oldest sizeable settlement in the county, located in its far southwest corner, was the county seat. It was originally called Stevens. It built a simple wooden courthouse in 1866 for $7,100. The sheriff and his family lived in the basement.

The 1870 census counted a population of 1,866, with most people living inland. The new population distribution and the remote location of Elk Rapids prompted a push for a more central county seat. In the end, the county voted 574

to 446 in April 1879 for a central location in the wilderness with little settlement at all.

The village of Bellaire was recorded in June 1879. Less than a week earlier, the post office there was established as Keno, a contradiction that was not corrected in Bellaire's favor until May 1880.

The name Bellaire is of unknown origin. Some say that an early surveyor chose it for the clearness and purity of the air. Others combine that theory with a story honoring Mrs. Bell Wadsworth, an early pioneer in the area.

Though Bellaire won the county seat, bitter wrangling continued for years before the courthouse cornerstone was laid November 11, 1904. Bellaire designated a courthouse square that stood empty for years except when it was used as a ball field and for fairs.

The county treasurer was sued for obstructing construction and for appropriating the county records, the earliest of which were never recovered. He resigned and was sued all the way to the Michigan Supreme Court. Justice Thomas Cooley wrote an opinion siding with Bellaire in 1880. Temporary facilities were used in Bellaire until 1883. Then the county rented office space in the town hall for $250 a year. Stone purchased for the courthouse stood unused until the school foundation needed material in 1890.

Logging companies moved to delay construction because they wanted to cut their trees and get out before a heavy tax burden for building a courthouse would be imposed. Indeed, many Michigan counties found the impetus and the funds for grand courthouses by imposing property taxes on itinerant industries that county leaders did not expect to remain permanently in the area.

Finally, on April 4, 1904, voters approved a loan of

$26,000 for the courthouse construction, to be paid off by a property tax. Total construction cost was about $30,000. Jens C. Peterson designed the building, and Waterman and Price built it.

Once constructed and dedicated, the grand late Victorian red brick building had an empty tower. Only in 1922, after the fire department led a fundraising drive, was a clock purchased. Inside the courthouse hanging in a frame are handwritten donation pledges that were collected. The clock was installed on December 14, 1922, and its hands were set in motion at 3:35 p.m. The forty-three-year struggle for Antrim's courthouse in Bellaire seemed complete, and the people had a new center for government, social events, and even childhood vaccinations.

But time and the elements presented new challenges. The four faces of the clock were independently set, which meant that wind and heavy snow would slow down one or more faces at different rates. Anyone late for an appointment or a curfew could take advantage of this phenomenon. A hand crank powered the clocks before they were made electric.

The courthouse once had a large glass rotunda. In the wintertime, townsfolk converted the inside of the courthouse into a greenhouse, keeping their plants indoors under the sunlight. The rotunda was eventually covered or removed, perhaps in 1935 when a steel ceiling likely meant for fireproofing was installed. Local historians are unsure of when or why the change happened.

But in the decades after that change, the building deteriorated and the county did little to stem the tide. Ironically, the lack of attention assisted in the renovation years later because it was clear which elements were original.

A new county building of modern design was completed in 1978 for $1.4 million. Court moved there, along with all the county offices. Besides storage, the old courthouse served no public function, other than perhaps reminding citizens of what once was.

A movement led by the local historical society gathered steam, prodding public officials to consider the fate of the old building and categorically opposing demolition. Voters approved a millage in 1990 to fund restoration.

The building was rededicated on August 8, 1992. Almost everything was returned to its original condition. The etched glass identifying each office and the court was replaced, but the originals for the circuit courtroom and the clerk's office were saved and are framed and displayed near their replacements.

On September 20, 2004, a 600-pound set of weights from the tower clock crashed through the ceiling near the entrance to the circuit courtroom, narrowly missing an attorney and her client, who were on a bench preparing for a civil case. Officials believe that a snapped cable was the cause, and the effect was a hole through the two-inch-thick wooden beams in the ceiling and a nearly two-foot-deep hole in the floor below. Up until that time, maintenance workers would wind the clock manually every week.

The circuit courtroom has a light and airy feel. The walls and the carpet have subdued colors. The wood is uniformly pale, and large vertical and arched windows let in ample light. Much of the furniture was replaced, and the original and reportedly uncomfortable juror chairs are no longer in use.

At the end of 2004 the county budgeted $3,600 for twelve to fourteen new chairs. Whether or not the occasional bored and uncomfortable juror senses an improvement, there should be at least some and perhaps a great deal of satisfaction in the story behind the resurrection of Antrim County's courthouse.

ARENAC COUNTY

STANDISH—One of Michigan's shortest used yet longest standing courthouses sought a place in the sand in Arenac County. The image is apt because Arenac's very name means "sandy place." It is the combination of "arena," where gladiators fought in the sand, and the suffix "ac," which means "place of."

This place was detached from Bay County and organized in its own right in 1883. The first courthouse was, according to the organizing act of the Legislature, located in Omer. Settlers intended to call the town Homer but had to register a different spelling because there was another Homer in Michigan. Omer won a subsequent election for the county seat over Standish and Sterling. The court was formerly the Gorrie house. The county purchased it for $1 and the promise to assume the $200 mortgage. Another $212.80 bought the land.

It burned on May 18, 1889. The county paid Angus McDowell $2,970.75 to build a new court, which he delivered on August 5, 1890. The white two-story wooden building is still standing, but it served as a courthouse for only a brief while. Arenac voted 831 to 609 on April 4, 1892, to move the county seat to Standish, which is named for an early settler, a few miles southwest of Omer down the Saginaw Bay. The move happened on May 10, 1892.

Standish temporarily located county offices and court in the opera house block. C. L. Judd and a local businessmen's association each donated $1,000 for a courthouse. The red brick courthouse went into use on December 27, 1892. It had an arched entrance and windows and a prominent tower atop one of its corners. It cost about $5,000.

The third courthouse served Arenac for seventy-two

years. It was demolished after the fourth and present courthouse was constructed on the same grounds. The old court had been in the courtyard area between the new building and the parking area. The Arenac County Building is a flat-roofed brick building designed by Ralph S. Gerganoff. The second story does not entirely cover the footprint of the first story. Four large stone-faced pillars stand near the front entrance. Reddish orange paneling runs the length of the front of the building, along with windows. A layer of sandstone lines part of the building too.

The building was dedicated October 2, 1965. The general contractor was Davison & Son Builders, Inc. Additional work was done on the building in 1985 to make it barrier-free. Its most noticeable connection to its predecessor is an old cabinet on display in the lobby. A sign explains its sig-

nificance as the only known original piece of furniture from the 1892 building that is in the possession of the county.

Meanwhile, in the same year (1892) the old courthouse in Omer sold for $500. It became Masonic lodge No. 377. Records indicate that over the years it survived a tornado, fires, flooding, and ice storms that all ravaged the immediate surrounding area. It served at various times as a temporary home for local firms, city hall, the post office, a pharmacy, and the newspaper.

Mounting maintenance costs burdened its owners, who sold it in 1997 to a local preservation-minded couple. They began working with the local historical society to convert it into a museum and a destination along a heritage route on the highway it abuts.

Inside the building one can see the old holding cell, a stairway to nowhere (it is believed that to make space it was walled off because there was another set of stairs), and the courtroom on the second floor. The courtroom contains some Masonic memorabilia, red drapes, a forty-eight-star American flag, and attractive carpeting with a floral design. The building, though creaky, is preserved remarkably well and has attracted its share of local news coverage as fundraising campaigns for its future have commenced. In September 2005, court proceedings occurred at the Omer courthouse for the first time in 115 years, as part of the historical society's campaign to generate interest in and funds for the courthouse. One good-natured defendant was quoted in a local newspaper joking that it was good he had yet to see any nooses, as friends quipped that hangings probably were happening back when court was last held in Omer.

The courthouse's short use in that capacity deprived it of the opportunity to hear many cases. Those went to Standish, like the case of the cussing canoeist who prevailed on appeal in invalidating a statute that some considered a Victorian relic for banning foul language in the presence of women and children. He, those within earshot, and the courthouse in Omer share at least one trait: a search for a pleasant place in the sands of Arenac.

BARAGA COUNTY

L'ANSE—Depending on what authority one consults, L'Anse is French for bay, arc, cove, or handle. It describes the location of L'Anse at the head of the Keweenaw Bay. Italian mapmaker Coronelli published a map in Paris in 1688 labeling today's L'Anse as "Ance de Kenonan." The last word was an early version of Keweenaw.

Baraga County came into being on February 19, 1875. Captain John Bendry, a prominent early resident, arrived much earlier. Born in England in 1822, he left at the ripe age of twelve to sail the seas. He first began sailing the Great Lakes in 1845. He was the wheelman of Independence, the first steam vessel on Lake Superior.

Bendry provided the first courthouse and county building for Baraga County. It was a narrow three-story frame building facing the bay. He brought it by boat down the bay from Hancock in 1872.

Ten years later, the county voted 158 to 95 to raise $10,000 for a new courthouse. The large brick building on a hill overlooking the bay was completed in 1884 at a cost of $11,945. A jail built in 1912 replaced the old one of 1883.

In addition to Bendry, Baraga County was home to the notable figure of Cara Anderson, Michigan's first female legislator. She was elected in 1925 and served one term.

But the most prominent person connected to the county is its namesake, Bishop Frederic Baraga. He was born on June 29, 1797, to a moderately wealthy family in Slovenia, a province at the time of the Austro-Hungarian Empire. Before the age of maturity, he was orphaned. He studied law, gained control of his family's estate, and was engaged to be married. But he met Clement Hofbauer.

Hofbauer was a revered priest who would be canon-ized a saint about a hundred years later. Due largely to Hofbauer's influence, Baraga broke off his engagement, gave away his estate, and entered the seminary. He was ordained on September 21, 1823.

For the first few years of his priesthood, Baraga worked as an assistant in parishes in his homeland. But mission-ary work called, and it led him to North America, where he arrived at the end of 1830.

His first two assignments were on the Lower Peninsula at the places that grew into Harbor Springs and Grand Rapids. Pierre Crebassa, a French fur trader in L'Anse, began writing to Baraga in 1840 and invited him to visit. In May 1843, Baraga came to the small settlement on the south shore of Lake Superior. He converted a number of natives and said that a permanent mission there would be success-ful. More pledged to be baptized if he would promise to reside in the area permanently.

Five months later, Baraga returned and stayed for a decade, though he did travel to missions he set up else-where around the Great Lakes. Baraga's travels are the stuff of local legend. There are accounts of treacherous canoe rides and Herculean hikes alone through blizzards wear-ing snowshoes and only carrying the instruments of his religion.

The church and government gave little to no finan-cial support to Baraga's projects. Instead, Baraga turned to his friends in Europe for assistance. He wrote articles for European journals about the plight of his many flocks, which persuaded some readers to send donations.

He was consecrated bishop of Upper Michigan on November 1, 1853, in Cincinnati. Fifteen years later he died in Marquette. When he died, there were twenty-one priests stationed around Lake Superior. He was the only one when he first came. Thirty-seven of his seventy years he spent living with Native Americans.

Outside of the center of L'Anse is a large shrine commemorating Bishop Baraga. The courthouse, an equally if not more prominent landmark, bears his name too. It stands prominently upon a hill, with its grassy portion bounded by a small retaining wall and black iron fence. The mainly red brick building stands atop a red stone foundation, with arched windows ringing the ground floor and rectangular ones on the second floor. Three black stripes run around the building. The upper and lower bands trace the window sills while the middle one curves around the archways of the lower windows and doors. Above the doors, the white curved areas frame stylized depictions of the scales of justice. The dark brown roof is peaked, a helpful design where winter snow can be plentiful. Large black lettering on a white background proclaims the name of the courthouse, but from afar the casual viewer might sense more house than court, as the architecture almost blends with surrounding residential areas.

Inside, the courtroom is functional, with modern ceiling paneling and rotating fans circulating the air above the yellow chairs for the jurors, witnesses, parties, and coun-

sel. A white background stands in contrast behind the dark brown judge's bench and chair. The lobby features a large carpeted wooden stairway, which shares space with historic black and white photographs on the wall, track lighting, a water fountain, and photocopier.

Though secular in its design and function, the courthouse is in a sense a cathedral named in honor of an uncommon clergyman who brought and gave so much to the relative wilderness he first found in 1843.

BARRY COUNTY

HASTINGS—Though Barry County and its seat bear the names of two prominent men who made names for themselves elsewhere, it forged an identity of its own over the years. William T. Barry was postmaster general under President Andrew Jackson, and Eurotas P. Hastings was president of the Bank of Michigan, with large land holdings in the area. Hastings donated the land for the courthouse square, where the county built its first wooden courthouse and jail in the summer of 1843 for $1,213.92. In 1908 a local newspaper eulogized James M. Hewes as the builder, who also made a living making coffins and working as a barber under opposite ends of the same roof.

Originally part of Kalamazoo County, Barry came into being in the spring of 1839. Court was first held in a schoolhouse in 1840. The sheriff spent several days scouring the wilderness to find jurors, who were kept in a log cabin two blocks from the court due to limited space. The first courthouse burned in 1846. John Lewis drew up the plans, and A. W. Bailey built its replacement, along with a jail, in 1847 for $2,381.09. It served until 1893. This court's white wooden frame stood two stories high.

The jail before 1843 was another matter. Local records indicate that a hole in the ground measuring six by ten feet and capped with a plank four feet above the surface was the first jail. It was understandably difficult to guard. After

fire destroyed the first proper jail, prisoners were sent to Kalamazoo until Barry built a brick jail in 1853.

Behind the wooden fence in the courthouse square was lush grass that residents would have their cows and horses graze from time to time. But in 1859 the county supervisors by unanimous consent instructed the sheriff not to allow any quadruped to graze on the square. Yet the county for years welcomed the annual fair of the local agricultural society on the square and in the courthouse itself.

Barry prides itself for its concerted effort to contribute to the Civil War. Apart from money, the county gave of its men. Though only 15,000 people lived in the county then, 1,632 men served in the army for an average of 102 per township and fully 11 percent of the total county population. For future war efforts, the Civil War cannon and a memorial fountain that adorned the lawn near the courthouse were donated as scrap metal. A 1942 newspaper article surmised that the fountain would not be missed should it take the form of shrapnel penetrating "vital portions of the anatomy of Premier Tojo of Japan, who ordered the sneak attack on Pearl Harbor." The Striker Memorial Fountain, so named for the late local judge who bequeathed it for the courthouse square in 1899, was restored in 1991.

After the Civil War, the next struggle Barry faced was a series of devastating fires, with the worst coming August

stone coursing of the second floor and just below the wood cornice line of the roof. The brick above each clock face is set as if emanating in rays from the center of the clock. Outwardly, the building looks very much like its older sister in Livingston County, with the exception of the large inscription reading "18 Barry County 92" and honoring the year the cornerstone was laid. Above it a decorative frieze lines the perimeter of the building.

Inside, a number of touches also distinguish Barry's courthouse. In particular, "B" and "BC" monogram some metal hardware on original doors and the bolted down folding chairs for the public in the courtroom, respectively. The courtroom is spacious and well lit by the large windows, which feature refinished original wooden blinds. The ceiling is coffered wood and plaster with round plaster reliefs centered in each coffer and designed to hold suspended light fixtures. The acoustics could be better, but visually the grandeur of the wainscot of original refinished wood paneling is difficult to match. The court was renovated in 1991. Its nearest neighbor is the old jail and the current annex building, which is home to, among other things, a drug court and veterans affairs.

In 1994 the courthouse welcomed a neighbor across the street, the Barry County Courts and Law Building. The new building houses probate court and a number of other county offices and functions.

As the ringing of the clock tower cascades down the court's busy neighbors and its humming square, one wonders if Messrs. Barry and Hastings and the many veterans of Barry County know for whom the 1,400-pound bell in that tower tolls.

13, 1886. It was in this context that a larger fire-resistant stone and brick courthouse was proposed. In January 1892 the supervisors and voters approved a $54,000 bond. Construction was completed in 1893 for $57,563.53. An area jeweler raised $420 by local subscription to purchase and install the 1,400-pound electric clock in the tower.

The four-story building is set half a story into the earth. Asphalt shingles replaced the original slate roof. Carpeting, four elevators, and a holding cell near the court were other modern alterations. A dedicated door to the elevator serves only those in custody. Occasionally officers neglect to flip the shut-off switch for the public door, which prompts to their amusement reactions from startled members of the public who insist on waiting for the next elevator.

The exterior of the eclectic Romanesque building begins at grade with rough stone to a height of nine feet capped by a coursing of cut stone. The cut stone also frames major entrances and the semicircular windows. The remaining wall material is brick. Decorative brick and tile accent the space between the bottoms of the windows and the cut stone. Brick corbelling appears below the cut

BAY
COUNTY

BAY CITY—Bay County throughout its history has shunned subservience as it sought ascendancy. From casting away the name Lower Saginaw for its county seat to erecting an eight-story art deco county building, action and aim coincide as upward they point.

Bay County was organized in 1857 in spite of opposition from Saginaw and Midland Counties, who stood to lose territory in the process. Bay County found itself in the opposite position when Arenac County was carved out of Bay's northern reaches. By 1883, Bay County's boundaries were settled.

Bay City took on its name in 1857 and dropped Lower Saginaw. From 1858 to 1868 it paid James Fraser $200 in annual rent for a wooden building on Water Street as its courthouse. The county's population in 1860 grew from 3,164 to 15,900 by 1870.

The county laid a cornerstone for a new courthouse on May 6, 1868. Cyrus Kinne Porter of Buffalo, New York, designed the building, which cost about $42,000. It was a square-domed structure almost identical to its younger twin in St. Johns, Clinton County's seat. The dome was about eighty feet from the base of the building, and the roof was slate. The basement was Kingston stone while yellow brick with sandstone trim made up the superstructure. George Watkins of Bay City was the general contractor. The two-story building, which also had an attic, had an interior of mainly white pine. The courtroom measured forty-eight by seventy-one feet, with a ceiling twenty-two feet high.

This building made way for the wrecking ball and its skyscraper art deco successor in 1933. The new county building came during difficult economic times as a jobs and public works project. The county invested a $375,000 bond plus a $165,000 sinking fund in the building.

Local architect Joseph C. Goddeyne, whose grandfather had done masonry work on the previous courthouse, designed the county building. Bay City Stone Company was the general contractor. Despite the headline-stealing escape and death of John Dillinger, the completion of the building on March 10, 1934, was also front-page news. It was said at the time of unveiling that the first-floor space went to offices the public most frequented and that welfare offices were in the basement near doorways to spare visitors undue embarrassment.

The building's steel frame supports limestone and granite. The lines of the outside walls emphasize a vertical effect, with upper stories set back from lower stories. The rectilinear design is unmistakably art deco.

The stylized geometrics characteristic of the art deco era appear liberally throughout the building's interior and exterior. Bright bronze elevator doors on the first floor welcome visitors. A small plaque with a map depicting the county and its townships appears on the elevator doors on the other floors, despite a typo that left the third "n" out of Pinconning Township. Fixtures such as wall-mounted lights invoke visions of Gotham City. Goddeyne placed four ornate vault doors from the old courthouse in the new building. A recent visit revealed that a break space with a refrigerator is behind one of them.

The building underwent about $2 million of renovation in 1984 through 1986. It included stairwell work and elevator modernization, new windows, revamping of wiring, and installation of a fire sprinkler system. The work stemmed in large part from sixteen fire code violations in 1981.

Despite its size, the building was not tall or wide enough to house all county functions. Some were already located in an annex, which was once a commercial center, a few blocks away when plans to relocate court functions emerged. A retired judge complained in a local article that the structure was more office building than courthouse. Its acoustics particularly concerned him, from invading outside noise that interrupted proceedings, to a lack of privacy for jury deliberations and privileged attorney-client communications.

Security was another primary concern, as the public, the accused, and employees had to share entrances, exits, hallways, and other space. There were also concerns that the books in the law library, which were accumulating at a rate of about five per day, would cave in the top floor, which was weak in the middle and not designed for such weight. Librarians were forced to disperse shelf weight away from the center to the perimeter walls and to remove an older book for every new one acquired.

The county spent $6 million creating a new court facility at Washington Park Plaza. Large lettering outside the one-story brick structure identifies it as the Bay County Court Facility. What it gave up in aesthetics it made up in security, efficiency, and better service to the public.

The old county building had squeezed a total of seven circuit, district, and probate courtrooms into a facility that originally only housed one. A combined session of the three courts held a farewell ceremony in the grand fourth-floor courtroom of the old building in August 1998.

This room is now the meeting place of the county commissioners. The chair sits at the judge's bench, and the remainder of the room is generally in its original state. The main exception is a curved table for the other commissioners in the space where opposing litigants had rectangular tables.

Behind the bench are two bas-relief figures that Robert L. Rischman shaped in three sections, with each clay slab weighing over a ton. Execution of justice is a male figure clutching a sword, whereas interpretation of justice is a female figure reading a book. Elsewhere, a bench a judge once used on the sixth floor is now the unusual desk of an equalization appraiser.

Unlike most courtrooms in the state, the old main courtroom has a large balcony on the fifth floor overlooking the action on the fourth floor. The theater-style seating, which is bolted down in rows, appears original by the look of its worn leather seats and fabric backs. The balcony is yet another example of how Bay County sought to elevate its citizenry.

In the lobby of the 1934 county building, the motive is clear in the inscription quoting Ruskin. It reads in part, "let us think, as we lay stone on stone, that a time is to come when those stones will be held sacred, because our hands have touched them, and that men will say as they look upon the labor and the wrought substance of them, 'See! This our fathers did for us.'"

Wherever one stands and lays eyes on the Bay County Building, one cannot help but look up, be it in the figurative or literal sense, or, probably, both.

BENZIE COUNTY

BEULAH—Like a partygoer hopping from one social affair to the next, the Benzie County Courthouse has made many stops throughout its history. It is only fitting that one of its incarnations was a former recreation and entertainment center called "The Grand."

But the origins of Benzie, like most other counties, were humble, not grand. It was organized on March 30, 1869, and about three weeks later the supervisors met in a schoolhouse in Benzonia. A group intent on founding a Christian center of higher education first settled the area, choosing a name from the Latin "bene" for "good" and the Greek "zonia" for "place" to indicate that they found a good place to live. For a time it was also called Herring Creek.

The name of the county began with the Native American name for the local river: Unszigozbee, which referred to a local duck species and meant Saw Bill or Merganserduck River. The French translated the name to Riviere Aux Bec Scies, which was corrupted in English to Betsie River, which is its present designation. For the county name, the more refined Benzie was preferred.

In July 1869 the vote for county seat gave Benzonia 75, Homestead 237, and Frankfort 194 votes, which meant no clear majority. In 1870 the county population was 2,184. Frankfort won the second round of voting in October 1869 over Homestead by 301 to 265. One account described the contest as "characterized by a great deal of bitterness and foolishness"—two vices that, according to some observers, would not soon leave Benzie's confines.

In Frankfort the supervisors met at the Victory Saterlee Hotel, a two-story frame building at the corner of Third and Main. The courthouse was another two-story frame building at Second and Main that the Doaby Brothers built.

Benzonia offered incentives if it were voted the new county seat. Some voters were willing to move out of Frankfort but not willing to relocate in Benzonia's township limits. So in 1872 the compromise location of a mile east of Benzonia, where nothing resembling civilization had taken root, won the vote. Frankfort won the first tally, but illegal ballots were allegedly cast, and the board of canvassers rejected the vote and certified a vote for removal. The legality of that action was questioned in protracted litigation, and the Michigan Supreme Court ultimately upheld it. By then the actual removal of county property to the new seat had already happened.

A contemporary account pulled no punches. "The present site furnishes a striking illustration of the follies men are capable of when prompted by a spirit of jealousy or spite." The L-shaped frame county building was in an isolated spot one mile from any hotel, post office, or place

of business. The circuit judge ordered that court would convene in a suitable place in the village of Benzonia. County business slowed during the seat struggle, with some board members, depending on their allegiance, meeting in different parts of the county and refusing to transact business in other parts.

After the judge's order, court held its sessions at Case's Hall in an upper floor in the heart of Benzonia's downtown. Benzonia held the seat for twenty years, but it was no honeymoon. Bond issues for a courthouse and other county buildings were rejected. In 1891 the board of supervisors considered nine different sites for a new county seat. The inconvenience of the seat's location and the ramshackle appearance of the county building precipitated in 1894 a vote of 1,060 to 795 in favor of removal to Frankfort at the western edge of the county.

Frankfort's public school, a frame building, was offered and converted into a court and county offices. A jail was built next door. There is a lighthearted story of an unsuccessful escape attempt at one of Benzie's many jails. The inmate viewed the ceiling as flimsy and therefore a good escape route. But he discovered more layers beyond the first one he penetrated, so he gave up the effort. When his attempt was discovered, he quipped that he just wanted to help the jail keeper dig his potatoes.

Benzie again grew weary of the location of its county seat and sought to dispatch the outlying Frankfort. An effort to move to Thompsonville, where the Ann Arbor and Pere Marquette Railroads intersected, but not in a central location in the county, failed in 1906 by a vote of 1,390 to 906.

Two years later the centrally located Honor won a vote for removal. An abandoned church on Platte Street was remodeled for county offices, and the court went to the second floor of a store on Main Street. A cement jail and sheriff's residence was constructed, but it was only used for eight years.

In October 1915 came Beulah, the latest contender. On the shores of Crystal Lake, it was once called Crystal City. Its name derives from Isaiah 62:4, which reads, "You shall no more be termed Forsaken and your land shall no more be termed Desolate; but you shall be called My Delight is in Her, and your land Beulah, that is Married." Beulah won the 1916 spring election handily, 1,371 to 670.

As an inducement, Beulah offered "The Grand," a three-story frame building downtown that was originally built in 1912 as a recreation and amusement center. Bowling alleys, billiard tables, a soda fountain, and slot machines were removed from the first floor, which was partitioned

into county offices. The second floor, which was used for public meetings, dancing, and roller-skating, became a courtroom and a sheriff's residence. Its eastern end connected to the jail, which was only a concrete box set in a clay bank and affectionately called "The County Root Cellar." The move on June 1, 1916, featured a procession of wagons and at least one early truck with hard-rubber tires. The blaring Benzonia Academy Boys' Band met the march halfway and escorted it into Beulah.

The exterior of the building was not very distinguished at first. But over the years it took on the air of a courthouse. The county rented the building from Beulah and then bought it for about $3,000 in 1942. Tall fluted columns, a contoured roof line, a longer porch, and a clock were some of the noteworthy exterior improvements. The shed-roofed, clapboard-sheathed structure boasted Flemish-gabled parapets at its front and side facades, a second-story open portico, and shed dormers that dot the sloping asphalt shingle roof. Inside, the court gained better lighting, heating, plumbing, and a high-beamed ceiling for the courtroom.

Entrance doors in the rear of the court were spring-hung louvered partial doors, which allowed one to punctuate an entrance or an exit with a spirited push. Passing freight trains came within one hundred feet of the building. They rattled the building and disrupted proceedings so consistently that by custom court would pause without recess until the train passed. A local attorney wrote that someone entering at that moment might mistake the location for a wax museum. A former district judge recalled with humor the case of the defendant with a loud muffler whose trial met the consecutive interruption of a passing train and downshifting trucks going up or down the nearby inclined road.

One could set a clock by the justice of the peace who invariably, even if a trial was running into the night, would enter court at 10:00 p.m. to check his watch against that of the court. Shortly before the county vacated the building, a stray cat named Benzie had the run of the place for eight months, sometimes shredding documents by night.

County leaders shrewdly took the proceeds from the sale of the county poor farm in 1967 and placed them in an interest-bearing account. In this manner they avoided turning to the electorate for funds for county buildings, which might have prompted another county seat move. Federal revenue-sharing funds were added to the account, which grew to $615,000 by 1975. The county was ready to build the Benzie County Government Center.

Blacklock and Schwartz of Midland prepared the plans, and Gust Construction Company of Cedar Springs did the work. Construction began in January 1975, and the $873,238 project was completed and dedicated on August 7, 1976. The 26,100-square-foot structure is made of brick and concrete with solar bronze trim and non-glare glass. It blends well with the topography of its hilly surroundings. In the late 1990s it welcomed an addition, which houses a family independence agency and unfinished office space for expansion.

The old court served myriad functions once the county moved out. It was home to stores such as an ice cream shop and a lady's dress boutique. A number of restaurants occupied its space and took advantage of the long porch overlooking Crystal Lake. For a time, it was an inn too, hearkening back to its early days when the third floor featured guest rooms. Recently it was converted into condominiums.

The present court complex is situated in such a way that it appears firmly rooted in, if not enveloped by, the ground, much like a bunker. Perhaps this characteristic is born of Benzie's history of shuffling county seats and a relatively recent desire to counteract that tendency.

BERRIEN COUNTY

ST. JOSEPH—The tug-of-war for the county seat of Berrien County pulled some communities apart, drew others together, and left another in the lurch with a courthouse that would serve various functions before preservationists prevailed upon the county to notice its historic value.

Named for John M. Berrien, attorney general to President Andrew Jackson, Berrien County was first part of Lenawee and then neighboring Cass County. It is among several counties in Michigan that make up the Cabinet Counties, as each was named for a different member of Jackson's cabinet. It was formally organized in 1831 with inaugural local elections shortly thereafter.

Court was first held in Niles, the principal settlement in the southeastern part of the county and near the Indiana border, at the "Council House," which was the home of Alamanson Huston. Spanish raiders in 1781 briefly occupied the area of Niles, which has also seen French, British, and American rule. Niles to this day prides itself as Michigan's only city of four flags, which the city seal reflects by bearing the words *terra de quattuor vexilli*.

By 1832 court moved to the coast of Lake Michigan at present-day St. Joseph, which at the time was called Newburyport. Court was first held in a log schoolhouse, then at the store of William Huff, and then finally in a building remembered as the "Old White Schoolhouse." It remained there until 1837 when it was moved to the less populous but more geographically central Berrien Springs.

One historical account recalls the maneuvering of the competing delegations appearing before a legislative com-mittee in Lansing. The Niles delegation secured the floor and spoke first at length, extolling in flowery oratory its virtues. The chair of the Berrien Springs delegation slipped out, went to the finest hotel in town, and arranged for a sumptuous banquet. He gave particular regard to having "a great plenty of wines and liquor." He returned in time for Niles to finish speaking and took the floor. All that was said in favor of Niles is equally true of Berrien Springs, he said. But he concluded that talking and listening were "dry work" and invited the committee to supper. The legislators enjoyed good food, drink, and laughter as the gape-jawed Niles delegation looked on with longing eyes. The next morning the committee voted against Niles, and Governor Stevens T. Mason later approved the act moving the county seat to Berrien Springs.

Gilbert Avery, a local master builder, built the 1839 Berrien Springs Courthouse. Its style is elegant Greek Revivalist featuring four large columns and mainly wooden materials painted white on the outside. It measures sixty by forty by twenty-four feet, with a sixteen-foot belfry capping the roof. Judge Epaphroditus Ransom presided over the first session, where a man was tried and convicted of stealing boots, socks, and mittens worth ten dollars and, ultimately, a sentence of one year.

By the 1870s grumblings about moving the county emerged. The courthouse grew shabby and could no longer hold all the county records. Muddy roads and no railroad between the county seat and the more populous Niles and the larger coastal towns of St. Joseph and Benton Harbor hastened the move of the county seat. Most of the legal talent of the county was on the coast, yet Niles seemed to prevail in the contest for the circuit judge.

Matters came to a head in the early 1890s. St. Joseph and Benton Harbor, sister cities who were originally competitors along with Niles for the county seat, came to an agreement. A joint commission decided that Benton Harbor would support St. Joseph provided that St. Joseph donated land for the court that was in view of Benton Harbor across the St. Joseph River. Plans for a site in the marsh between the two towns were abandoned as impracticable. It was also rumored that St. Joseph made a side deal as well when it promised not to compete with Benton Harbor for a mutually desired chapter of the Knights Templar.

The county required $25,000 to secure a site. Niles objected to the legality of St. Joseph's proffered bond because St. Joseph was already heavily in debt due to bonds already taken out for other municipal improvements. Select citizens of St. Joseph came through with personal bonds, and the first battle was won.

A heated campaign for the vote ensued. Voters in St. Joseph and Benton Harbor carried the day over the opposition of Niles and Berrien Springs, prevailing by a margin of 242 out of over 11,000 votes cast. Berrien Springs promptly challenged the vote in court, arguing that the ballot was illegally worded.

Judge Coolidge of Niles agreed and invalidated the vote. The Michigan Supreme Court reversed, and St. Joseph won the war, but not before a few parting skirmishes.

Only two ox teams had been needed to move the county records to Berrien Springs in 1838. Over thirty were needed for the return trip to St. Joseph in 1894. The victors styled the move as a grand procession filled with music, cheering, pomp and circumstance. A man playing an organ grinder looking to find tips instead found the boots of enraged Berrien Springs citizens who kicked him a mile down the road, where he waited for the parade to arrive. Another man decked out in a stovepipe hat lingered too long in his celebration at Berrien Springs. Local boys knocked the hat over his eyes and beat him while he was blinded. The final snag in the move to the court's temporary confines at the Music Academy was when the treasurer's safe tumbled down the stairs.

For a final cost of $104,007.42, a grand stone courthouse and a separate jail and sheriff's residence were dedicated on February 20, 1896. Meanwhile, the 1839 courthouse became at different points a dance hall, a militia drill hall, a church, a college campus, and, briefly, a vacant target for demolition. In 1967 local historical organizations united to preserve the courthouse square, which is now jointly owned with the county. Restoration commenced. Lightning struck in 1989, severely damaging the northwest corner of the building. But removal of debris revealed details that guided continued restoration.

The 1839 courthouse stands today as the oldest courthouse in Michigan and, along with its historic adjacent buildings, as one of the finest early government squares in the Midwest, like the nearly contemporaneous seat of local government in Lapeer County. Technically and legally speaking, the building still functions as a courthouse, though trials are rare and the building typically houses other community events, such as recitals. For ceremonies such as the swearing in of a new judge, the court still occasionally attracts standing-room-only crowds.

Meanwhile, the stone edifice that replaced the wooden one fell victim to its multistory concrete successor of 1966, which is also on the river overlooking Benton Harbor, and the wrecking ball. Niles had a last laugh of its own when it

unveiled in 2004 an addition and renovated courtrooms in its South County Building.

The county that is home to the city of four flags is also the land of multiple county seats, courthouses, and presently operating courts. It is an example of a county seat struggle that produced no clear winners or losers, for the prize was split even though some figured the whole trophy was carted away forever.

BRANCH COUNTY

COLDWATER—Branch County's new courthouse captures the essence of its predecessor, which succumbed to the tragedy of fire. A band of motivated and historically minded citizens worked to erect a new bell tower in memory of the old one, finally succeeding several years after the modern facility was completed.

The county is named for John Branch of North Carolina, who was President Andrew Jackson's secretary of the navy. It was laid out in 1829 and first attached to Lenawee and then St. Joseph County for judicial purposes. Coldwater, the county seat since 1842, was first called Lyons for a place in New York and then Masonville for Governor Stevens T. Mason. It was then named for the township in which it is located, which is named for the Coldwater River.

The seat was first at Masonville but it moved to the town of Branch in 1831. Judge William Fletcher first held court in Branch in 1833 in a schoolhouse. Criminals were sent to St. Joseph. Stephen Bates built a modest structure for $383. Six years after the seat moved to Coldwater, whose residents offered an inducement of $300, a courthouse was erected. Court met in Coldwater for a time in the brick residence of K. H. Beach.

In the spring of 1847 the county approved a new build-ing by a vote of 834 to 794. It was by the same margin in 1887 that the county approved a second courthouse in a vote with a significantly higher total number of voters. G. W. Davis built the $5,000 building, and the county occupied it in December 1848. The building had a Greek Revivalist design, with four large round columns supporting a portico and a small square tower. A picture of it hangs in the present courthouse.

Branch County grew weary of its courthouse and its space limitations several decades later. However, voters in 1886 rejected a proposal for a new building. The county tried again and in April 1887 won a close vote of 2,791 to 2,764. M. H. Parker of Coldwater designed the High Victorian building. Armory Hall housed the circuit court during construction after the old building was razed.

Crocker and Hudnutt of Big Rapids constructed the building, completing its work in the summer of 1888. The building cost $52,098.99. It was mainly red brick, with an imposing clock and bell tower visible for miles. It carried the heavy load of a 3,500-pound bell from the C. H. Meneely Company of New York. The clock was from Howard Company of Boston.

A midnight fire on December 5, 1972, destroyed the

courthouse, gutting the second floor and causing extensive water damage to the first floor. A juvenile already in the local criminal justice system was later convicted in Ingham Circuit Court of arson. Shortly after 1:00 a.m., wood and metal from the tower came crashing down. The bell was salvaged, as were the clock parts, which sold at auction in disassembled form for $35.

For almost three years county offices and the courts operated out of temporary facilities. The circuit judge worked in a former nursery that had images of Walt Disney cartoon characters on the wall. The local press quoted him as glumly saying, in response to a question about his thoughts on his new quarters, "I don't like them." Temporary courtrooms were arranged in local banks. One of the buildings of the Coldwater State Home and Training School later became a temporary courthouse.

On April 16, 1974, the county voted 2,880 to 1,933 to erect a new courthouse on the site of the old one. A $1.9 million bond issue paid for the modern two-story facility, which Haughey, Black and Associates of Battle Creek

designed. Wagner-Flook of Grand Rapids was the contractor. The county moved in during January 1976, and the dedication happened in late March.

The flat gray stone facades and shiny glass of the new building bear little resemblance on their own to the old courthouse. The Branch County Clock Committee sought to change the skyline and connect the building better to its heritage. Organized in 1974 and reorganized thirteen years later, it doggedly collected funds and located the old bell and clock. No public money was used for the project.

On July 30, 1988, the county dedicated the new clock tower on the southwest corner of the courthouse square. Apart from the old bell and clock, it also features the original finial tops of the cupola. A large display at the tower's base commemorates the 1972 fire.

Like its predecessor, the tower of the courthouse dominates its profile. The right angle and gaze manage to blend old and new as the spirit of the past morphs the form of the present into one quintessence that is the courthouse of Branch County.

CALHOUN COUNTY

MARSHALL—A number of chief justices have made their mark on Calhoun County. The seat is named for U.S. Chief Justice John Marshall, a friend of an early settler. Three plaques in the entranceway of the impressive new courthouse in Battle Creek commemorate three Calhoun residents who served as chief justice of the Michigan Supreme Court: Walter H. North, Benjamin F. Graves, and Mary S. Coleman.

The county is named for John C. Calhoun, the senator from South Carolina and vice president under Andrew Jackson. It was set off in 1829 with Marshall as the county seat in 1831. For judicial purposes it was organized on March 6, 1833. Marshall for a time was viewed as the heir apparent as the state prepared to move the capital from Detroit. In anticipation of the switch, prominent citizens of the state built many stately homes in Marshall, which still grace the city even though unsettled Lansing won the coveted designation.

The first court sessions in Marshall were held in schoolhouses and hotels. The state authorized Calhoun to borrow up to $12,000 for public buildings. The county laid a cornerstone on July 22, 1837, for a brick structure. The foundation was Marshall sandstone. It had a colonial portico and columns at its front and rear, as well as a square cupola. The columns on the west were round, whereas those on the east were square. In 1855 one of them fell and shattered a window. The building was completed in 1838 and actually cost over $25,000.

The extravagance of the building led many to oppose separate construction of a jail or sheriff's residence. The basement of the court became the jail, but it proved inef-

fective when a general escape of nine prisoners happened in 1850. They heated an iron on a stove and used it to burn through the logs and the lock fastenings that confined them. They freed a fellow inmate bound to an oak log by burning out the staples in the log.

An early murder trial featured some theatrics by the defense counsel that would give a modern ethicist pause. The defendant was a wife accused of killing her husband with a poisoned cake. The prosecutor offered the remainder of the cake into evidence. The defense attorney approached it and calmly ate a large piece of it in front of the jury to show that it was harmless. A short while later he went to a private room in the courthouse and used a strong emetic to induce vomiting and to rid his body of the cake. His client was acquitted.

With time the soft Marshall sandstone foundation began to give way. In 1872 the board of supervisors approved a ballot proposal asking for $50,000 for a new courthouse. Voters approved the measure in the spring of 1873 by a majority of 475 among 5,311 votes cast. E. E. Myers of Detroit drew up the plans, which called for mainly pressed brick. Boulder stone made up the basement walls, and the trim was Marshall and Ohio sandstone. The attractive building was rectangular and measured about 4,500 square feet. A large cupola thrust out of the center of the roof skyward. Atop the peaked roof well above the steps to the main entrance stood a figure of a lady holding scales in her left hand and a sword in her right.

She watched in the 1950s when her building's successor was born hugging the contours of its predecessor. The county laid the cornerstone of the Calhoun County

The courtroom in the county building in Marshall now houses meetings for the county commissioners.

Building in 1953. The structure was completed in 1955 for a price of $1,550,000. It is modern in design, with very utilitarian straight lines and right angles—unmistakable for its era. The interior is functional, with the exception of a large mural of the county and its notable buildings behind the statue of old Lady Justice. The circuit courtroom is now primarily a meeting room for the board of commissioners, though the building does still house some district court functions. The jail is empty.

Battle Creek is now in many ways the de facto county seat. Circuit court and the county correctional facilities are located there in a large new facility. Battle Creek's special status dates back at least as far as a 1905 law requiring the court to sit at least two terms per year there.

In mid-February 1979 the county and city began holding court in the old post office building after the federal government moved operations. Albert Kahn designed the building, which had been dedicated on May 5, 1907. An addition closely matching the original doubled its size in 1930–31.

The county and the city spent nearly $2 million renovating the structure. Federal funds and a city-county building authority bond issue paid for the lion's share. Grants covered some costs, too. Soon, the old post office was the Hall of Justice.

But the county's presence in the building was relatively short-lived. Security problems, including the theft in 1982 of a $2,500 dedication plaque, emerged. In 1984 somebody smeared a judge's bench with red paint.

A nearby parking lot and railroad shipping yard became the site of the new Calhoun County Justice and Correctional Center. In 1989 the county voted 6,818 to 6,326 for a $20.5 million bond. The county agreed only after Battle Creek gave land and promised to clean contamination at the site. The city also purchased the Hall of Justice for $5.5 million. Some criticized the new 303,000-square-foot correctional facility as a Taj Mahal, with its televisions, air conditioning, and microwaves stocked with popcorn for the inmates. It was dedicated on June 22, 1994, and it cost $39,100,000. Cain Associates designed it, and Walbridge Aldinger managed the construction. The court moved in that August.

At the dedication, Michael Cavanaugh, Michigan's newest chief justice at the time, spoke. He noted the apparent beauty of the new facility and said that it "will come to life as it connects people and institutions." In like manner, Calhoun County connects the lives of no fewer than five chief justices.

CASS COUNTY

CASSOPOLIS—Though the historic courthouse of Cass County now stands empty, a rich and venerable history fills the land that surrounds it: from a dramatic confrontation against raiding Kentucky slaveholders in 1847 to the discovery of the only diamond ever found in Michigan's rough.

The Michigan Territory first set off Cass County and named it for Governor Lewis Cass. The governor had a long tenure serving Michigan followed by several years of federal service as secretary of state and U.S. senator. He won the Democratic nomination for president in 1848.

County commissioners first selected Geneva on Diamond Lake as the county seat. The county quickly had the action reversed due to public outcry after the self-dealing of two of the commissioners who reportedly bought tracts of land near the seat before their decision was made public.

Court first met at the house of Ezra Beardsley in Edwardsburg on August 9, 1831, as did the board of supervisors about two months later. One source contends that court was actually first held at Cassapolis, which changed spelling in 1865 to Cassopolis, "under an oak tree just south of the public square." Cassopolis offered half of its village plats for the county seat designation, which the governor approved on December 19, 1831.

The first public building was a jail that Eber Root and John Flewwelling built in early 1834 for about $350. Hewn logs made up the thirty-by-fifteen-foot frame one-story structure. The county accepted the building and modified the plank floors by having them bound with strap iron and driven full of nails. A newer jail by James Taylor came

in 1852, which in turn was replaced by a structure built in 1878–79 by W. H. Myers of Fort Wayne to the plan of T. J. Nolan & Son of the same place for $17,770. It was said of Taylor's jail that the "back door was shrunk and could be opened from the outside with a shingle."

The first courthouse came on May 1, 1835, and was used until 1841. A newer structure costing about $12,000 replaced it. Specifications called for a stone wall foundation and a wooden structure painted white and measuring fifty-four by forty-six by twenty-four feet. It combined Greek Revival and colonial architecture with four large columns and an unusual exterior stairway behind them that appeared like an inverted letter V. A small belfry capped the structure. The interior plans were elaborate, requiring "good pine siding" throughout and a sixteen-by-seventeen-foot brick safe.

A fireproof building for county offices was erected in 1860. It was called "The Fort."

The courthouse was the scene of part of a memorable dispute recalled as the Kentucky Raid of 1847. Cass County contained the intersection point of two lines of the Underground Railroad: the Illinois Line from the Mississippi River near St. Louis and the Quaker Line from Kentucky and the Ohio River. By 1848 the sympathetic Quaker population in the county had assisted an estimated 1,500 fugitive slaves in reaching refuge in Canada.

A good number of the fugitive slaves in Cass County in 1847 were from Bourbon County, Kentucky. Several slaveholders from there organized and sought to reclaim the persons they considered their legal property. A scout presented himself as an abolitionist and worked for a lawyer in Kalamazoo while secretly gathering information on where to find the runaway slaves.

The posse entered Michigan on August 1, 1847, and was foiled in Battle Creek. They regrouped in Indiana and decided to target Cass County. They captured nine fugitive slaves there, but an angry white mob confronted them and would not allow them to depart. Before any violence erupted, some Quakers persuaded the Kentuckians to seek a court hearing in Cassopolis. The court dismissed their claim on the technical grounds that they failed to offer into evidence a certified copy of Kentucky statutes that proved the legal existence of slavery in that state. The slaves at the center of the controversy were quickly whisked to Canada before the losing parties could seek recourse. The episode was one of many nationally that led to the Fugitive Slave Act of 1850, a controversial piece of legislation that the Civil War and the Thirteenth Amendment ultimately rendered null and void. Recently, the state bar dedicated a plaque commemorating how Cass County assisted fugitive slaves.

The dual location of the courthouse and the county offices beginning in 1860 led to difficulties that prompted larger construction on the public square. In 1898 the county laid the cornerstone. The wood frame structure with its limestone exterior was completed in 1899 by contractors James Rowson and A. W. Mohnke. The architects were Rush, Bowman & Rush, who selected a Richardsonian Romanesque style characteristic of the time. A red roof tops the building and its large central clock tower. A bust of Lewis Cass adorns the exterior wall near a large archway, which is flanked on the other side by a scowling gargoyle-like face.

In the early 1900s the county found another gem to go along with its new courthouse: the Dowagiac diamond, which was found in a gravel pit north of its namesake town. Fittingly, the name is from the Potawatami word "Ndowagayuk," which means "foraging ground." The find weighed in at nearly eleven and a half carats.

In 1976 the county built an additional wing along one end of the building, where county offices such as the clerk and county administrator's office are now located. On July 23, 2003, the county dedicated a new Law and Courts Building on the outskirts of Cassopolis. The Troyer Group designed the modern-inspired one-story brick building. Miller-Davis Company was the construction manager. Security concerns and cost issues motivated county leaders to explore and approve a new facility away from the old courthouse. There are no firm plans for the third courthouse, which stands empty, locked, and stripped inside of all but the courtroom furnishings.

Behind a plaque in the fourth courthouse is a time capsule. Unlike the 1899 building, it is not an empty vessel, for it holds a small part of the full and plentiful history of Cass County, where foraging the terrain for a diamond in the rough has proven successful in more than the obvious way.

CHARLEVOIX COUNTY

CHARLEVOIX—The county named for a peaceful Jesuit has had some turbulent times in its history. Pierre Francois-Xavier de Charlevoix was born in 1682 in northern France. At age sixteen he entered as a Jesuit novitiate, and after his studies he taught at a college in Quebec from 1705 until 1709.

He returned to Paris to finish his education and was ordained in 1713, again becoming a professor and teaching a young Voltaire. King Louis XV wanted to know how deeply Britain had penetrated the Great Lakes and sent Father Charlevoix to find out. He also gave Charlevoix the clandestine mission to search for a northwest passage to the Pacific. Charlevoix landed at Mackinac on July 29, 1721. It is probable but uncertain that he headed southwest and landed on the territory now named for him.

Over a century later the first permanent settlers arrived. The county was split from Emmet County and organized in 1867. A ramshackle wood building of 1870 was Charlevoix County's first courthouse. When Judge J. G. Ramsdell presided over the first court session, it was so crowded that the floor gave way. No one was injured because the floor was less than two feet above the ground.

In the stormy period of 1867 to 1897, the county seat moved between the three principal communities in the county: Charlevoix, East Jordan, and Boyne City. While attached to Emmet County, Charlevoix had won an early vote to get the county seat from Little Traverse (now called Harbor Springs), but a judge invalidated the vote on the technicality that the order for removal said "county site" and not "county seat."

With its influx of settlers, East Jordan gained a majority

and the seat in 1884. But immediately county business was muddled and the seat moved to Boyne City. Tax officials from Lansing were reportedly so confused by the situation that they returned to Lansing and washed their hands of the matter. Matters normalized in 1887, but shifting political sands gave the city of Charlevoix another chance for the seat.

The city of Charlevoix gained votes with the dissolution of Manitou County, which gave Charlevoix County the Beaver Islands. Plus, townships in the northeastern part of the county were lost to Emmet County, which weakened the vote against the city of Charlevoix. A vote decided the matter in April 1895.

The city of Charlevoix had built a town hall in 1885 for $5,865 and offered it as a county court. Only in 1897 was the offer accepted. The brick and stone building with a dark roof had three prominent features: a belfry, a hose tower (where fire hoses were hung to dry), and a cupola. All three were lost when a fire severely damaged the second floor in the early 1900s. The jail space inside was converted to offices when the county built a new jail in 1920.

In 1932 the deteriorating building was condemned for the first time. Charlevoix County was forced to pump money into the structure simply to keep it operating. An ultimatum from the state fire marshal bought matters to a head in 1956.

A vote on constructing a new county building and, perhaps to quell old grudges, to keep the county seat in Charlevoix passed with a large majority. The old courthouse was razed in 1957, and a new modern structure built around the old jail was dedicated on August 30, 1959, at a cost of

$259,259.40. Ralph S. Gerganoff was the architect, and Lake Waster Construction Company was the contractor.

Charlevoix County had finally reached a point of tranquility. That point stands in stark contrast to July 17, 1853, when the shores and waters of Charlevoix County witnessed perhaps the only land-sea battle in the history of the Great Lakes.

At that time the Mormon community on Beaver Island held political power over the area. The mainland was home to fishermen who did not get along with the Mormons. In 1851 Lansing passed a law banning the gift or sale of liquor to Native Americans. It was a measure that most traders ignored, but the Mormons took it seriously and began to enforce it. The bad blood was ready to boil over.

What happened at the Battle of Pine River is difficult to know because there are three accounts: that of the Mormons, of the fishermen, and of a captain on a passing ship who gave the fleeing Mormons sanctuary. Sheriff Miller, a Mormon sheriff from Beaver Island, embarked on some business to the mainland. He was either out to summon three men for jury duty or to apprehend three fugitives. He came expecting trouble, and therefore a flotilla of two small boats and fourteen to eighteen mostly unarmed men accompanied him.

The territory was hostile. Any Mormon setting foot on the mainland to serve process was told in no uncertain terms to expect death. A heated discussion ensued on the beach when suddenly a shot rang out. No one knows who fired or if it was accidental.

The shot sparked a hail of bullets from the fishermen, some of whom were hiding in wooded bluffs above the shore. One fisherman was wounded in the knee, and six Mormons were wounded nonfatally.

The Mormons fled and the chase was on. The angry fishermen were in hot pursuit for ten or more miles when wind conditions changed and the Mormons were within range of the guns, which riddled the boats with bullets.

Just then an upbound ship from Buffalo appeared and the captain responded to the distress call. He took the Mormons aboard and refused to turn them over to the fishermen, who returned to their shore.

The matter went to court, and indictments were sworn out against the fishermen. Fearing retribution at the hands of larger Mormon numbers, the fishermen quickly abandoned the area. And the shore where it is believed gentle Father Charlevoix landed was peaceful yet again, but only until battles for the county seat raged.

CHEBOYGAN COUNTY

CHEBOYGAN—There is an old joke purporting to explain the origin of Cheboygan's name. A Native American chief who fathered many sons was anxious for a daughter. He emerged from a wigwam as his newborn babe cried for the first time and said to those present, "she boy again."

In actuality, the name comes from "Cha-boia-gan" and means, depending on the chosen authority, place of entry, place of portage, place of harbor, or water passage. Historians surmise that the locale earned its name for being the eastern entry point of an inland waterway where canoe paddlers could travel from Lake Huron to Lake Michigan and avoid the sometimes rough and treacherous Straits of Mackinac.

The county and its seat bear the same name. For a time, the city had the nickname of "Hub City" and "Gateway to the North." Presently, it also goes by "Old Rivertown."

A county for the area was authorized in 1840. Surveyors by the name of Burt and Mullett surveyed the region in 1840–43. Two large inland lakes bear their names. Alexander McLeod, one of the first nonnative settlers, came in 1844–45 from Mackinac Island. Jacob Sammons was another early pioneer. Soon, there were log cabins, a dam, and a water-powered sawmill, foreshadowing what would become a large lumber boom.

The settlement grew into Duncan City, the first county seat of Cheboygan County that now is a ghost town. The county was organized in 1853. A simple wooden building was the courthouse until 1869. The seat was moved to Inverness Township in 1860, where a small wooden courthouse was constructed.

For $3,000, James Watson built the county's second courthouse, a mainly wood twenty-eight-by-fifty-five-foot structure completed in 1869. Court was held there on the second floor for thirty years, with county offices on the first floor. The building continues to stand and has since served many purposes: firehouse; disabled veterans' facility; community center for churches, scouting groups, and the American Red Cross; a boxing gym; city storage; and, presently, private law offices. Before the law offices moved in, the building was extensively renovated in 1983.

In September 1898 a cornerstone for a grander county courthouse with room for the sheriff and jail was laid in the city of Cheboygan, the new county seat. Located west of old

Cheboygan's second courthouse currently houses law offices.

Images of Cheboygan's predecessor courthouses hang inside their modern counterpart.

Duncan City, Cheboygan was a village in 1877 and gained the status of city in 1889.

The courthouse was a large stone and red brick building completed in February 1900 for $35,000. The roof was dark, and in the center jutted out a large and intricate clock tower. Its replacement, a modern building outside of the center of town, was complete in 1969, and the stone building was sold to a paper company, which razed the building in 1970 to create parking spaces for its employees.

Inside the current courthouse is a large graphic depiction of the 1898 courthouse with small likenesses of its two predecessors in the upper corners. Two other items connecting the current courthouse to its past are the monuments moved from the 1898 location to the new site.

The first is a war memorial capped with a large gold star. The second is a 9,035-pound cannon from the *Hartford*—the Civil War flagship of Admiral Farragut, which saw action at the Battles of New Orleans, Vicksburg, Port Hudson, and Mobile. It was first put in place in Petoskey in 1904. Finally, portraits of past circuit judges hanging behind the gallery in the current circuit courtroom suggest continuity in Cheboygan County's administration of justice.

There has been less continuity in Cheboygan's commerce and industry. A lumber boom fueled the initial rise of the area. For a time, Cheboygan's primary distinction was the world's largest sawdust pile. Town coffers swelled, and a city-owned Town Hall and Opera Theater, one of the few in the country, was built in 1877. Fire destroyed the opulent building in 1886, but it was replaced with a structure that still serves the community. Arrival of the railroad in 1882 made the area less dependent on boats.

A steep decline occurred due in large part to depletion of area forests and the effect of a tariff. In the short six years between 1894 and 1900, Cheboygan County's population fell from 9,574 to 6,489 people. The last vestige of lumbering in the area vanished when the final operating mill burned down on November 15, 1928. Since then, local industry has diversified, with an emphasis on fishing and tourism.

As long as fish and tourists find reason to flock to the land of the water passage, they will be the lifeblood of the local economy.

CHIPPEWA COUNTY

SAULT STE. MARIE—The first European settlement in Michigan is Sault Ste. Marie, county seat of Chippewa County. French settlers chose the moniker in 1641 because the spot overlooked rapids ("sault" in French) and to honor the Virgin Mary. In 1750 King Louis XIV granted title to the area to Louis le Gardeur, Sieur de Repentigny, who fell under British jurisdiction after resolution of the French and Indian War. He became Michigan's only soldier in the Revolutionary War when he refused allegiance to King George III.

But the story goes back even earlier. A local Ojibwa (also called Chippewa, for which the county is named) myth of the boys and the crane explains the founding of the settlement on the south shore of the river now called St. Marys. Two boys were fleeing their mother, who was intent on killing them. At the north shore they met a crane who heard their ordeal and agreed to fly them across the rapids.

The crane later agreed to fly the mother across but dropped her purposely in midflight into the rapids. She cracked her skull on the rocks, and her brains became the whitefish that continue to populate the waters. The crane adopted the boys and one of them married the crane's daughter and founded the settlement.

The story is very similar to the myth behind the founding of Rome, which centered on a she-wolf nursing two boys named Romulus and Remus. Two statues in front of the courthouse depict both myths. The statue of the myth of Rome is a replica of a famous statue in Italy. Chase S. Osborn, a Sault resident and governor of Michigan in 1911–12, donated the statue. His widow donated the crane myth statue.

Chippewa County was originally part of Michilimackinaw County, established in 1818 by territorial governor Lewis Cass and encompassing all of the Upper Peninsula and part of the Lower Peninsula. In 1826 Chippewa County was formed, and Sault Ste. Marie ("the Soo" for short) has been the county seat ever since.

In 1853 the first canal to Lake Superior was completed, sparking a population boom leading to the incorporation of Sault Ste. Marie in 1874. The courthouse was constructed in 1877 from sandstone extracted from the second canal. Limestone from nearby Drummond Island was also used. It is one of the oldest courthouses in Michigan that has been in continuous use. It was built on land where Reverend Abel Bingham established a Baptist mission in the 1820s. Adjoining Bingham Avenue was named for him.

William and John Scott, a local father-and-son team, were the architects, and the building was one of John's first large projects. He designed it in the Second Empire style. The stone walls are two feet thick. The tower features a clock and a bell tower with steep sloping roofs that were once covered in slate but now are capped with asphalt shingles.

Additions were completed in 1904 and in the mid-1930s with care taken both times to match the new space to the existing building. Another local architect, R. C. Sweat of Marquette, designed the 1904 addition, which at a cost of $25,000 exceeded in absolute terms the original building construction cost of $20,000. The 1877 cornerstone was opened in 1904, revealing newspapers, calling cards of county officials and local politicians, coins, a two-ounce bottle of champagne, and other items. Though capped with a cork and sealed in wax, the champagne bottle leaked,

rior were revamped. Layers of paint were removed from the judge's bench, revealing the original oak finish. Two large pillars inside the courtroom bear ornate cast iron capitals. Intricate metalworking also adorns radiators in the courtroom. A great challenge was installing an elevator to make the building barrier-free. New doors and windows were installed.

Finally, the face of the clock tower was restored, along with the wooden statue of Justice, a blind lady in a tunic holding a sword in her right hand and scales in her left hand. A professional woodcarver who also happened to be the chair of the Chippewa County Board of Commissioners restored the scales.

At the top of the tower, a flagpole was placed with an electronic sensor to automatically raise and lower the third country's flag to fly over Sault Ste. Marie, like the mythically inspired crane.

giving the papers a strong odor. After being resealed and again interred, the box was reopened and its items put on permanent display in the courthouse after rededication on November 11, 1989.

The courthouse was rededicated after a large renovation project costing over $1.2 million. The interior and exte-

HARRISON—The early part of Clare County's history had one prominent characteristic: lawlessness. From the arson of the county courthouse to the corrupt dealings of county officials, a future observer could not help but wonder how the Wild West got such a foothold in central Michigan.

Along with Antrim, Emmet, Roscommon, and Wexford Counties, Clare is named for a county in Ireland. Some attribute the name to large numbers of Irish pioneers, whereas others look to the surveyor Henry Nicholson as a native son of that part of the old country. Originally the land was called Kaykakee for a chief mentioned in an 1826 treaty. Not much else is known about him other than that his name meant "Pigeon Hawk," which was an appropriate name for the territory given that before lumbering its western townships had large pigeon flocks.

The Legislature changed the name to Clare in 1843 and attached its territory to Saginaw and then Isabella County. Clare had its first board meeting on May 1, 1871, at Farwell, the first county seat, and already trouble seemed to brew. There were allegations that itinerant lumberjacks voted illegally, often in exchange for beer. Farwell was a lumberjack town that drew the ire of farmers and homesteaders who lived elsewhere in the county and viewed the tree-fellers as uninterested in the long-term future of the county. Allegations, mainly from the newspaper in the rival town of Clare, accused the "Courthouse Ring" of corruption.

The county approved $400 for a court, later earmarking an additional $100. In 1877 the court went up in flames, and $2,000 of property was lost, as were some county records. It was widely alleged that disaffected citizens from

Clare set the fire because the court represented all that they hated about Farwell as a lumber town.

A. N. Gebhart built a temporary facility and received a contract for rent with the provision that he would get the building once the court moved. He did not wait long, for in April 1879 a vote of 439 to 106 removed the seat from Farwell to an undeveloped area near Budd Lake. The Flint and Pere Marquette Railroad donated the land, which was in the north of the county where rail lines and lumbering activity were expanding. Construction of a courthouse began on September 20, 1879, and a town sprung up almost overnight. It was called Harrison for President William Henry Harrison. The court cost a total of $2,689.06, which included $99 for stump removal to E. Unicume and $2,125 to I. Hanna for construction.

There was no jail until 1885, which contributed to the portending lawlessness about to descend on Clare County. The county's strict oversight of transportation costs for moving wrongdoers to holding facilities in neighboring counties meant that the sheriff would personally lose money on such transactions. Juries reportedly were not shy about turning defendants loose.

The environment was ripe for James Carr and his ilk. He arrived in 1880, and for the next few years his liquor and lust business ravaged law and order in Clare County. He set up a saloon kitty-corner to the courthouse. Outside of the county seat, a hard-drinking town home to numerous houses of ill repute set up shop near the Gladwin County line. For a few years in the 1880s Meredith was a booming vice town that operated with relative impunity.

At the end of December 1884, the Meredith Sharpshooter arrived. He proved to be an expert shot as he drank and shot between bystanders' feet and otherwise "in unpleasant proximity to the victim of his sport." A policeman tried to arrest him, but the shooter quickly knocked him senseless. Another officer arrived and the shooter teased him, making him take a drink and exit at the point of a gun. Then the shooter made every able-bodied man within earshot take back whatever he may have thought or said and he quietly left. The next morning the sheriff came from Harrison and arrested the shooter without incident, figuring that the shooter acted as he did "in order to get set up for the winter."

A few months earlier the county treasurer had been robbed of about $8,000 while the circus was in town. Suspicion immediately turned to one of the transient entertainers, but he was eventually exonerated. The treasurer later confessed to embezzling $1,000, and it was believed that the robbery was an inside job, but the allegedly corrupt county officials were never brought to justice. Arrival of a new sheriff and prosecutor in 1884 in an upset election meant that the outlaws' days were numbered. Three grand juries were called to look into killings, robberies, and arson.

Attention turned to Carr and his "soiled doves," some of whom were arrested and convicted in 1885. He was tried for the death of a female employee, whom Carr beat with brass knuckles. He allegedly turned to his bouncer when she was prone and said, "Finish her." While his case wound its way through different venues in Midland and Gratiot Counties, as well as the Michigan Supreme Court, Carr turned to arson.

He decided that he could not abide by his competition and set out to torch a rival's establishment, which led to a comical scene of women fleeing in their "working clothes" while men ran and buttoned their trousers. No one was killed.

Mounting legal bills and law enforcement pressure convinced Carr to move his operation to another jurisdiction. He dragged his saloon across the street to Gladwin County, which prompted a quick backlash. His buildings were raided and torn down on October 7, 1887. He died a social outcast fewer than five years later, succumbing to alcoholism and venereal disease.

Clare County moved on and busied itself with more lawful pursuits. Another colorful character entered the picture in the twentieth century. John E. "Spikehorn" Meyer opened his famous bear den and wildlife park, which ran for thirty-five years. He was a rugged individualist with a long white beard, an aversion to government regulation, and a nose for publicity. He appeared as a plaintiff or a defendant no less than thirteen separate times, all in the courts of Clare County. No one else could feed his bears, so the few times he was held in custody he was released once a day to do the job.

On July 22, 1967, Clare County dedicated its one-story brick courthouse. Brysselbout-Starke-Hacker & Simon, Inc., the architects, selected a modern and utilitarian design, which Gregory Construction Co. erected. Expansions in the rear of the building occurred in 1994 and 1998. An annex and space within a lower level were added, as was a second story.

But no amount of ingenuity could recreate the lawlessness that this region suffered as a result of rivalry with lumbermen and at the hands of Carr and his cabal. Clare County probably likes it better that way, for its courthouse complex stands in sharp contrast and opposition to those times.

CLINTON COUNTY

ST. JOHNS—Evolving metamorphosis characterizes the elusive location and appearance of the many versions of Clinton County's courthouse. But beneath the seemingly perpetual change was an abiding and permanent desire of the people to have a courthouse to call their own. Whatever its form, they always gave it the same name.

First organized independently in April 1839, the county fell under the successive realms of Wayne, Oakland, Kalamazoo, Kent, and finally Shiawassee County. Clinton County's namesake was DeWitt Clinton, the governor of New York who was a driving force behind the Erie Canal, which helped to bring much commerce and immigration to Michigan. For a time, the county seat was the settlement that bears his first name. Court was first held in the home of David Scott from 1840 until 1847. A schoolhouse was rented from 1847 to 1855 for county offices.

Court moved around private rooms and a Baptist church after 1847. In 1855 county leaders considered a motion to move the county seat to St. Johns, a centrally located town along the Detroit & Milwaukee Railroad. It was named for John Swegles, one of the state officials who examined the proposed right of way. A Baptist minister added the prefix.

An unfriendly amendment to the motion sought to replace St. Johns with "centre of Muskrat Lake." The amendment and the original resolution failed, as did more resolutions until 1857. St. Johns agreed to up the ante: donated land for a public square and $2,000 for construction. By a margin of 1,423 to 689 voters approved the move on April 6, 1857. In December the county offices moved to Plumstead Hall in St. Johns until the following year, when a more permanent brick building measuring twenty by twenty-five feet was erected and occupied.

The court had a nomadic existence in multiple private residences until the new court, which was modeled after Bay County's, was completed in October 1871 for $35,344.58, significantly over the original budget of $24,000. Part of the reason was the decision of the county to reject as too high all bids after the foundation was laid and to supervise the rest of the construction itself. On March 15, 1871, the dome was struck by lightning, which blew out some windows and completely destroyed the southeast corner at a cost of at least $500.

Oliver Hidden of Bay City was the architect. He also designed the red brick jail and sheriff's residence, which was completed in October 1876 for $10,015.53. Its modern successor was unveiled on October 23, 1950. It was state of the art at the time. Local residents could boast in its early tenure that Jackson State Prison could not handle "Crazy Jack" Hyatt and for a few weeks sent him to St. Johns. Between 1862 and 1876 there is no record of a jail in the county, leading some observers to opine tongue in cheek that perhaps people were especially law abiding in those years.

The 1871 courthouse was stone with arched windows, friezes, and a gable stationed below its distinctive cupola. A large flagpole rose from the top. A local newspaper in 1899 welcomed the prospect of a cannon for the court's lawn with an enthusiastic headline—"Hurrah! Bif! Bang!" In 1904, on December 31, a $1,000 eight-day four-faced Seth Thomas clock set was unveiled and rang in the New Year for the first time.

A hodgepodge of improvements and additions

would follow. Extensive interior remodeling happened in 1927, including the installation of fire-resistant vaults for $35,000. Another $20,000 in general renovations, including sandblasting of the full exterior, occurred in the spring of 1957. The following year a new entrance was built for $59,089.51 and judges' chambers were added. A west wing costing $165,765.56 was completed in 1965. The next year a matching east wing was unveiled. It cost $246,000. In 1969 the circuit courtroom shrunk by two rows in the rear to make room for conference and office space.

At the close of the twentieth century Clinton County grappled with its growth and the need for larger court facilities and county offices. It considered seven proposals, polled the public, and decided that razing the old structure and replacing it with a new one would be best. Demolition happened in October 1998. Beginning August 21, 1998, court moved to a temporary facility in the Southpoint Mall until a week before the unveiling of the new $17.4 million courthouse on June 22, 2000.

Its trapezoidal roof and classically inspired cupola hearken back perhaps more than any other modern Michigan courthouse to its nineteenth-century heritage. The 17,000-pound cupola of the 117,000-square-foot structure was fabricated in Kentucky. It was reassembled on the ground in St. Johns and lifted into place by a massive crane as hundreds of schoolchildren and adults looked on in the rain. It contains the original clock, which long before had been electrified. It was refurbished along with the original bell. The spiral access stairs salvaged from the old building were also placed in the new courthouse.

Photographs of the exterior and interior of the 1871 courthouse adorn the hallways of the new building. The wooden bench, jury box, courtroom trim, and some furniture were preserved and installed in the new courtroom along with art and photographs that hang on the walls.

In naming the expanded building, which houses myriad offices and functions, county leaders insisted on Clinton County Courthouse. They recognized that "courthouse" is what people would naturally call the place. The architecture of the structure exudes a dignified design proclaiming that the red-brick and green-trimmed edifice gazing down at the public is first and foremost a court.

CRAWFORD COUNTY

GRAYLING—The history of Crawford County demonstrates that a river's headwaters can be rough. Crawford's Au Sable River flows from Grayling to Lake Huron, and the Manistee River heads the other way to Lake Michigan. The valley between these rivers has seen its ups and down.

Crawford County was organized in 1879. For a short while, the area was called Brown County. In 1840, the name was changed to Shawono, which means southerner, a name given by others to the Shawnee tribe. This name was short-lived, as Crawford was chosen for good in 1843. Historians are unsure if the county name traces to different land in what was then the Wisconsin Territory, or if the intent was to honor Colonel William Crawford. A friend of George Washington, the colonel had been captured and burned at the stake near Sandusky, Ohio, in 1782. The county was at various times attached to Cheboygan, Antrim, and Kalkaska Counties.

At first the county seat was in Pere Cheney, a village that grew around the sawmill of G. M. Cheney. Now a ghost town, it was also called Cheney and Center Plains. When the seat moved to Grayling, the railroad gave land for the courthouse.

Grayling was platted in 1874 by the Saginaw & Jackson Railroad. It was named after the grayling trout, an abundant fish in the Au Sable River. The town was formerly called Crawford and Crawford Station. It was incorporated as a city in 1935. Fishermen flock to the county's rivers every season, contributing to the tourism industry that took root locally.

The first courthouse was built in 1879. Around this time, the county had a population of 1,159. An early photograph shows that the wooden building stood on a large lawn surrounded by a wooden fence. It was three stories with a dark angled roof, several chimneys, and a tall flagpole rising from behind a small tower atop the building. Its lifespan was brief, as it was burned down on a dark winter's night in 1902. The culprit was inmate Mrs. Henderson, who reportedly set her straw mattress on fire.

A red brick courthouse with a gray roof was erected in 1909. Its two stories featured arched and rectangular windows. Centered atop the structure was a multilevel bell tower, which dominated the building's silhouette. Bold white letters above the second story and just below the triangular portico spelled "Crawford." Visitors can see photographs and paintings of this old courthouse in Grayling.

The present courthouse was built in 1969 according to the specifications of architects and engineers Harley Ellington Cowin and Stirton, Inc. The general contractor was Elzinga and Volker, Inc. The utilitarian one-story building stands on prime sloped land near the river. The light brown exterior is capped with dark brown bands. One of those bands is the background for reminiscent bold white lettering that declares "County Building." A large flagpole anchors the front of the building complex, where a sign directs the public in opposite directions to "Inmate Receiving" and "Jail Visiting." Toward the rear of the building, the flagpole finds its counterpart in a tall communications tower.

Inside, the main courtroom is spartan, with functional tables, benches, and orange chairs. A simple state seal and the flags of America and Michigan frame the modest bench, which looks down upon a minimalist podium and, along the wall, a chalkboard. A small aesthetic touch strikes a geometric note behind the bench: protruding wall blocks arrayed in isolated areas with no particular pattern. A younger demographic might be reminded of the elements of the video game Tetris.

The 46th Circuit Court found itself in a different courtroom in the summer of 2003, when it participated as plaintiff in a six-day trial in Kent County. The defendants were Crawford County, its board of commissioners, and Kalkaska County. Otsego County was also involved in the litigation, though its role ended before the trial on the merits. The dispute centered upon the funding of court employee health and pension benefits. Fourteen witnesses testified, and 300 exhibits, which measured over 200 inches tall when stacked, were entered into the record. The estimated legal fees were over a million dollars. The plaintiff court won at trial, releasing a posttrial comment quoting Lincoln, who believed "in a short statute of limitations in political matters." The statement ended, "Enough is enough."

With the conclusion of the appellate process, the political headwaters of Crawford County again grew calm, as another chapter of the history of the Au Sable River Valley closed.

DELTA
COUNTY

ESCANABA—The Delta County Courthouse of today stands in stark contrast to the one it replaced in 1961. Its predecessor was valued at $20,000 when it was dedicated in 1882 at a time when the county had a population of 6,812. Today's courthouse cost millions if one adds its original cost to renovation and expansion expenditures, and the county population has grown to over 38,000.

The old courthouse was built mainly of brick and wood in the Victorian style. It boasted high ceilings, tall windows, and a circular staircase. The current courthouse is modern in design, measuring 263 by 109 feet, and was built at a cost of $680,000, including a $50,000 bequest in the will of the late Catherine Bonifas. Its masonry walls and floor and steel-frame roof are meant to be fire resistant. In many ways, the new courthouse took its design cues from the failings of the old courthouse.

Time was not kind to the old courthouse. After World War II, its grand tower was removed because of increasing structural weakness. In 1957, a local newspaper article indicted the building for passing "its useful days." The writer described a lack of vault space and fireproofing, inadequate electrical wiring, limited restroom facilities, poor lighting and ventilation, and a shabby appearance due to cracked

steps, crumbling mortar, and warped doors. Indeed, it was reported that rainwater damage caused plaster to fall in one of the courtrooms during proceedings. Two years later, Delta County broke ground for its new courthouse and would, before long, raze the old one.

G. Arntzen, Architect, & Co. prepared the final plans for the courthouse with an eye toward avoiding the shortfalls of the old courthouse. For instance, the courthouse has large fireproof vault rooms in its basement for storage of county records. The interior liberally employs glass, stone, and wood rather than the plastered walls and dark woodwork of the old building. The construction contract went to Erling Arntzen, an Escanaba contractor. Groundbreaking occurred in 1959.

There had been much building beforehand. Delta County was first surveyed in April 1843. In addition to its present territory, it included all of Menominee County and parts of Dickinson, Iron, and Marquette Counties. The county name is due to its original triangular shape, like the capital Greek letter delta. L. A. Roberts, a fur trader, was the first recorded European settler, arriving in 1830.

Historians believe that Etienne Brule, the first European known to have visited the Upper Peninsula, may have tra-

This photograph depicts the 1882 courthouse of Delta County.

public building was a jail for its first convict and a residence for its sheriff.

Justice was swift in those days. One historical account of the county mentions a horse thief who stole on a Monday and was duly convicted and sentenced by the following Monday. Pragmatism, not passion or prejudice, motivated such haste. Travel was difficult for witnesses and jurors, and circuit-riding judges had busy schedules.

Though perhaps at a different pace, Delta County continues to dispense justice, now in a well-appointed facility. To alleviate overcrowding, work began in 1994 for a second floor for the courthouse. The first floor was also updated at this time in order to bring it up to code. The price of construction and renovation topped out at over $5 million. The second-floor hallway displays photographs of the old county jail and artwork depicting the original courthouse.

But the most prominent artwork appears outside on the south wall of the courthouse facing Ludington Street. It is a massive bas-relief sculpture of Delta County. The Delta County Board commissioned T. D. Vinette to create and mount the ten-by-eleven-and-a-half-foot bronze sheet sculpture. Falling ill in 1999, Mr. Vinette received the help of Ritch Branstrom.

At its unveiling on November 1, 2000, the chairman of the county board presented the sculpture to local citizens as a symbol representing tribute to local talent and inspiration for future generations in Delta County. For the casual visitor, the sculpture ensures that there is no mistaking Delta County's courthouse for that of any other Michigan county.

versed the Delta County area in 1618. In 1634, Jean Nicolet passed by as he looked for a northwest passage to China. French Jesuit missionaries reported in 1659 that there were Native American villages at the head of Little Bay de Noc near Rapid River. The Nokay Native Americans and Bay de Noc derive their names from the French who called both Nocquet.

It was only a matter of time before more settlement and industry arrived in Delta County. Much of it was and is in Escanaba, the county seat, which sits on the northern shore of Lake Michigan. The origin of Escanaba's name is unclear. There are Ojibwa words sounding like Escanaba that mean "land of the red buck" and also "flat rock." E. P. Royce, who first platted the city in 1864, said that it was named after the Escanaba River, which he was told meant "flat rock." A Native American treaty from approximately 1830 called the river Skonawby.

Daniel Goodwin of the Michigan Supreme Court was the first judge in the area. He rode circuit throughout the Upper Peninsula before creation of the present judicial districts. In May 1865, he presided over the trial of Timothy Donovan. Donovan killed a man, and the jury convicted him of assault without intent to murder. Judge Goodwin imposed a sentence of one year in the county jail.

But there was a slight problem. Delta County had no jail. In fact, Delta County had no public buildings whatsoever. Court and other public functions were held in private buildings, or outside. Accordingly, Delta County's first

DICKINSON COUNTY

IRON MOUNTAIN—The proud home of sports figures Tom Izzo and Steve Marriuci is also home to a more-than-presentable courthouse. Dickinson County was the last of Michigan's eighty-three counties to organize, which it did in 1891. It was named for Donald M. Dickinson, a prominent Detroit attorney who served as postmaster general during the first administration of Grover Cleveland (1885–89). Iron Mountain was the center of commerce and was the natural choice for the county seat.

Within five years of its organization, Dickinson County erected its courthouse and jail. The jail, a castlelike wing attached to the courthouse, was in a state of disrepair in the early 1970s when the Michigan Department of Corrections threatened condemnation.

The jail moved to a new facility in 1975, leaving the old jail abandoned and crumbling. Dickinson County let it languish until 1979, when water damage and general disrepair posed a safety threat. The county made a fateful choice. It decided to renovate rather than to raze.

At a final cost of over $1.8 million, which included federal funding, the jail was spared, and it now houses county administrative offices. On May 15, 1980, the courthouse and jail were added to the National Register of Historic Places.

The exterior is made of rock-faced brick trimmed with Portage entry sandstone and a slate roof. Massive granite columns support the grand archway above the front entrance. The architectural style is Richardsonian Romanesque. The interior at the time of unveiling featured hardwood finishing and oak doors. Presently, the interior is significantly modernized.

Upon completion of the courthouse, a local newspaper reported on the first seventeen cases on the court's docket.

The cryptic reports listed the names of the parties and the type of case. Among them were a divorce action, a charge of violation of liquor laws, and "bastardy."

More detail was provided for a case that the author deemed the "most interesting and sensational." It was a slander action: *Ex-Editor Fitzgibbon v. Ed. Harvey.* The

author commented on the caliber of the lawyers on both sides, writing that the arguments would be interesting to hear, which may have prompted some readers to attend and visit Dickinson County's newest venue for trial practice, which some consider a performing art.

Dickinson County nearly made one of the workers who helped to build the courthouse and jail the first inhabitant of the latter. Doro Bussetti was found guilty of assault and battery and ordered to pay a fine and costs in the amount of $8.75. He had no money and appealed to friends in court for assistance, which was not forthcoming. After an hourlong search he, according to a local newspaper, "grew despondent and informed the officer in charge that he might as well lock him up."

But Bussetti happened upon a friend in front of the courthouse who paid Bussetti's fine. Instead, the honor of inaugurating Dickinson County's jail fell upon an unfortunate lumberjack named Edward Goodrich.

Goodrich was found late one night wandering the streets dazed and covered in frozen blood from deep gashes on his head and face. He apparently squandered in the span of three hours the money that he had earned and saved in the past three months. He was found guilty of being drunk and disorderly. Unable to pay the fine, he was sentenced to fifteen days in jail. The account ran under the following headlines: "First Boarder . . . He Was Howling Drunk."

Sheriff Charles Anderson required early prisoners to earn their day's rations of mush, milk, cold turkey, and mince pie. While wearing a ball and chain, each prisoner helped to clear the debris left behind by the builders of the court and jail. A local report lamented the fact that the ball and chain limited the work that each prisoner could do, yet concluded, "the amount of labor accomplished by the prisoners is very gratifying when the cost is taken into consideration." Later, prisoners assisted in the landscaping of the grounds surrounding the complex.

In February 1912 the courthouse nearly burned to the ground. The fire was detected in the basement and originated at or near the furnace. The whole building filled with a dense smoke. When it cleared after the fire was extinguished, damage was estimated to total $2,150 to $3,200, well under the $49,000 of insurance covering the building at the time.

In spite of the threat of fire and water, the historic Dickinson County Courthouse still stands on the grounds gently sloping down toward Stephenson Avenue, pride manifest on a hill for Iron Mountain and the rest of the county.

EATON COUNTY

CHARLOTTE—Fire kissed the heels of the statue of the goddess clutching the scales of justice when the bell on Eaton County's second courthouse struck its death knell. The damage was extensive, but the county repaired the courthouse and did not vacate it until 1976. Still it stands, now in the hands of a private nonprofit organization working to make it a museum and educational center, but it remains for the public.

Michigan named Eaton County in honor of John Eaton, the secretary of war for President Jackson. Charlotte is the county seat, and it commemorates the wife of an early landholder from New York. A visitor who fails to pronounce the name with an accent on the second syllable reveals his or her status to anyone within earshot, who might politely respond that they are a far cry from North Carolina.

Originally attached to St. Joseph and then Kalamazoo Counties, Eaton was organized in its own right on December 12, 1837. In the prior year, three appointed commissioners selected a large poplar tree in the center of a prairie and wrote upon its trunk in red chalk "county site." Until 1840 court met in Bellevue at a house but then moved to Eaton Centre, which evolved into Charlotte.

The Eagle Hotel made room for the court and jail. William Stoddard was both the host and the jailer. The county approved $500 for a court in 1844. S. E. Millett and Lewis Scour built the simple Greek Revival structure, which was completed in 1846 for closer to $1,000. The first benches cost seventy-five cents each. The main room measured twenty-four by forty-two feet and had an arched plaster ceiling. Two wings measuring eighteen by fourteen feet later created space for jury rooms. The building moved locations at least five times before it ended up in Bennett Park, where restoration could happen. It is rented for occasions such as weddings.

A small belfry was added to accommodate a reluctantly accepted bell. Ohio businessman John P. Reznor donated a bell and paid to have it shipped to the place where he was party to a number of collection actions. The commissioners first rejected the gift, with some reasoning that their constituents lived too far away to hear the bell. The opposite side, with help from a local newspaper editor, pressed the matter and prevailed upon the county to accept the bell. A different bell replaced it in the second courthouse, but the original bell found space mounted on a pedestal in the current courthouse lobby.

In 1867 authorities declared the court unsafe. It was moved and used as a church, school, library, carriage house, and garage before settling in its current confines. The county in the meanwhile used Sampson Hall, a recently completed brick building that would later become an opera hall.

By a majority of about three thousand votes the county in 1882 approved $40,000 for a new courthouse. The county laid a 2,000-pound Berea sandstone cornerstone on July 4, 1883. David W. Gibbs of Toledo designed the three-and-a-half-story Renaissance Revival brick building, which was dedicated in 1886. Miles, Cramer and Horn of the same city built it. The final price was $71,306.79. It measures one hundred four by ninety-seven feet. The height to the base of the tower is sixty-four feet, with the tower itself measuring thirty-eight feet. The nine-foot pressed zinc figure of Lady Justice brings the total height to one hundred eleven feet. Local subscription paid for the bell and clock.

Rough-cut fieldstone makes up the basement walls. Red brick forms the upper stories, with galvanized iron for the cornices, pediments, portico ceiling, and tower covering. The tower has three levels—a square base, a columned open belfry, and an octagonal domed tower. Below it inside is a rotunda with a colored skylight.

Earthen color tiles and black-and-white marble make up much of the interior floors. The wood trim, which is often hand-carved, is native black walnut and butternut. Romeo Berra of Toledo painted the frescoes in the courtroom on the second floor. Original vents above the chandeliers, formerly gas and now electric, as of 1898, make for high winter heating bills, according to an employee who works at the courthouse.

A fire on July 4, 1894, threatened the building. At least two theories explain the cause of the fire. One account claims that painters using a lamp to burn old paint off the

cornice of the belfry started the fire. Another account suggests that spontaneous combustion was the cause. Three hollow spread-winged eagle figurines atop globes once stood on the roof of the building. They attracted birds, who deposited flammable nesting materials inside the gossamer zinc sculptures.

Whatever the origin of the fire, there were heroes who climbed atop the roof and courageously fought the blaze. An observer likened one of them to "a pea on a hot griddle." As the flames crawled up toward the goddess of justice, the six thousand-pound bell chimed six times for the evening hour and then promptly crashed to the ground along with much of the roof and the lady and eagle figurines. The bell was beyond repair, and the eagles were not replaced, but Lady Justice was restored, though she no longer holds her scales, which are instead on display in the building.

Josephine Johnson, a local poet, found inspiration in the ill-fated bell and penned the following: "With true courage and hope, like the clock let us stand / And strike for the right."

The county had to spend about $24,000 to restore the building, which also suffered some water damage. The tile floor below the rotunda slopes due to the impact of the falling bell and debris. The tile manufacturer had discontinued some of the colors needed for replacement, which is visible in the different appearance of part of the floor. The building gained a number of improvements, including a steel frame for the roof and tower, as well as steel lath on all-new walls and ceilings.

In 1952 a remodeling project sealed off the west entrance and added a jury room. It was one of the final changes to the courthouse before the county vacated it. The building is now home to displays on local history, from political organization of the county, to a schoolroom, to a vintage doctor's office.

Eaton County broke ground on January 24, 1975, for a new court facility on the outskirts of town. The previous year it acquired a seventy-four-acre site for $63,000. The new building was dedicated on July 4, 1976. It is 87,700 square feet and cost about $4 million. Robert Cain & Associates of Kalamazoo designed the modern brick building, which also houses the offices of many county departments. TerHorst & Rinzema Construction Company of Grand Rapids built it.

The bell on display in the lobby is the one Reznor gave to Eaton. It connects the first courthouse to the third. The second finds its connection in the bell and clock tower before the entrance of the new courthouse. Its disconnected design and use of fireproof materials may betray a desire to not repeat the fate of the bellowing but broken second bell of Eaton County.

EMMET COUNTY

PETOSKEY—The only constant for Emmet County is change. Originally part of Mackinac County, Lansing in 1840 carved out Tonedagana County. It was named in honor of an Ottawa chief who signed a number of treaties ceding parts of Michigan to the United States.

The name was changed in 1843 to Emmet. The namesake is Robert Emmet, an Irish patriot who led a revolt in 1803 resulting in the assassination of the Lord Chief Justice. Britain tried him, and he was hung and then beheaded for treason.

Though independent on paper, Emmet County did not organize until 1853. Robert Strang, the Mormon leader from Beaver Island, convinced Lansing to fold Charlevoix into Emmet County that same year. Its first elections were in 1855, and the Mormon vote carried the day.

Non-Mormons on the mainland did not approve of the situation and soon got the Legislature to create a different county for Beaver Island. Though Emmet's county seat was formally in Mackinaw City, county business was transacted in Little Traverse (which in 1881 was renamed Harbor Springs) until 1867.

On April 1 of that year, Charlevoix lost a vote of ninety-nine to eighty-five to move the county seat to Charlevoix. Bitter feelings lingered, and the politics got dirty. County records and the county seal mysteriously disappeared. Suspicion centered on the county clerk, and a warrant for embezzlement was sworn out against him. But before the court could do much with the case Lansing granted Charlevoix its own county and declared that Little Traverse would be the seat of what remained of Emmet County. The records suddenly reappeared.

Several years later a growing population in Petoskey and a decade of agitation finally persuaded Little Traverse to allow a public vote on moving the county seat. Only when Petoskey offered offices in its new city hall for fifty years for one dollar a year did Little Traverse assent. Charlevoix campaigned against the idea because it feared losing some of its northern townships to Emmet County if the seat moved to nearby Petoskey.

The vote carried on April 7, 1902, and the county seat officially moved to where it has been ever since: Petoskey. The name originates from "Pe-to-se-ga"—a native word for "the rising sun." Neyas Petosega (1787–1888) was born to his Ojibwa mother as his father, an employee of the Astor Fur Company, saw shafts of light from the morning sun penetrate the sky. His name changed to Ignatius Petoskey after he became Catholic and Jesuits convinced him that Ignatius, the name of the founder of their priestly order, was the same as Neyas. Petoskey was among the first to settle on the west side of Traverse Bay, and the settlement that grew around him came to bear his name.

Petoskey's first courthouse was completed in 1902 for $40,000. It was brick and stone with an angular roof and an imposing square tower capped with a four-sided clock and a cupola. Private money purchased the clock at the 1902 Buffalo Exposition. Though the building was razed in 1968 to make way for its modern replacement, the clock was put in storage before it was placed atop the historical museum and former depot building.

The 500-pound clock and Liberty Bell replica weighed down the top of the old depot and threatened structural damage. A new home was found for it when the county designated space on the bayfront and acquired a steel tower for the clock in 1996. Standing sixty-two feet tall and weighing in at thirteen tons, it is quite the landmark. It stands near the harbor that saw Emmet County grow explosively once the land opened up to private acquisition in 1874. By 1882, Petoskey was a booming lumber town of 2,500.

The third lawyer to set up shop in Petoskey was Charles J. Pailthorp, age twenty-seven and a graduate of the Law Department at the University of Michigan, on April 23, 1875. He had a distinguished career that ended when he argued his last case in 1940 at the age of 92 before the Michigan Supreme Court.

In the 1890s he was the circuit judge for Emmet and three neighboring counties. He reportedly enjoyed telling how he would hold court at Tim Rafferty's saloon in St. James on Beaver Island. The bar was his bench, and the jurors, witnesses, attorneys, parties, and public sat on beer kegs.

His daughter described in an unpublished memoir a particularly bad scene in Cheboygan. Pailthorp was presiding over court, and the conditions were intolerable—sawdust on the floor, people chewing and spitting tobacco without a spittoon, a burning furnace, and, consequently, an awful odor. Judge Pailthorp grew sick and vowed to never return until Cheboygan cleaned up the place.

Another notable character connected to Emmet County is Ernest Hemingway. His family had a summer cottage at Walloon Lake where they would bring young Ernest every summer. Researchers have found that much of his literature was based on his youthful experiences and that he did not bother to change the names of some of the characters in his work. He probably rarely found occasion to visit the courthouse, but the historical museum has a copy of his will that went through Emmet County Probate Court.

Shortly before Hemingway died, Emmet County unveiled its new courthouse and county building in 1960.

Its exterior is mainly brick with narrow vertical and horizontal windows. The county and city seal appear on one corner of the building, which was renovated in 1990. In December 2005, Emmet County unveiled a substantial new wing, which houses the district court and an expansion of the jail. It is connected to its predecessor, and demolition of an Elks lodge made room for the project. The wavy exterior of the building undulates as it contrasts itself with its angular counterpart.

Since 1975 the foyer of the 1960 building has been home to a Civil War cannon made by the Revere Copper Co. of Boston. Petoskey businessmen bought it in 1882. Four days after it arrived, it was fired on June 30, 1826, when President Garfield's assassin was hung. Less than a week later it took part in a hundred-gun reveille for Independence Day. Earlier, the cannon had been on display in a public park. The cannon's migration, like that of the county seat, the people who came and went, and the shifting borders of Emmet County, is but another example of ever-changing Emmet County.

GENESEE COUNTY

FLINT—There are two sides to the present Genesee County Courthouse: old and new, twentieth and twenty-first century, respectively. Such is the consequence of the decision to build a modern addition to the historic building and to meticulously restore the interior. The connection

between past and present is by no means seamless, but there is an intended and obvious level of continuity.

Genesee derives its name from Genesee County, New York, the original home of many early settlers. The Flint River was named for its rocky bed, which Native Americans called Pawanunking. The town got its current name in 1836, having been called at various times Grand Traverse, Todd's Crossing, and Flint River. The territorial government created Genesee County on March 28, 1835. For judicial purposes, it initially remained attached to Oakland County. During 1837 and 1838, Genesee County used for court purposes the upper story of Stage & Wright's store and hall above the store that Benjamin Pearson owned.

The first courthouse was built in 1838 on the land where the current one stands. An early illustration depicts it as a simple light-colored two-story building with a peaked roof and two chimneys. It was made of solid oak logs with a jail on the ground floor and the courtroom above it. A fire that an inmate likely started burned it to the ground on February 21, 1866.

Over the coming months the county built the second courthouse, which was completed in 1867 for $50,244. It was brick with two stories and a bell tower. It remained in use until 1903. The following year the county completed work on a Renaissance Revival building with a large dome as its most prominent feature. It was completed on April 24, 1905, just under the budgeted $100,000 by Reed Brothers Contracting. It was dedicated during Flint's golden jubilee, with vice president Charles W. Fairbanks attending.

This building too succumbed to fire on March 14, 1920. Photographs on display depict the old courthouse in ruins, gutted and covered in ice from the spewing fire hoses. In its wake on the Ides of March came the eve of several years of debate surrounding plans for a new courthouse.

Finally the county, after rejecting other proposals, approved $750,000 for the new building, which was built in 1925 and 1926. It came in under budget at $710,000 and three weeks early. Frederick D. Madison of Royal Oak designed the neoclassical structure, which looks very much like several federal courthouses in Michigan that were built during the same architectural era.

At the building's completion, the board of supervisors released a resolution that read in part:

> Behold! Here it is, an ornate, finished product of cumulative intelligence, culture, and character; modern, massive and distinctive, without rotunda or dome, enclosing useless space; built for service, being composed of corridors, and rooms, spacious and commodious, harmoniously arranged into groups of mutual relations, suited to complex Public functions and usefulness . . . .

The full resolution is on display inside the courthouse.

The building is five stories and has a concrete-frame structure that is faced with Indiana limestone. It also features marble wainscoting, American walnut woodwork, and wrought iron handrails. Two large bronze standards are near the Saginaw Street entrance. They hold glass globes, beneath which are light fixtures.

Thirty years after this building's unveiling, it welcomed a neighbor on the southwest corner that would house probate court. The Frank L. MacAvinchey Building stood four stories tall, was modern and utilitarian in design, and was razed to make way for the courthouse's current addition.

CHMP, Inc., designed the curved-face but otherwise polygonal addition. Sorensen Gross Construction Co., Inc.,

broke ground on September 28, 1999, the seventy-fourth anniversary of the groundbreaking for the 1926 building. The new addition was dedicated on July 10, 2001.

The hallmark of the courthouse is its art. The courtrooms on the old side of the building have murals, whereas the modern addition does not. They survived in spite of renovations in the 1970s that added air conditioning, lowered ceilings, and painted over or carted away the artwork of Edgar Spier Cameron of Illinois. Recent restorations have faithfully returned the courtroom murals. Planning for the renovation began in 1990, and work was completed after several stages with rededication events on September 12–14, 2003.

Courtroom 2 was spared the most and remained truest to its historical appearance. Above the bench from left to right are three figures in separate sections depicting Mosaic, Natural, and Roman law. There are also two fasces, a Roman symbol of authority, which are bundles of rods bound around an ax. Portraits of judges who presided here appear elsewhere on the walls of the courtroom.

Courtroom 1 relied on black-and-white photographs and the few remaining sections of mural that were left above the lowered ceiling. The county raised the ceiling again and restored the mural behind the bench, which featured the industries that brought economic development to Genesee: lumbering, agriculture, and manufacturing.

Courtroom 3 was the largest in the building, extending almost the complete length of the building to Saginaw Street. The courtroom was shortened and its ceiling lowered. A partial wall capped with a banister separates the smaller courtroom from its new office space. The mural is a scene of the crossing of the Flint River at Saginaw Street. At this spot Jacob Smith, the founder of Flint, established his trading post.

The last historic courtroom is the original probate courtroom. It was altered rather significantly, beginning with the addition of a jury box shortly after construction. The most recent renovation restored the light fixtures, raised the ceiling again, and gold-leafed the eagle behind the bench. Portraits of the Big Four, prominent justices of the Michigan Supreme Court who served together, are also behind the bench. Where larger portraits of Thomas Jefferson and John Marshall once existed are now two artistic renderings of Lady Justice. The images of Jefferson and Marshall were not original to the courtroom and had deteriorated.

Old gave way to new in the case of the portraits in the original probate courtroom. But elsewhere in the Genesee Courthouse, what was, what is, and what shall be find a way to share common space.

GLADWIN COUNTY

GLADWIN—Major Henry Gladwin is the namesake of this county and its seat. He was the British military leader who held Fort Detroit during an uprising led by Chief Pontiac in 1763 to 1764. A large portrait of him by a local artist hangs in the courthouse.

Elias Steel's barn is where Gladwin County first conducted its government business beginning in 1875. Chappel Dam and Cedar vied for designation as the county seat. The struggle was one-sided after the former burned down in a fire of unknown origin. In 1883 Cedar changed the name of its post office to Gladwin, as there was another Cedar elsewhere in Michigan.

The cornerstone for the first proper court was laid in early 1876. The county occupied it in October 1878 at a cost of $17,000. Fred Hollister of Saginaw replaced the first unrecorded contractor. The contract was assigned to two other contractors before the project was finally finished. It was three stories of brick measuring forty-five by sixty feet. It also featured four fireproof vaults. The county paid J. A. Wells for the job of "slicking up and fencing the Court House grounds." Some called the building "a rank extravagance," but there it stood and served until it was razed in the shadow of its replacement in 1941. In its time it would also serve the purpose of church, regular and Sunday schoolhouse, and dance hall.

The old cornerstone was unsealed on September 18, 1939. Its contents included a copy of the *Midland Sun* dated October 18, 1876, a *New York Illustrated Times* from three days later, an 1863 penny, a piece of rock, and a horse chestnut. The newspapers were badly deteriorated. Some of the items were placed in the new cornerstone along with contemporary newspapers and a photograph of the old courthouse.

An oil boom in the late 1930s paid for the new courthouse. Unlike neighboring counties, Gladwin held its oil tax revenue in a reserve fund for the express purpose of funding a new courthouse. The money did not quite suffice, however, and voters rejected a bond proposal for another $30,000 in April 1940. To protect his interest and that of his employees, Charles Engelhardt, the general contractor, served notice that he would lock the doors to the unfinished building until the county was able to pay him to complete the work. It took some doing because of state law limiting tax millages, but the matter was solved when a compromise bond for $16,000 passed in September 1940. In total, the building cost $82,000.

In its foundation are large granite slabs bearing the inscribed names of Gladwin's sixteen townships. Higher up there are etchings depicting some popular county activities: farming, commerce, bricklaying, hunting, lumbering, and skiing. Interspersed throughout the facades of the building are decorative bricks with simple designs. Facing north, a large inscription tells passersby to make no mistake, for they gaze upon the Gladwin County Court House.

Inside, the court has an attractive lobby area with a decorative ceiling and a floor depicting a Native American chief in profile. This lobby is no longer used as an entrance. A 1976 addition to the rear added new space and a different entrance near the parking lot. It is here where visitors meet Major Gladwin's portrait. Elsewhere visitors see a different portrait of Gladwin the county in the form of a mural depicting a number of Gladwin scenes. This mural was added to a wall along the main stairway where expansion removed an earlier window.

The courtroom on the second floor is unmistakably art deco in design, particularly in its decorative plaster and ribbed faux stone columns. Above the bench there is an octagonal bas-relief of Lady Justice, who holds scales in one hand and a sword in the other. Jurors sit in original wooden swivel chairs that are bolted to the floor. They appear to at least have newer cushions for comfort.

Outside, an imposing brick war memorial lists names of local citizens who served and died in American wars. A pair of twelve-pound howitzer cannons from a Civil War boat sunk in Pensacola, Florida, adorns the memorial. A plaque indicates that they were stolen in 1988 and returned "after an extensive search nation-wide." They greet both friend and foe, standing guard much like the artillery on which Major Gladwin depended when he repelled warring

Chief Pontiac. Though distant in time and space from this county seat, one can only guess what ruling order might have taken root here had Gladwin not held his fortress.

GOGEBIC COUNTY

BESSEMER—Farther west than St. Louis, Missouri, and wholly within the Central Time Zone, Gogebic County may qualify as the Wild West of Michigan. The most celebrated murder trial within the county reportedly was the last stagecoach robbery east of the Mississippi River.

It happened on Stagecoach Road on the south shore of Lake Gogebic, a popular resort area that, among others, bankers from nearby states frequented. One unfortunate group of four such bankers crossed paths with Rheinhardt "Reimund" Holzhey, a twenty-two-year-old German immigrant who spoke broken English but was fluent in the universal language of violence.

He met the four when he guided them on a fishing trip. Later, in the morning of August 26, 1889, when they were riding in a modified covered wagon on their way to catch a train home, Holzhey flagged them down and they stopped. Thinking he was joking when he demanded a "little kollection dis morning," he was asked how much he wanted. Revealing a revolver in each hand, Holzhey said, "I vill take $500."

Pretending to comply, a member of the party reached into his pocket but brandished a pistol and shot at Holzhey, who then let loose with both revolvers. He struck the

shooter in the mouth and the knee and hit Adolph G. Fleischbein twice above the right hip as the latter tried to step off the coach. The horses spooked and fled with the remaining passengers.

Help arrived for Fleischbein, who was left on the road, and he was brought to the Gogebic Hospital in Bessemer at 4:30 p.m. He died of blood loss the following morning at 6:15 a.m. Meanwhile, a massive manhunt was on for Holzhey. He spent three days walking the woods before he boarded a train and again traveled by foot to the town of Republic. When he signed in as Henry Plant and gave no residence at the Republic House, the son of the owner grew suspicious. Authorities were waiting on August 31 when Holzhey checked out, whereupon he was apprehended.

The "personable young desperado" (according to one record) called "Black Bart" became a bit of a folk hero. Whitesides Studio of Ironwood had him hold a rifle and dressed him in a cartridge-laden vest and a cowboy hat, mimicking the famous photograph of Billy the Kid.

He was quickly brought to trial, convicted of first-degree murder, and sentenced to life in prison at Marquette, where he arrived on November 16, 1889. Six months into his sentence, he fought with another prisoner and threatened to cut his throat. The warden shot a knife out of Holzhey's hand, taking four fingers with it. The troubled prisoner was sent to Ionia, where he reportedly underwent brain surgery.

After the surgery, the headaches about which Holzhey complained were gone. He became a model prisoner, working as the prison librarian, newspaper editor, and photographer. Governor Fred Warner commuted his sentence in 1911 to forty years. Holzhey was eligible for parole and was quickly released. He committed suicide in 1952.

That Gogebic County would have such a sensational trial so early in its history is unusual. The county was drawn off Ontonagon County and organized in 1887. Its name is native in origin ("a-go-je-bic" or "gogebing" or "gu-gwa-ga-bing"), meaning "rocky dividing lake" or "place of dividing." The county seat is named for Henry Bessemer, the English inventor who created the iron reduction process that bears his name. Ironwood, a larger city called Michigan's western gateway, alleged ballot tampering after the election awarding the county seat to Bessemer.

The courthouse, jail, and sheriff's office were completed in 1888 for about $50,000 by architects Charlton and Kuenzli and contractor Herman Gundlach. The exterior is red Lake Superior sandstone, though some spots appear green due to years of dripping rainwater. The rock was quarried from a mountainside a half mile away. Some criticized the courthouse for being in a valley rather than on a nearby hilltop.

In 1915 the courthouse was enlarged. The original jail and sheriff's office were demolished and replaced in 1965. Restoration and refurbishment of the courthouse occurred in 1974, along with an addition on the north side to connect the complex to the social services building. The project cost $650,000.

Inside the circuit courtroom where Holzhey was tried is an arch-shaped mural behind the judge's bench. It depicts three female figures representing Law, Mercy, and Justice. One can only hope that Gogebic County did its best at an early age to deliver Holzhey, his victims, and the citizens at large all three.

GRAND TRAVERSE COUNTY

TRAVERSE CITY—The Grand Traverse Courthouse stands atop a hill where time literally and figuratively stood still. When the wrecking ball threatened, a confluence of dedicated people proved that the building could be saved cost effectively. The clock stopped for this court, and its life was extended indefinitely. Earlier when the clock in its tower gave out and stood motionless for a decade, a local engineer volunteered his labor to repair it.

Grand Traverse County came to be in 1853. The name originates from a French reference to the long bay of Lake Michigan that penetrates the northwest coast of the Lower Peninsula. Earlier, it was called Omeena. Traverse City as the largest population center has always been the county seat and the commercial capital of the area. Its name was registered with the postal service on February 7, 1854, replacing the name Wequetong, or Head of the Bay. It became a village in 1881 and a city in 1895.

The county board of supervisors first met at the Peninsula store of Cowles and Campbell on July 27, 1853. At an early meeting they considered and tabled banning the dumping of sawdust in the water, which years later was passed. Parts or all of relatively unsettled Antrim, Kalkaska, Leelanau, Manistee, Missaukee, and Wexford Counties fell under their jurisdiction. Hannah Lay Mercantile Company donated land in 1854 for the governmental seat, along with $600 and later another $300 to construct public buildings. Perry Hannah is widely regarded as the father of Traverse City.

The county built a wooden jail, court, and county offices, but they burned down eight years later. No records

or lives were lost, and a replacement jail was quickly made. County offices rented space in the growing town, and Hon. D. C. Leach built a business building on the corner of Front and Park Streets and provided a courtroom, office space, and a fireproof safe for county use. In 1884 the county unveiled a brick jail that cost about $20,000.

The contract with Leach ended after the jail was built and county offices moved in there. The county contracted separately with the Patrons of Husbandry to build and rent a court facility on Cass Street.

But growing pains connected to an increasing population requiring service from the fragmented county spaces led to calls for a more developed governmental center. A committee visited courts across the state and recommended a budget of $40,000. Voters in April 1898 approved $35,000 in bonds. The county hired architects Rush, Bowman and Rush of Grand Rapids and builder J. E. Gibson of Logansport, Indiana.

Gibson's bid was a lump sum, so when he began submitting itemized bill items, progress on construction was slowed. Moreover, the politics surrounding the election year of 1898 did not help matters. A compromise was reached on November 10, 1898. A new committee in charge of construction was installed, C. M. Pratt became the new architect, and the builder accepted $4,643.50 to settle a contested bill of $6,732.20. The building was completed for a total cost of $35,664.90 and accepted on March 20, 1900. The locally made furniture cost $1,065. Circuit court had its first session in the new building on April 16, 1900.

In spite of the greatness of the occasion, no formal

dedication ceremony was held. The board of supervisors passed a flowery resolution calling for such a ceremony, but it stated that popular subscription and not county funds should pay for it.

The building's architectural style is Richardsonian Romanesque, and it is made primarily of brick with a rusticated base. It features round arches, castellated turrets, and some Gothic elements. The steps are made of Portage entry red stone. Stone trimming is Amherst sandstone. The wooden trimmings were hemlock, except for the trusses, which were white pine. The casings, jamb facings, and cornice were all made of galvanized iron.

The prominent clock tower was completed in September 1901 when Nels Johnson of Manistee set the clock, which had an eight-foot pendulum with a 137-pound ball, in motion. The 1,500-pound bell was cast in Pittsburgh. In the 1970s a local engineer donated many hours of labor to restart the clock, which had stood motionless for about a decade. His work included lugging heavy gears down a narrow spiral staircase.

The landscaping was another touch that was completed after the building was accepted. It was graded and beautified, while the interior was adorned with vault fixtures and some portraits. One of the portraits honored recently assassinated President William McKinley. Predating the courthouse was a Civil War memorial, which was first unveiled in connection with Memorial Day festivities in 1890. At its dedication before a crowd of three thousand, the presenter declared, "Let no foul hand mutilate it!" The grounds, which locals called Jail Hill, welcomed the oration of presidential candidate William Jennings Bryan in 1896.

The statue moved about the lawn over the years. It was restored and rededicated on its 115th anniversary in 2005. Near it sits a 9,800-pound parrot gun cannon. A Civil War buff packed it with three-quarters of a pound of black powder and fired it at the court's rededication in 1981. Granite slabs for casualties of the Spanish-American War and World War I were installed in 1924. A friendship statue from Soviet Georgia was installed on another side of the grounds in 1991. It depicts a girl holding up her long flowing hair, which contains a ribbon, bunches of grapes, and other fruit.

The court underwent some changes over the years. In 1905 the courtroom was reconfigured because of complaints about how sunlight entered the room directly into people's eyes. A fire in the 1930s damaged part of the interior, which had to be rebuilt. The double stairway to the second floor was reduced to one, and terrazzo was placed over wooden hallway floors. Around this same time conservation officers hauled in interesting exhibits to secure convictions of wood-hungry thieves. The court was shown how pieces of wood matched stumps that were presented to the court. To make office space, the main entrance was bricked up. The circuit court shrank to make room for a jury room after the original one was converted into an office.

A new jail was built south of the courthouse and the old one demolished in 1963. Many began to view the courthouse as inadequate. But voters rejected a new courthouse proposal in 1968. In 1975, by a vote of 1,603 to 1,316, the public recommended that the county renovate the courthouse, which back in 1972 faced twenty-nine fire code violations. The circuit court at one point ordered that until fire detectors were installed fire checks would be made every fifteen minutes when the building was not occupied. An exterior fire escape was added, though subsequent renovation removed it.

The overcrowding and fire hazard convinced county leaders to approach the problem with a two-stage solution. First, a new governmental center building adjacent to the courthouse was built in 1979. County offices moved there. The second stage was to renovate the courthouse and keep it for judicial purposes. The county spent $1.5 million dollars on the project. Architects International of Chicago worked with Tezak Company, the local general contractor.

They gutted the building's interior. Restrooms on each floor, an elevator, soundproofing, modern heating and air conditioning, carpeting, ramps, and fire detection were added. The creation of a third floor, which along with the second houses the circuit court, added 4,049 square feet.

A new law library was placed in refurbished attic space on the fourth floor. In it one can see the spiral staircase to the clock tower. District court is on the first floor, along with a cramped security entrance. The county has plans to build a separate facility for district and probate court. Less noticeable exterior improvements were made too, such as a new lightning rod, storm windows, weather stripping, and brick remortaring.

Rededication occurred on July 4, 1981, which was only fitting. The courthouse was free of its earlier overcrowding and dilapidation, free from the threat of demolition, and free for any visitor to appreciate. It was thus indeed Independence Day for the courthouse. Above all, even though technically it is an inanimate object, it was free to turn back the clock and enjoy its new lease on life.

GRATIOT COUNTY

ITHACA—Atop the many columns of the Gratiot County Courthouse, one might expect Ionic capitals. The Ionian Sea, after all, is home to the Greek island of Ithaca. But only the most ornate Corinthian capitals would do for this structure, where there is no shortage of structural and aesthetic columns to top.

Gratiot County is named for Captain Charles Gratiot, a distinguished officer who served during the War of 1812 under William Henry Harrison. In 1814, Gratiot, who eventually attained the rank of brigadier general, built Fort Gratiot at the head of the St. Clair River in present-day Port Huron. He died in 1855, the same year that Gratiot County was organized.

Gratiot Center, located naturally in the center of the county, has always been the county seat, though in 1857 it was renamed Ithaca for the New York hometown of John Jeffery, an early settler. One account states that, after vigorous debate about the location, "a large concourse of people" went to the appointed spot to place the county stake, with each supervisor striking it into the ground with an axe. Then the county seal was affixed to the stake.

In exchange for locating the courthouse on his property, Jeffery built at his own expense a two-story log cabin that the county accepted in autumn 1856. The city built in 1861 a separate one-story wooden office building measuring sixteen by thirty-two feet. Another two-story wooden structure replaced the old courthouse on the same plot of land in 1870 at a cost of $10,000. The new building, which featured an open cupola, measured thirty-six by sixty feet; its builder was William C. Beckwith. Voters approved part of the funding in a close 872 to 854 vote. The county board

authorized additional funds on the condition that Ithaca would grade the grounds.

The countywide vote in 1900 for $34,000 for a stone courthouse was a landslide: 4,058 to 2,311. The school district bought the second wooden courthouse, but the building would never serve as a school. It was eventually sold to Archie McCall, who took it apart and used the lumber to build his home at 207 N. Pine Street.

In 1900, the county broke ground on July 24 and laid the cornerstone on September 18. By winter, work stopped as the general contractor demanded more money. The county lost $11,000 and filed suit against the bondsmen, who then countersued. The lawsuits were dropped and construction was completed, with the building dedicated on September 10, 1902. Total cost, including furnishings, ballooned to $74,103.23. Claire Allen (the cornerstone reads "Clare")

of Jackson designed the ornate Beaux-Arts classical building, which measures seventy-six by one hundred twelve feet. The builder was A. W. Mohnke of Grand Rapids, and Jere. Marks of St. Louis supervised the construction.

The yellow-brown Berea sandstone is ornate in its details, from panels with figurative relief carvings to the spiral-fluted columns near the entrances of the courthouse. The octagonal domed roof stands one hundred twenty feet above the ground. In 1905 a clock by N. Johnson of Manistee was installed in the tower.

A rotunda anchors the inside of the building, as it is the central point of reference for most interior features. Oak and marble dominate the indoor environment. In the large courtroom, dark wood and a deep blue carpet contrast the cream-colored walls and ceiling. Inlaid in the wood behind the judge's bench are twin wreathed symbols: scales and a law book.

The building was nearly lost in 1978, two years after it was placed on the National Register of Historic Places. Local fire departments saved the building, but the second floor required extensive renovation. In the 1990s more change came—planned this time. A "connector building" was constructed, which offered, among other things, barrier-free entry for all visitors. Additional renovation came with the new construction, which cost over $3 million. John Dziurman, the historic architect, collaborated with Giffels Consultants, Inc., of Southfield, architects and engineers who served as construction managers. Heartland PCS, Inc., of Lansing was the general contractor.

In a nod to the wooden counterpart in its older appendage, the new building hints at a rotunda-centered design with its circular metal banister above a lobby area. Outside, the light-colored brick and gray roof blend with the old building's visual cues. Alas, there are no new Corinthian columns. But it may be that the predecessor, pregnant with that element, has enough for two.

HILLSDALE COUNTY

HILLSDALE—Hillsdale County's second courthouse was muse to one of Michigan's poet laureates. Before his career blossomed he attended proceedings inside the building the community called the Old Stone Pile.

Hillsdale is named for the hills and dales that mark its topography. Originally part of Lenawee County, it was set off in 1829 and organized on February 11, 1835. The first county seat was Jonesville, which was selected in 1831. Hillsdale began to press for the seat in 1839. One tactic Jonesville used to thwart efforts aimed at a move was to create the new village of Osseo on paper to divide and conquer the opposition.

The strategy backfired when the Legislature chose the practically nonexistent Osseo as the county seat. But the designation was for three years only on paper, for no county buildings or business ever took root in Osseo. Hillsdale prevailed by act of the Legislature in January 1843.

The county hastily erected an unsuitable frame structure for a courthouse, which the builders Cook and Ferris quickly replaced with a better thirty-by-fifty-foot frame structure. A group of Presbyterians paid for the structure on the condition that it would have joint use of the facility with the court and county offices.

A local newspaper on November 13, 1849, reported that the courthouse burned by an incendiary device based on evidence that the treasurer's office was broken into and ransacked. His records were lost, but those of the register of deeds and the probate court were saved.

Next came the Old Stone Pile, a sandstone courthouse that was completed in January 1851. It featured large columns and a cupola. The building's dimensions were forty-five by seventy-five feet. The building cost $6,250, which was slightly over the $6,000 budget. Native lumber and brick made up part of the building, as well as stone bought locally for three dollars per cord. A bell and furniture each cost $150. Baldwin and Boles were paid $12.50 for the architectural plans. McAdam & Stimson were the contractors. In October 1852 the county drove several large iron rods through the building to keep it from spreading apart. A year later it approved $45 for lightning rods.

Inside this building young Will Carlton attended court sessions on the second floor. He was destined to become a nationally recognized writer who was for many years poet laureate of Michigan. He penned "Betsey and I Are Out" after witnessing a divorce proceeding. The *Toledo Blade* first published it in 1871. Carlton's name and work circulated, and he developed a reputation as a commentator on the humble man's way of life.

He is also noted for "Over the Hill to the Poorhouse." In it he expresses concern for the elderly with uncaring children. Many view the poem as a point of origin for local and state reform aimed at protecting the aged and needy.

The building was torn down in 1899 with the advent of Hillsdale's third and current courthouse. The cornerstone bears two dates—1850 for the Old Stone Pile and 1898 for the year the new cornerstone was laid. Claire Allen of Jackson designed the building, which has a twin in Van Buren County. Both feature a prominent double-level cupola with a copper roof. Hillsdale's Berea sandstone building was dedicated on September 6, 1899. It cost $45,000, which voters did not approve until after a fourth try in 1898 by a majority of 172, with the first unsuccessful vote dating back to 1887. Geake & Henry of Fort Wayne, Indiana, was the general contractor. The Renaissance Revival style of the building is characteristic of the late Victorian period.

It took ten years to add a clock to the tower. The mechanism is by Seth Thomas, and the bells, which are Meneely, are said to come very close to mimicking the chime of

London's Westminster Abbey. In 1985 repairs restored the chime to every quarter hour.

Hillsdale's county flag has a white field with a yellow border and four circular symbols in each corner. They represent the religious, agricultural, educational, and industrial aspects of the county. In the center an emblem depicts a maple tree and a sap bucket.

Slowly and steadily, like the sap's sure flow, Hillsdale built courthouses that left their mark—from the tower that physically dominates its skyline to the poignant words of a poet who found his inspiration in the human drama he witnessed below a more modest community beacon.

HOUGHTON COUNTY

HOUGHTON—There is no mistaking the polychromatic Victorian building atop the hill overlooking the Keweenaw Canal. It is the Houghton County Courthouse. Its opulent style is witness to the copper boom that happened in the area in the late nineteenth century. But unlike many of the industrial installations that were razed or abandoned after the copper heydays, the courthouse stands largely in its original form.

Houghton County was organized in 1845. In its early history, the county seat was rather transient. The offices of the Lake Superior Company housed county meetings from 1849 until 1853. Then they were held in the Phoenix Copper Company building outside of its mine. Eagle River, the current county seat of Keweenaw County, was the seat of Houghton County from 1853 until 1861, when the Legislature split off the northern territory as Keweenaw County.

A contract was struck in 1862 for a frame structure courthouse on the site of the present facility. It was replaced by its grand successor in 1887. As Houghton's population grew, from 456 in 1850 to several thousand, it decided to spend $75,568 on its new courthouse. The cornerstone, featuring a miner's coat of arms and containing a copper box filled with artifacts, was laid on July 24, 1886. Due to extreme heat, the planned winding procession was cut short, and everyone walked instead in a straight line to the construction site.

J. B. Sweatt, an architect working in Marquette, designed the building. His style was a Midwestern interpretation of the Second Empire school, revived from the classicism used in French architecture in the seventeenth century. The large tower and the wide wings of the two-and-a-half-story

building create a tension between horizontal and vertical. Chimneys and the pointed gables of the dormers add to this feature.

There are contrasting yet complementary colors too. The bulk of the exterior is yellow, or Milwaukee cream, brick. Local red sandstone lines the windows and parts of the walls. The oxidized copper roofing tosses in a mellow green. An intricately carved wooden cornice also encircles the building.

Inside, the courthouse features a number of quaint touches, including a round cage filled with lottery balls for jury selection and engraved signs instructing persons not to light matches on the woodwork or walls. In 1913, noted advocate Clarence Darrow appeared in the courthouse because of a large labor strike in the area.

Tucked away in the southwest corner of the building are a 6,000-foot five-story addition and a parking deck. Covered parking can come at a premium in the winter when heavy snow falls. The addition is virtually hidden by the front of the building, which, except for surrounding development, is just as it appeared at the dedication in 1887. Along with the addition, Houghton County undertook a considerable renovation of the interior and exterior existing structure.

To coincide with the centennial of the courthouse and the sesquicentennial of Michigan's admission to the Union as the twenty-sixth state, the courthouse was rededicated in 1987. A U.S. flag with twenty-six stars that flew over the U.S. House of Representatives in Washington and the State Capitol in Lansing was raised over the courthouse.

It was an event that no doubt would have impressed the namesake of the county, Professor Douglass Houghton. Dr. Houghton was appointed the first state geologist in 1837, and his geological investigations are credited for bringing people and money to the region when he discovered evidence of vast deposits of valuable minerals.

He made voluminous annual reports of his findings, focusing most of his time in the Upper Peninsula between 1838 and 1845. He drowned at the age of thirty-six on the morning of October 13, 1845, when water overcame his open row-and-sail boat in Lake Superior off the coast of Eagle River. His remains were found the next spring, and he was buried in Detroit's Elmwood Cemetery.

Within a mile of where he met his fate, the Keweenaw Historical Society, the Home Fortnightly Club of Calumet, and others from both Houghton and Keweenaw County erected a monument in his honor at Eagle River. It is composed of a number of irregularly shaped Upper Peninsula stones bonded together, along with a copper plaque commemorating his untimely death.

Several miles down the Keweenaw Peninsula stands Dr. Houghton's other great monument, built of stone, copper, and wood for the county that bears his name: the unique Houghton County Courthouse.

HURON COUNTY

BAD AXE—Perhaps no other county in Michigan has a more unique and memorable name for its county seat. Bad Axe proved a good place to be when the county suffered a great fire in 1881. The new brick courthouse sheltered about four hundred people from the flames, giving the idea of finding refuge in the court system an entirely new meaning. More than just a vault protecting records, the courthouse stood as a firewall preserving the human lives that would be the future of the county.

Huron County was organized on January 25, 1859. This tip of Michigan's Thumb was earlier attached to Tuscola and Sanilac Counties. Its name derives from the French word for head: "hures." An early French observer's statement "inelles hures" or "what heads" referred to the manner in which local Native Americans dressed their hair.

The first county seat was at Sand Beach, now Harbor Beach, where it remained until 1865. After the court in Sand Beach burned on June 25, 1864, Port Austin offered free use of county buildings for ten years. The board of supervisors accepted, though earlier it approved $4,000 for county buildings in Bad Axe. Voters chose Port Austin in April 1865 by a vote of 320 to 162.

Bad Axe received its name from two early surveyors who visited a lumber camp. This camp had a broken axe. History did not clearly record if the handle or the head was defective, though current city signs depict a broken handle. The surveyors coined the name Bad Axe, which stuck despite the Legislature's efforts decades later in 1909 to change the name to Huron, which local voters rejected in favor of the old name.

Voters by a large margin selected centrally located Bad Axe as the county seat in April 1873. Woods & Company donated forty acres of land for county buildings. Septimus Irwin cleared land and erected a frame building in time for the October meeting of the board of supervisors. The records were moved on October 1. The supervisors brought bedding and slept on the floor of the courtroom after their meeting. They had a shanty "eating-house" and were surrounded by dense forest. The building cost $1,877.89 and measured sixty by forty by twelve feet.

In time Irwin would build a hotel and the county would fund a two-story brick building with a basement. The old courthouse was demolished when the county moved into the new one in 1875. The new structure and its contents cost $24,275.89.

The value of the building and its contents was immeasurable on September 5, 1881, when a great fire swept through virtually the whole county. Drought and windy conditions set the stage for a staggering fire that swept in from the southwest. Only the western edge and a few enclaves on the eastern shore of the county were spared.

The fire reportedly appeared as "a giant, whirling ball of spitting flames that moved high in the treetops, igniting one clump and passing another." Survivors who buried themselves in cornfields, crawled in wells, and in one remarkable case, burrowed inside an elk carcass lived to tell their tales. About four hundred people saved themselves by scurrying into the brick courthouse.

The building's east side had a well, which was shielded from the flames on the west side. Men pumped water to

drench the building as temperatures inside it soared above 110 degrees. The fire claimed 282 known casualties and 3,400 buildings, leaving over 15,000 people homeless. Help poured in from around the country, including the first disaster services of the Red Cross within America's borders. Locally, cows were taken to the courthouse to provide milk for infants.

Bent but not broken by the fire, the courthouse continued to serve, gaining an addition to its rear in 1930. A young attorney named Frank B. Murphy first practiced in the old courthouse. He would later serve as judge and mayor in Detroit, U.S. attorney general, and U.S. Supreme Court justice.

In 1965 a building authority began exploring options for a replacement of the courthouse. It entered an agreement with the county to construct the new building and rent it for $86,000 a year until the $1,225,000 in bonds and interest were repaid, at which time the county would gain the deed to the property. Several years later, the county had a bond burning ceremony to mark the occasion.

The project cost $1,360,000, and the two-story brick L-shaped building was dedicated on June 1, 1968. Ralph S. and Steve T. Gerganoff designed the modern structure, and Granger Brothers, Inc., was the general contractor.

A plaque at the front of the building states Richard Nixon "on April 10, 1974, and on this spot made his last campaign appearance as president." Whether he sought it or not, he found inside the courthouse no refuge from the firestorm, unlike Huron County's residents about a century earlier.

INGHAM COUNTY

MASON—The courthouse in Mason is the forgotten sister of Ingham County, which is home to the State Capitol Building in Lansing. Being in the shadow of Lansing gives Mason a unique distinction, however. In no other state in the Union is the capital city not also the county seat.

Mason won the seat before the Legislature decided to designate unsettled Lansing as the state capital. The capital was first called Biddle City, for Major John Biddle of the War of 1812, who was also a delegate for Michigan to Congress. For a time, it was also called Michigan, Michigan, but finally the name rested on Lansing, the surname of a noted Revolutionary War figure from New York. Mason, on the other hand, commemorates Governor Stevens T. Mason, who led Michigan in its border dispute with Ohio. Ingham is for Samuel D. Ingham, the secretary of the treasury under President Jackson.

The county, which was first part of Wayne and then Washtenaw County, was organized on April 5, 1838. The seat was at Ingham, which was also called Jefferson City, beginning in 1836, but the location was complained of and no public buildings were ever erected there. One historian noted that "the embryo village died ere it had donned its swaddling clothes." The seat moved to Mason on March 6, 1840. Court first met there in a schoolhouse. Emmons White erected in 1840 to 1841 a one-story frame building for public purposes. It measured sixteen by twenty-four feet and cost $325. Another $6 bought a platform and steps.

In 1842 the county approved $800—$600 in bonds and $200 in real estate—for a new building. William Hammond & Company won the contract, erecting the two-story frame structure, which boasted eighteen-foot posts and measured twenty-eight by thirty-four feet. It had a yellow fence with white trimmings. The county spent $100 to paint the structure and forty-two dollars for stoves and piping, including installation. Here the public gathered for all sorts of functions, until population growth necessitated a larger structure.

That building came in 1858 at a price of $12,229.19 after voters in April 1856 approved $5,000 in a tax and loan to fund it. Matthew Elder of Lansing designed and built the two-story brick edifice. A wide hallway on the first floor separated the offices while the courtroom was on the second floor. The building would serve for forty-five years.

Voters approved $40,000 for a new courthouse in April 1902 by a vote of 5,691 to 3,503. Mason voted overwhelmingly in favor, 546 to 3. The massive cornerstone was laid on May 5, 1903. On October 26, 2004, it was opened and the time capsule and its contents of over sixty artifacts were recovered, some of which are on display inside the courthouse. On November 3, 1903, voters approved another $36,000 by a vote of 2,885 to 1,332 after an initial unsuccessful vote due to low turnout. Mason again weighed heavily in favor of the expenditure, voting 577 to 9.

In the end, the building cost $96,678. Edwin A. Bowd of Lansing designed the structure in the federal style. The general contractor was George Rickman and Sons Company. Construction began in the autumn of 1902, and the building was dedicated on May 9, 1905. The exterior is saw-cut Berea sandstone from Amherst, Ohio. The roof is black slate, which was recently restored. Four large columns

straddle the main entrance and grab visitors' attention, along with the clock and bell tower. The Seth Thomas clock and McShane bell were purchased in 1912. A new clock came in 1995. The original glass of the clock faces was removed. Sunlight interacted with the magnesium in the white glass to turn it a subdued shade of orchid, which can be seen in one of the display cases inside the building.

In 1919 the county added interior decorations. In particular, authorities commissioned murals. Four arch-shaped scenes appear below the rotunda on the second floor outside of the courtroom. The south wall depicts an early street scene in Mason, including the first courthouse and jail and their stockade fence. The east wall has a likeness of Chief John Okemos, a notable figure who traded with early settlers. The north wall features a pastoral sketch of Jefferson City, which was originally intended to be the county seat and capital. Finally, the west wall blends images of marching Civil War and World War I soldiers guided under Lady Liberty.

The courtroom is expansive, grand, full of wooden furnishings and home to some frescoes of its own. The most distinctive feature is its two large jury boxes, a rarity among Michigan courtrooms that usually have only one. A second box is useful in the event of a trial in which co-defendants face separate juries but share some of the same proceedings.

The exterior of the building has a number of distinct touches. Near the entrance is a memorial plaque honoring veterans of World War I. One corner of the lawn features a large monument bearing similar plaques for subsequent wars. A large Civil War cannon and a smaller antipirate cannon from Cuba as a gift in the wake of the Spanish-American War adorn another spot on the lawn. Between the cannons are forty cannonballs that are totally or partly encased in concrete. None of them fit either of the cannons. Elsewhere, a large cement horse trough marks how locals once gave water to their means of transportation. Every summer it is filled with flowers.

Atop the tower is the Golden Eagle. Its height and wingspan are each about three feet. A traveling salesman first sold it to the county. Some taxpayers viewed it as an unnecessary extravagance and protested. A storm blew it off and the county put it in storage. Years later a mainte-nance man discovered it, asked to repair and reinstall it—and he did just that. It reportedly has three bullet holes in it, for weathervanes historically were popular targets. Getting one to spin would supposedly get a rise out of observers.

In 1971 the building was placed on the National Register of Historic Places. Nine years later the county completed a renovation study aimed at preserving the courthouse. Fifteen years of such work ended in 1995, costing a total of $7 million.

INGHAM COUNTY

On November 24, 2001, Ingham County dedicated in downtown Lansing the Veteran's Memorial Courthouse. Wigen Tincknell Meyer and Associates designed the multistory modern building. Clark Construction managed the construction, and the engineer was MacMillan & Associates. The project cost $24 million. Lansing has the majority of the circuit judges of Ingham County and handles about three-quarters of the docket.

But forgotten Mason, which recently celebrated the centennial of its courthouse, proudly and stubbornly retains its county seat designation. It is the only county seat in the nation that stands apart from yet in the same county as the state capital. It thus demonstrates that the reason it is like a forgotten bridesmaid nonetheless makes it a special and memorable place.

IONIA COUNTY

IONIA—Lady Justice stands atop the Ionia County Courthouse looking down over her people 120 feet below. Originally, her skin was painted white, her tunic gray, and her tiara, sword, and scales were covered in gold leaf. Alas, her gilded accoutrements lost their luster and were not refinished in the latest round of restoration.

But her garb continues to suit her, for her county like her fashion has deep roots. Ionia is a name for an ancient civilization along the western coast of Asia Minor. It boasted twelve cities known collectively as the Ionian Dodecapolis.

Ionia in Michigan did not quite boast so many cities at its founding. Its county seat was called Washington Center, then Ionia County Seat, and then finally just Ionia. The village became a city in 1873.

The county was part of a long succession of other counties—Wayne, Oakland, Lenawee, St. Joseph, and then Kalamazoo. Ionia was organized in its own right in 1837, with its first election and circuit court occurring that spring. Judge Epaphoditus Ransom presided. An inexperienced prosecutor and a confused grand jury meant that he had to excuse himself from court to go solve their problems. Historical accounts joke that it was a rare example of a judge being called from the bench to appear before a grand jury. Ransom was described as "a man of commanding presence" at six feet tall, over two hundred pounds, and with a massive head and powerful voice. He initially presided over court in a schoolhouse.

Later, court moved to the store of Daniel Ball. From as early as 1845 until 1850, Avel Avery furnished rooms for court and the county supervisors. Then the county rented Smith's hall for about eighteen years until Dr. Bayard's hall was called into service. The final temporary location was Armory hall of the Ionia Light-Guard Association, beginning in May 1879. Part of the reason for the delay in constructing a permanent courthouse was the opposition of Lyon and Portage, two locales that lost out in the contest for the county seat.

The county did construct a small building for offices and record storage in 1843 after a countywide vote of 152 to 117. No description of it exists, but it was probably made of brick because it is recorded that kegs of lime for the mortar to build it were purchased from Grand Rapids. In 1874 Ionia spent $1,100 for an addition and repairs.

The first jail was completed in 1851 and then replaced in 1881. The new jail was made of brick and Ionia sandstone. An early account that no doubt lamented the lack of a proper court described the jail as "commodious, substantial in appearance and adding somewhat to the hitherto desolate aspect of the 'Public Square.'" The deed for the western half of the square, incidentally, was never recorded.

On April 2, 1883, a vote of 3,426 to 1,483 approved courthouse construction at a cost of $45,000. A remarkable margin of 996 to 1 was officially reported in the city of Ionia, prompting one local writer to comment years later on how unusual it was to see such "management of the ballots" in rural America. Even the revered Mayor Fred W. Green did not get such unanimous support when he ran for governor.

Construction began in the summer of 1883 and went on for three long years. The contractor went bankrupt.

County supervisor Chauncey Waterbury lost his seat but remained on as chairman and manager of the project. The cost overruns were tremendous, bringing the final price tag to nearly $70,000, which was well above the original budget of $45,000. As homage to or perhaps umbrage against him, there is an inscription above the south entrance that reads "Waterbury's white elephant."

David W. Gibbs of Toledo was the architect. He also designed the courthouse in nearby Eaton County, as well as the capitol of Wyoming. The style may be called Italianate or Renaissance Revival. An Ionia sandstone exterior was applied to the brick walls. All outside steps and piers are made of Ohio bluestone. The dome is a wooden frame covered by bent and formed galvanized sheet iron. The gable of the front portico features the state coat of arms, grape leaves, cannon balls, and thirteen stars for, presumably, the original colonies.

A tin and lead cast assembly eagle with a twelve-foot wingspan once perched just above the gable. Eleven different feather molds made up the bulk of its surface. Its hollow interior filled with dirt, moisture, and, ironically, birds. It was beyond repair when the county undertook $140,000 worth of building restoration in 1994. The noble bird was removed and unceremoniously put in storage. There is hope but no firm plan for replacing it.

The restoration also stripped the interior of the court of its lead paint and plugged its leaks. The grand interior stairway, which is made of oak and cherry, was also refurbished. One quirk that was left unchanged was the upside-down leg post five down from the top of the first landing on the right side.

Earlier efforts brought other changes. A telephone was first installed in 1888. Wiring for electricity was added in

1920. A boiler was added in 1956, rendering the fireplaces ornamental. No two are alike, and they are slate painted to look like marble. In 1976 the skylight below the dome was covered due to the fire marshal's safety concerns. Because the thickness of the walls decreases as one climbs the building, the installation of an elevator in 1981 proved difficult because measuring the boundaries for where to cut the shaft required fixed points. After a prank involving youngsters and water in the 1950s, the board of supervisors voted to remove the dome and replace it with a flat roof. The vote was reversed a few days later. In 2000, a clock was added to the south face of the tower for $3,375 thanks in large part to a sewing group that raised money. The roman numerals cost $900. Ionia hopes to someday have a clock for each of the tower's four faces.

Smoking was banned inside the courthouse, but not tobacco chewing at first. Early in the life of the courthouse, the county spent $89.48 for 126 cuspidors for chewing tobacco. One wonders where they all might have fit. Within a week of circuit court's first session in its new building, the local newspaper reported that the "decorative beauties of tobacco tints are already plentifully displayed upon the floor of the new courtroom."

The dedication on July 3, 1886, was an event to remember that attracted a record crowd. The program listed eight addresses, including one each on behalf of farmers of the eastern and western parts of the county. After all the speeches came running races, bicycle races, long-distance throwing, and a "fat man's race." Another competition was substituted when it was clear that judges were unwilling out of politeness or perhaps genuine fear to name "the handsomest country girl."

Given the great expense of the building and the risk of fire, the county supervisors categorically forbade a fireworks display of "our court house" on the roof. The fireworks show went on without that detail, though organizers managed to somehow spread and ignite in red, white, and blue those words across the front of the building.

According to a newspaper report, "when the last spark of the brilliant light had vanished, the people plodded homeward, retired to their various couches, and peace reigned supreme." Presiding over that serenity was the steadfast symbol of justice atop the courthouse dome. One can only imagine its glistening gold leaf reflecting the flickering, flashing, and fantastic fireworks frolicking among and above the festooned fair.

IOSCO COUNTY

TAWAS CITY—The original name of Iosco County, Kanotin, means "in the path of the big wind." It derives from a Native American legend about an upset great spirit blowing through the land and uprooting trees. That same wind may have been unleashed when a small boat from Iosco carried, ironically, the murdered corpse of the county's most notorious convicted murderer all the way around the Thumb and into Canada some 130 miles away.

In 1843 Kanotin was changed to Iosco, which means "water of light." It was organized as a county on February 16, 1857, with the seat at Ottawas Bay. The name either referred to the Ottawa tribe or to the Ojibwa chief named Otawas. Its name was later changed to its current form, Tawas City.

The board of supervisors in 1859 ordered that circuit court would meet in the second story of G. O. Whittemore & Company store. The Whittemore family was prominent in the early history of Iosco, at one time holding six of the seven county offices. It donated land for public use on which the current courthouse sits overlooking the bay.

The county spent $1,750 on stone and brick in 1863 for a courthouse, but work gave way to votes rejecting the project. Finally voters approved a scaled-back project, at least in terms of building materials. A wooden court was built on the high land by the shore. It was finished on February 17, 1869. The jail was in the basement, which was made of limestone from Kelly's Island in Lake Erie. Offices were on the first floor. The lofty and spacious circuit courtroom with chandeliers was on the second floor. It was in session whenever judges from Bay City could catch a sailboat. Vaults of brick that stood on independent foundations were said to

be fireproof because of double doors of boiler iron and four inches of air space on all sides. The exterior featured front and rear porticos, arched windows, a triplet east window, and a dome capped with a flagpole.

An effort to move the county seat to East Tawas failed on April 5, 1875, by a vote of 557 to 444. Up to that date the county spent about $18,000 on its buildings. The twelve steps below an entrance to the courthouse were used for many group photographs over the years. The courtroom also served as a community gathering place for events such as graduation exercises. The first county fair was on the courthouse grounds in 1875. Between 1891 and March 1895, it split circuit court sessions with the O'Toole Block in Au Sable.

Several years earlier, grisly murder visited the county. The murderer years later turned murder victim and was discovered in dramatic fashion. Henry B. Farrington was a jeweler in the area who reportedly did not do much legitimate business. He was convicted of killing a local butcher, whose head was split by a single blow from an axe on October 25, 1875. Though the butcher was robbed of $1,000 he had just collected from a lumber camp, the motive for the murder reportedly emerged from a love triangle.

Suspicion turned to Farrington, and a local deputy sheriff found a frozen pool of blood and red icicles below Farrington's kitchen floor, which had been scrubbed clean. Officers discovered the murder weapon, which fit the wound it gouged in the victim. Farrington was convicted despite his claims of innocence and his "rabid outburst" after the verdict was read. He received a sentence of life in prison. He made a number of desperate escapes that led to recapture before he was sent to Jackson prison for solitary confinement.

Governor Begole, believing that only manslaughter was proven and that Farrington had served enough time, pardoned him. With a record expunged of his murder conviction, he returned to Tawas City in May 1884. He was arrested again on the word of a saloon keeper for conspiracy to kill the old jailer who had foiled Farrington's earlier escape attempts.

Back in jail, Farrington befriended his cellmate, and the two escaped on the morning of June 2, 1885. It is believed that Farrington fashioned a spoon into a key to break out. The next day a fisherman reported his rowboat stolen from Tawas Bay. That same boat washed ashore in a storm over a hundred miles away in Forest, Ontario, which means that it had to have looped around the Thumb.

Farrington's corpse was inside, tied to the boat. At first his discoverers figured that he tied his midsection to the boat to stay afloat and was killed by the violent thrashing that beat his head and body about the boat. But that theory could not explain his tied hands and feet. His murder was never solved and his cellmate never found.

A few years later the Iosco courthouse heard the slip-and-fall case of Lotta Lombar, who injured herself on a faulty wooden sidewalk plank on June 8, 1888. She sued and prevailed in the Michigan Supreme Court in May 1891. Key evidence was the plank, which was immediately replaced but left nearby for the plaintiff to recover. The village was strapped for cash and took over thirteen years to resolve the case, by which time cement was quickly replacing old plank sidewalks.

The old courthouse served well beyond its useful life, as failed bond proposals, wartime scarcity, and tight budgets emerged in the beginning of the twentieth century. In 1941 the basement was remodeled for offices, which brought

structural changes that weakened supporting walls and created a roller coaster effect in the main corridor of the first floor. Architect Joseph Goddeyne of Bay City drew up plans in 1944 for a three-story brick building. Over his objections the voters finally approved $250,000 for a one-story design in 1952. Shade trees planted in 1875 were removed so that construction could happen up to the setback line on Lake Street, allowing the old courthouse to function through construction, transition, and eventual demolition.

Arthur Vollmer Construction Company completed work in December 1954. New work was completed in the 1970s, but the one-story brick and stone building is substantially the same. A bicentennial time capsule to be opened in 2076 is buried near the cornerstone. Next to both is a rock and plaque erected in 1923 commemorating the county and the establishment of its first post office.

The plaque quotes Carlyle, who said, "history is the essence of innumerable biographies." For Iosco County, two of those biographies consist of a patient slip-and-fall plaintiff and an axe murderer turned seaward murder victim.

IRON COUNTY

CRYSTAL FALLS—Any lawyer worth his or her salt will tell you that larceny is a crime against someone's personal property, not real property. But many an inhabitant of nearby Iron River will contend that Iron County's magnificent courthouse in Crystal Falls was stolen. The resentment runs deep for some, who reportedly continue to mutter and shake their fists at the sight of the old building at the top of Superior Street.

The state Legislature set off Iron County from Marquette and Menominee Counties in 1885 and named it after the ample iron deposits located in its territory. The iron ore was the first mined in the Menominee Range, and shipment began with the arrival of trains in 1882. Lansing designated Iron River, a small mining and lumber town in the western part of the new county, the temporary county seat. Meanwhile, Crystal Falls in the eastern part of the county was about as old and as large in population and wanted the county seat designation too.

A clever plot was hatched. After a County Board of Supervisors' meeting in Iron River, a contingent from Crystal Falls proposed a high-stakes poker game. The Iron Riverites quickly accepted, and news spread through town. People gathered at the Old Boyington Hotel and watched in delight as the boys from Crystal Falls had a bad night of gambling. The diversion was set.

Two members of the Crystal Falls delegation feigned fatigue and excused themselves upstairs to go to bed. Instead, they sneaked out the back through a window into waist-deep snow and temperatures that dipped to twelve degrees below zero. The streets were deserted. One of them left propped open the back door of the shack that then was the courthouse. They gathered the county record books, packed them in a hand sled, and made off for the railroad yards. There they bribed a conductor, who happened to be from Crystal Falls, to stow the records in a freight car. They waited an anxious hour before the train left, worrying that at any moment an angry crowd would seek them out.

Where the records were kept safe for Crystal Falls is unclear. Some accounts say that the local sheriff guarded them, while others maintain that the records were hidden in a mine or in a hollow pine tree.

For a while, Iron River threatened armed invasion. Cooler heads prevailed, and efforts turned to a public referendum in the spring of 1889. But the fight was by no means clean. Loggers and miners from surrounding areas reportedly voted in the election, along with many deceased persons. Other irregularities call the validity of the ballot into question.

In the end, Crystal Falls won the election by a scant margin of 1,142 to 1,051. This "measly" margin "gave us the legal right to have the county courthouse," said one of the original conspirators. He added, "To rub things in a bit, we built the best in the Upper Peninsula."

The courthouse is indeed exceptional and is prominently situated on a hill overlooking the surrounding area. Iron County's average elevation is 1,500 feet above sea level, ranging from a high of 1,860 to a low of 1,120 feet.

The building was completed in 1890 at a cost of about $40,000. Its architectural style is Romanesque, featuring a high-pitched roof, high windows, deeply arched doorways, and exterior ornamentation. J. C. Clancy of Wisconsin was the architect. Most notable are the seventeen-foot tall statues representing Law, Mercy, and Justice, which were added in 1910 along with the nearby clock tower. On a clear day, the bell can be heard up to four miles away.

Iron County broke ground in 2003 for a new wing for county administrative offices. The project included extensive renovation of the interior and exterior of the old building. The exterior was sandblasted to return the stone to its original lemon color. The wooden bell tower was temporarily removed and placed on the ground to allow for refurbishing of the bricks supporting it. The deterioration was bad enough to prompt Iron County to stop ringing the bell because its vibrations were believed to exacerbate the crumbling of the bricks.

The new wing is not the first one added to the courthouse. In 1955 Iron County dedicated an expanded wing containing offices such as the county treasurer. A more recent modernly designed building housing the prosecutor's office is across the street.

The circuit courtroom on the second floor is impressive in its scale and detail. At the time of construction, it was the largest auditorium in the Upper Peninsula. At the center of the high dome-shaped ceiling is a massive chandelier. Facing out from above the bench behind the chandelier is decora-

tive detail proclaiming, "In God We Trust." The ceiling itself is embossed octagonal tin featuring intricate designs. The recent renovation refinished the tin's paint job. Elsewhere inside one can find fine oak doors with decorative hinges and an elegant staircase featuring an oak balustrade with pointed newel posts. Another old touch some may find less quaint are the sinks located in the hallway outside of the restrooms for men and women alike to share.

But because the location of the courthouse itself cannot be shared, the "Jewel of Iron County"—as it is known locally—for some of the county's approximately 13,000 residents will forever be a crown jewel pilfered from Iron River. It is a jewel just the same.

ISABELLA COUNTY

MT. PLEASANT—The tribal heritage of Isabella County is apparent in its everyday business and in its primary symbol: the county seal. The seal depicts a bearded man shaking hands with a figure wearing two feathers in his hair. The oil derrick and shafts of wheat recall two important local industries. The oil lamp symbolizes the enlightenment spread every day at the county's educational centers, most notably at Central Michigan University. The year 1856 holds a prominent place in the seal too.

Local historians when they prepared for the county's sesquicentennial found the date puzzling, however. The Legislature organized the county three years later in 1859, and its earliest board of supervisor minutes reach that far. The first county expenditure came in the same year: an order to pay M. D. Davis or the bearer seventy-five cents for services in gathering a jury. The first money paid into the treasury was a fine in the same amount against L. C. Bright for assault and battery.

There is, however, a record in 1856 of the first lawsuit. It happened in Coe Township when two neighbors, David Brickley and D. Childs, aired a dispute about sap troughs that amounted to only four dollars, which may be why they represented themselves and the outcome was not memorialized.

Judge Wilbur F. Woodworth presided over the first circuit court session in 1858 at Isabella Center. Its name and that of the county are for Queen Isabella of Spain, the benefactor of Christopher Columbus, who set in motion the events that brought Europeans to the indigenous people of the Americas. Woodworth came to the log courthouse of a Dr. Jeffries, who never did succeed in getting the perma-

nent county seat. The building was also used as a residence, a store, and a hotel.

Its location was central but uninhabited. It was moved a mile down the river in April 1860, when the county population was 1,433, by a vote of 156 to 103, to the only commercial center in the county. Supporters of the move curried favor with local Native Americans by giving them land near the new seat. Mt. Pleasant has since remained the county seat.

The county met difficulty in raising money for county buildings. David Ward donated five acres for county buildings. W. H. Nelson built a modest court for $140. A later writer speculated on the atmosphere of early court sessions in Isabella County. Because of unfavorable crops, people in the area were subsisting on wild leeks and maple sugar. He imagined a room with "no more ventilation than Noah's Ark," with heat from a box stove filling the air along with the smoke of pipes and cheap cigars, and "the breath of a room full of stomachs loaded with leeks and maple sugar gulping up gas."

Another early story was not nearly so pungent. A good-looking local widow enjoyed the company of her twelve-year-old son. Her widower neighbor had a boy of similar age. The two children went together to shoot at robins, and her son was accidentally killed. She went to a lawyer for advice and to draw up papers for a manslaughter arrest. The widower came, leading his boy by the hand. He heard her plea and offered her his boy to make her whole. She did not care for the lad and rejected the offer. So the widower offered himself. The widow joyfully accepted and the new family returned home to bury the dead boy.

Similar spontaneity is found in local lore about abrupt weddings. A man needed a housekeeper and went to a local farm to hire a woman he had never before met. Before the end of the carriage ride home he proposed, she accepted, and they by chance met a reverend on the highway. They requested that he marry them on the spot, without them having to even step off the wagon, which might have been the first drive-through wedding ever conceived. The reverend prevailed upon them to go to a nearby house, which hastily welcomed the couple, and vows were exchanged without haste. Another couple riding horses searching for a justice of the peace found the back roads unforgiving. They "borrowed" a wagon and had it returned after their quick ceremony.

Lack of thought did not end so happily for the beaver glove thief. He was a rough itinerant seen stealing the goods from the pocket of a hotel guest. Without delay he appeared before a jury and heard some testimony. Thinking the trial was a joke, he arose, drew the gloves from his pocket, and suggested everyone have a drink. He was found guilty and sentenced to six months in the county jail.

In 1876 the county received a windfall of $10,486.76 from Lansing by special act due to an error of the state auditor when Clare County was detached from Isabella. The county earmarked $10,000 for a courthouse, with an additional $2,000 from citizens and $1,000 from taxation.

The contract was awarded to Hemmeter & Kaiser, and the cornerstone was laid on July 28, 1876. It was completed on October 26 of the following year, and with furniture it cost $16,190.49, which was fully paid at the time of opening. The red brick building was attractive in design, with a cupola gracing its crest. Due to deterioration and cramped space, a new county building was unveiled in 1972, and its predecessor was subsequently razed. Its cupola was saved and later placed on nearby fairgrounds. Some have expressed a desire to display it permanently on the grounds of the current courthouse.

The courts did not stay long at the 1972 building. Quickly the limited space of the 45,500-square-foot structure became apparent. Moreover, its traffic flow patterns did not take into account concerns for security and efficiency. The public, the accused, jurors, staff, judges, and everyone else had to use the same corridors. The building was renovated and held on to many county offices, including the clerk, after the courts moved next door into the new modernly designed Isabella County Courthouse in 2000.

The new court building is about 48,600 square feet and cost approximately $6 million, of which $1 million came from revenue sharing with the local tribal casino.

Additional funds from the casino proceeds helped to pay for local art that adorns the many corners of the building. Its theme reflects the area's Native American heritage, and the bulk of it is by the hand of local artists.

Behind one court's bench a simple dreamcatcher serves as a nod to the local Native American community. Similarly, next to the hanging American flag in the lobby is a mobile that wafts as it displays the flags of Michigan, Isabella County, the Saginaw Chippewa Tribe, and the Isabella County Trial Court. The court administrator attests that the latter is the first of its kind in Michigan. Elsewhere, four works of art by a local artist depict the family of four courthouses in Isabella County.

A few miles away, there is yet another court hearing cases and settling disputes: the tribal court. Outwardly and inwardly, it looks much like any other court in the state built in the last twenty years or so. The architecture, the

furniture, and the recording technology are the trappings of a trial court. But the name and artwork set this place apart, as does the circular configuration of the courtroom, which is of particular significance in the tribal culture. The jurisdiction of this court is distinct too. Often federal, state, and tribal courts must decide questions of fact and law to determine which sovereign has jurisdiction over a particular case.

Somehow, they coexist peacefully and perhaps even happily ever after, just like some memorable couples throughout the history of Isabella County.

JACKSON COUNTY

JACKSON—Some notable protracted litigation in Michigan's history finds its origins in Jackson County. Named for President Andrew Jackson, this county was organized on August 1, 1832, and attached judicially to its neighbor to the east, Washtenaw County.

The county seat was also named for the president, though it had a number of variations including Jacksonburgh and Jacksonopolis before locals settled on simply Jackson. The first court convened at the log house of Horace Blackman, a prominent early settler, on the first Tuesday of September 1832.

The judge addressed the grand jury and the people gathered for the inaugural session. "We are just emerging from the barbarous period of our lives, and that is comprised of the four months which have passed away since we left our Eastern homes in search of Western ones." He charged the jurors with their duties and admonished all present to give each case its due consideration.

In 1836 the Legislature authorized the county to borrow $10,000 for a court and clerk's office, both of which the county quickly erected in stone. Sheriff A. B. Gibson was the superintendent of the work, while David Porter did the masonry and Leonard House the carpentry. The ground was too soft in the original spot designated for the building, so it was moved slightly to the east. The Greek Revivalist structure with a columned porch across its front was completed in 1837. It was not replaced until the 1870s.

In the meanwhile, Jackson County became the birthplace of the Republican Party, a distinction that road signs and a historical marker commemorate to this day. No hall could accommodate the crowds, so the convention adjourned to an oak grove, where a platform and seating were temporarily placed.

Around the same time, less peaceful agents of change were at work in Jackson County. Railroad accidents claiming the lives of cattle and the economic well-being of their owners gave rise to some bad blood. Many resented the railroads for not erecting enough safety measures such as fences and for not settling cases at a fair level of compensation.

Bands of men began tampering with the tracks and disrupting the business of the railroads, who sought their remedy in court. The situation led to the indictment of thirty-seven men, who were tried in Wayne County. It was a four-month trial with 240 witnesses for the plaintiffs over twenty-seven days and 249 witnesses over forty days for the defendants. Some were acquitted, others were convicted, and many voiced lingering dissatisfaction over the whole affair for years.

Jackson County erected a new court in 1871. It was a large four-story stone structure with ample windows and a small cupola centered over the main entrance. Its address was 1 Michigan Avenue. Commercial development grew around it, encroaching on the square to the point where, judging by vintage black-and-white photographs, it looked like little more than another large storefront. Fittingly, it became just that years later when J.C. Penney Company bought and razed it to construct a department store.

Before then, the courthouse was the center of great media attention when it dealt with the murder of local millionaire Jacob Crouch, his pregnant daughter, her husband, and a house guest. They were shot on a cold and stormy night on November 21, 1883, in Spring Arbor Township.

Suspicion turned to Crouch's allegedly estranged and resentful son, Jason D. ("Judd"), and Daniel S. Holcomb, the man who with his wife raised Judd because Judd's mother died within a week of childbirth. It was a sensational trial lasting over three months and leading to the acquittal of Holcomb and the dismissal of charges against Judd.

Witnesses and suspected coconspirators were turning up dead, some by apparent suicide, but not if one asked skeptics. Days into the presentation of his circumstantial case, the prosecutor died too. Austin Blair, the sixty-six-year-old former governor from the Civil War years, took over the case. More than 140 witnesses testified. The county spent about $13,000 trying the case, and the defense reportedly spent nearly $20,000, princely sums at that time.

Decades later the same amount of money could have financed a significant portion of the new courthouse. The five-story brick and stone building was first constructed in 1927 to 1928 as an Elks lodge. The elaborate recreational facility soon fell victim to difficult economic times and stood empty several years for lack of funds. In 1935 the county bought it from bondholders for $27,000, which included $17,500 in delinquent taxes. The county spent $360,000 remodeling it and moved in during the spring of 1937.

Etched prominently on the walls are the words "Jackson County Building." Much lower on the street level newer lettering reflects that the building is now solely the "Jackson Court Building." It features several courtrooms, some of which suffer from occlusion by load-bearing columns. But typically the view of the trial by the public is all that is partly obstructed, not that of the judge, jury, or litigants.

Apart from its courthouses, Jackson boasts the Jackson State Prison. The county sought and won the institution early in its history in 1838, hoping that it would be a step toward winning the state capital, which legislators were considering moving from Detroit to a more central location. About thirty joint sessions were required before Jackson and other contenders lost out in 1847 to what would become Lansing.

The first jail was made of oak plank. Prison labor was a boon to the community until it was outlawed in 1909. The last contract under the old system expired shortly after World War I, at which point the oak planks were long gone, and a much more modern facility had taken its place.

Perhaps the most daring escape from the prison was the inmate who hopped into a hijacked helicopter that landed in the prison yard on June 6, 1975. He was captured the following day. Historical accounts do not mention if the escape led to charges in a court of law and, if so, how long the trial lasted compared to Jackson's other epic courtroom contests.

KALAMAZOO COUNTY

KALAMAZOO—On the banks of a boiling river, Kalamazoo County was founded. As with any steaming teacup, there is a saucer that has both a cooling and a calming effect. The courthouses of Kalamazoo County are that saucer, points of stability for a land with a name suggesting quite the opposite.

Kalamazoo County, which was once attached to St. Joseph County, was established on October 29, 1829, and organized in its own right the following year. Bronson was the seat of justice, named for Titus Bronson, the founder of Kalamazoo who first hosted court in his log cabin. In 1836 the Legislature changed the name of the seat to match that of the county. Kalamazoo means "it boils like pot" or "the boiling pot"—a moniker that signifies the many boiling-like eddies that were early observed on the surface of the river of the same name.

On the third Tuesday of October 1831, Abraham I. Shaver hosted court in his house. Court adjourned to the schoolhouse near John Insley's in Brady Township. An early court record delicately described the charge against Hannah Carpenter as "the crime of the woman whom Jesus of Nazareth bade 'go, and sin no more.'" She did not appear in court and was fined $25. In 1837, records indicate that the court held session inside the shop of a blacksmith.

On April 28, 1836, the county passed a resolution to build a courthouse for $6,000. Local lore attributes the architectural work to Ammi B. Young of Montpelier, Vermont, but other sources credit E. R. Ball, who had already built one local mansion. The clapboard Greek Revival structure featured double-hung windows made of multiple panes with moldings atop and shutters astride them. The forty-two-by-fifty-five-foot structure had pilasters at each corner and a twenty-foot tower or cupola in the rear. Offices were on the first floor, and a courtroom with a capacity for about 300 was on the upper floor.

In 1866 contractors Bush and Paterson removed the tower and moved the building back a few feet. They rebuilt the courtroom, extended the building's two entrances, and added central roof pediments. Their work cost about $8,000.

The building would migrate in 1884 to the extreme northwest corner of its lot, to make room for the large stone edifice that would succeed it. Voters approved $60,000 for the project designed by Edward O. Fallis of Toledo, Ohio. The Renaissance Revival style brick building had long narrow windows, pedimented entries, brick pilasters, and a large cornice. The main central tower was framed by four rounded corner towers with mansard roofs. The first session of court in the new structure occurred on October 26, 1885.

After construction, the original courthouse sold for $100 and was moved to another location, where it later gained a brick veneer. It was a laundry and then a livery stable before it was razed in 1921. The successor met the same fate in 1935 to make way for the Kalamazoo County Building. Cries for a newer, more secure jail preceded the wrecking ball. Lady Justice, however, was spared. She stood atop the central tower and was placed in storage. She is now on display at the Kalamazoo Valley Museum, where visitors can read how local businessman Donald O. Boudeman saved her from the scrap heap during World War II. He claimed that the worth of her tin paled in comparison to her historical value. He pledged to give money to the county scrap metal drive if authorities would agree to save the statue.

The latest courthouse found its genesis in the Public Works Administration, which in June 1934 approved a loan and grant totaling $731,000. In September voters approved $565,000 in bonds. Local architect M. J. C. Billingham conceptualized the art deco design for the 91,000-square-foot steel reinforced concrete monolith. The exterior walls are Mankato limestone, and the base is dark granite. Corrado Joseph Parducci carved several figures in relief representing Justice, Law, and Vigilance, including, above the main entrances, a bearded man in a tunic holding two tablets.

Lions' faces and swags adorn the cornice line. There are six stories, though the top floor is only the fifth floor because the first floor is above the ground floor, where Veteran's Hall is located. Ornate bronze doors and marble-paneled lobbies welcome visitors waiting to board the elevators. The long-awaited jail was once at the top, where now the prosecutor's office occupies the space. In 1972, the jail moved about four miles away to the eastern outskirts of town.

There are two large original courtrooms and two additional courtrooms that are more modern in appearance. Dark oak paneling surrounds the former, where well-appointed benches impose their authority from every angle. The building was officially dedicated on October 16, 1937.

Several offices left the County Building in 1978 for the 83,500-square-foot administration building on nearby Kalamazoo Street. Cain Associates designed this newest building. Contractors Whitaker Construction Company and Miller-Davis Company completed the project for about $4.18 million. The county has since also built a juvenile court building. In 2002, however, voters rejected a proposal for a new jail, juvenile home, and single-site court building.

So the saucer remains in its current state, as a counterpoint to boiling rivers and other volatility, whatever their form.

KALKASKA COUNTY

KALKASKA—Depending on one's source, the land of Kalkaska is either fertile or fallow. Literal translation of its name means "table land" or "burned over land." On the other hand, the county has succeeded in its own right, even in gaining the designation in 1990 of Kalkaska soil, which is located in at least twenty-eight other counties, as Michigan's state soil. The honor is all the more notable, considering that Michigan has over 450 different soils.

From 1840 to 1843, this unsettled territory was called Wabassee for a Potawatami chief whose name means "Swan." He signed the Treaty of 1821. Before reaching its current form, the county name was spelled Calcasca and Kalcaska. The village of Kalkaska was incorporated on March 10, 1887, though it was first settled in 1871. The Legislature organized the county on January 27, 1871. Previously, Grand Traverse and Antrim Counties administered Kalkaska.

County supervisors first met on April 25, 1871, in a schoolhouse in Round Lake. There they approved the following annual salaries: sheriff ($100), clerk ($150), prosecutor ($200), and probate judge ($100). The house of A. C. Beebe was designated the circuit court. At the second meeting on June 14, the supervisors voted to prohibit swine from running loose between April 1 and September 1.

Kalkaska was chosen as the county seat on July 14, 1873. In October the county authorized $1,000 for a courthouse. It was slightly above budget at $1,075.51 when it was completed in January 1874. The building contract went to H. L. Birdsall, and lathing and plastering was the responsibility of A. W. Jones.

A larger and more impressive brick court was constructed for about $20,000 in 1883. It remained in use until its successor was completed across town in 1976. After records and other materials were transferred, the 1883 building was razed.

A framed illustration of the old building is in the current clerk's office. It was three stories, with the sheriff's quarters on the top floor and prisoners in basement cells. The remaining floors housed county offices and the circuit courtroom. Rows of rectangular windows lined the walls. The roof was pitched with a tower above the front entrance of the building. The courtroom had an arched and embossed ceiling. The courthouse faced Cherry Street at Third. Its grounds are the current site of a senior citizens' center. The judge's bench, the railing, and the jurors' swivel chairs were saved and placed in the new courtroom.

Behind the bench is an impressive set of Fairbanks scales. They reportedly sat on a shelf near the bench in the older building. In the new building, they dominate the view of the bench, standing behind it and between the flags of America and Michigan in a circular recess painted a sharp blue. They are perhaps the finest symbol in the 1976 Kalkaska Governmental Center, which is made up of the courts building and the adjacent county offices building. The modern one-story buildings are not quite twins, but they are born of the same time and style.

In 1987 Kalkaska got a new jail for $750,000. The old jail was declared unfit long before in 1970. Annual expenditures in the neighborhood of $250,000 had been required to send inmates to neighboring counties, which did not include the cost of transporting deputies.

The main geographical feature of the county is a plateau separating the watershed of the Manistee River to the southeast from the Boardman and Rapid Rivers in the northwest. They welcome more than a few recreational

fishers, who travel to Kalkaska for its annual trout festival. Locals joke that Kalkaska has the largest trout in the state, a sculpture in the middle of town.

The ground gave birth to controversial oil and natural gas exploitation in the 1970s. Local unions did not care for Shell Oil Company's contract with a nonunion Texas engineering firm to construct in Kalkaska a $20 million processing plant. Tensions were so high and state trooper presence so prevalent that a local newspaper described the situation as a "military occupation." To smooth matters over, the two companies as a goodwill gesture offered a $250,000 gift to the township, which was ten times its annual budget. Local unions pitched in free labor to construct a new fire hall.

Whatever the state of Kalkaska's soil, its public buildings, particularly its three courthouses, demonstrate that when good things take root, they tend to stay in one form or another.

KENT COUNTY

GRAND RAPIDS—The county that is home to Michigan's second largest city also boasts perhaps its most user-friendly modern courthouse. Television screens akin to those in an airport give the public updates on matters before the court. Citizens facing often stressful experiences as witnesses, litigants, criminal defendants, jurors, and spectators find comfort in wide corridors and ample light filtered through blue-tinged windows that grant some of the finest views of the city. Different elevators, hallways, and bathrooms separate the public from the personnel and from those in custody.

Built for $60 million and unveiled on September 5, 2001, the twelve-story building is one of the newest landmarks downtown. It stands as one edifice measuring 323,626 square feet, but close inspection of its design reveals that it is really two towers connected by a V-shaped elevator lobby and vestibule.

It is hardly the first symbol of justice in Grand Rapids. Kent County was first drawn and named on March 2, 1831, for Chancellor James Kent, a celebrated New York jurist who died in 1817. By 1836 it was separated from Kalamazoo County and organized in its own right.

The first courthouse was erected in 1836 at present-day Fulton Street (Veteran's) Park at a cost of about $5,000. It was a two-story frame structure measuring about thirty by forty feet. Columns at the front of the building faced south, and a cupola capped by a gilded ball graced the top of the building. Fire destroyed it on July 12, 1844.

A few months before, perhaps the most dramatic murder trial in Kent County history was recorded. The victim was Nega, a Native American woman found dead on December 21, 1842. E. M. Miller, the suspect, fled toward the lakeshore and then down the frozen ice toward Chicago. Nega's mourners cried foul after they lost his trail in Muskegon. Prominent white citizens of Grand Rapids promised to help, and T. D. Gilbert, the newly elected sheriff of Ottawa County, left in pursuit.

Gilbert figured that Miller was bound for Chicago, but there were no tracks on the snow-covered trail along the shore. Gilbert walked out onto the ice and finally found a clue—frozen tobacco juice, which was the mark of a white man because Native Americans typically did not chew. He followed the trail into the night, pushing on until he reached the lighthouse at the mouth of the Kalamazoo River. He learned that no one had passed that day. The keeper was instructed to send his boy to Saugatuck should anyone pass.

The boy came the next morning. Gilbert made haste

and apprehended Miller, who said, "I suppose I must go with you." Miller revealed that he camped on shore the night before, which is why Gilbert lost his trail.

Intense excitement over the trial filled Grand Rapids. A steady stream of visitors came to lay eyes on Miller. Proceedings began on May 17, 1843. A packed courtroom listened to several days of testimony, which closed on May 24.

The jury began deliberation at 3:00 p.m. as a massive storm struck the area. A particularly colorful account recalls that the court was shaken to its foundations as the people stood aghast. "It seemed to be the storm-king giving warning to do justice, and the jury took the hint." Thunderclaps continued to ring out as lighting struck and rain poured down "until it seemed that heaven was at war with the earth."

Nature did not subside even as the foreman at 11:00 p.m. read a verdict of guilty with a recommendation for executive clemency. Fully aware that a bill was pending that would ban capital punishment, Judge Ransom sentenced Miller to hang on February 25, 1844.

The bill did not pass that year. A scaffold was erected, but friends of Miller secured for him a reprieve. In the meanwhile the ban passed after another attempt, and his death sentence was set aside for life imprisonment. Years later he was pardoned after the prosecution's star witness on his deathbed confessed to the murder.

Another source asserts that Sheriff Gilbert was convinced of Miller's innocence, worked to have the ban passed, and assiduously delayed completion of the scaffold even though many good oaks with low branches were near the court.

After the court that saw Nega's murder trial burned down, a $300 makeshift replacement building was erected. It was serviceable for only six years. The growing records were scattered about the city in clothes baskets, flour barrels, and vacant rooms. The county government and court moved about town, with the latter landing on the west side of the Grand River for some time before returning east in 1852.

The county and city would later enter a protracted dispute over who owned the land at the old courthouse square. The state supreme court eventually ruled in favor of the city in 1887. All told, the grand new stone courthouse would cost $277,610.98 when it opened on July 4, 1892.

Exactly three years earlier, Judge Marsden C. Burch had given an address at the laying of the cornerstone. Noting the anniversary of the Declaration of Independence, he said that everyone was gathered "on liberty's birthday to plant in freedom's soil the cornerstone of a temple to justice."

He also dubbed the planned building "a citadel of equal rights." At the 2001 dedication, the mayor quoted the following words of Burch. "There should be some place in a great municipality where all classes of citizens may meet upon equal terms with equal rights. Such . . . is being provided here."

One wonders if a man arrested for drunkenness in 1908 felt the same sentiment. He fought the policeman every step of the way to the courthouse. When the judge heard the charge and remarked that the man was not drunk, the officer quipped that he was two hours ago.

The courthouse fell victim to the city's plan for urban renewal. In 1969 the modernly designed Kent County Hall of Justice opened, and its predecessor was razed. In turn, the replacement was itself replaced in 2001 and, according to some, not missed for a moment.

While there was no going back for Kent County, a few small touches connect the new courthouse to its architectural past. Historical displays inside the courthouse include a judge's chair and desk from the 1892 courthouse. Above one jury box are several portraits tracing the judicial family tree of the county's oldest circuit judgeship.

Outside the building is a clock tower preserved from the demolished 1888 city hall and standing in a spot very close to its original footprint. Bordering stone and corner elements from city hall stand at the base of the new clock tower, which lights the face of the clock different colors at night. The four stainless steel turrets arc away from the new building as an homage to the tearing down of the original tower turrets.

Perhaps the greatest tribute is that the legacy of service to Kent County's inhabitants lives on, whatever form the venue for it might take. Its current user-friendly shape is sure to endure for some time, particularly because some floors were left unfinished in anticipation of future needs.

KEWEENAW COUNTY

EAGLE RIVER—Keweenaw has yet to outgrow its simple and elegant wooden courthouse overlooking Lake Superior. Since the creation of the county in 1861, which is named for a native word meaning "place of portage," the total population reached its peak of 7,156 in the Census of 1910. Presently the population stands at about 2,300.

Keweenaw is Michigan's least populated county, as well as the northernmost. It lies closer to the North Pole than to Quebec, Canada. Its large territory includes Isle Royale National Park, the emerald isle of Lake Superior forty-eight miles northwest of the tip of the rugged Keweenaw Peninsula.

Eagle River was one of the earliest settlements along the Keweenaw Point, founded in 1843. Travelers called the gathering point "Eagle's Nest River" due to the abundance of the bird in the area then. French settlers called it "La riviere nid d'aigle."

Keweenaw County's first court was a room rented at the Phoenix Hotel for $50 a day. When court was not in session, the space was a billiard and barroom. Luminaries such as President James A. Garfield and John Bagley, mayor of Detroit, appeared on the register.

The courthouse was built in 1866 for $6,578. Like elsewhere in Michigan, controversy surrounded the approval

of funds for construction. The minutes of the County Supervisor indicated much squabbling. The sheriff and his deputy were paid extra to quell riots at most of the county's early meetings. Eventually a countywide vote carried the day 414 to 372. Opponents sought to invalidate the vote, alleging illegally cast votes in Sherman Township. There were still sore feelings as construction neared its end when the undersheriff was paid $15 to bring in two supervisors who had failed to attend an important meeting.

An 1883 publication described the courthouse as "a commodious wooden structure, two stories high, with the county offices being on the first floor." Keweenaw was renting a local attic as its jail, which gave the writer some pause. "The building used as a jail is a rented structure, and is not a very secure place to hold professional 'cracksmen.'"

The story of Jemmie Tresize perhaps best illustrates the problem with the jail. Tresize was a miner who worked hard six days a week, reportedly loading a kibble faster than any ten men who worked together. Sundays he reserved for heavy drinking. No one begrudged him his day of leisure, especially because he provided such valuable labor most of the week. County officials were typically mining officials too, which put them in the awkward position of choosing between dispensing justice and getting rock out of their

shafts. Plus, Tresize was hardly an exception because conflicts between Methodists from Cornwall and Catholics from Ireland were regularly weekly occurrences in the streets and saloons.

The calculus changed when Tresize began licking whole groups of men. On Monday morning, half of a given mine may have been missing its underground crew, which fell the day before under the legendary fists of Tresize. Because the situation could not long endure, a standing order to lock up Tresize before he could inflict any more mayhem was issued.

On a particularly riotous Sunday, the jail was already filled with brawlers and could hardly fit the large Tresize. The city council had a special meeting to address the sheriff's difficulty. The next day, Eagle River sent to Detroit for a solid iron ball and chain weighing 200 pounds.

The new device worked well for the first few weeks. But one Sunday after a long day presiding over regular Sunday special court, the justice of peace eyed quite a sight. Through the window of a popular Cornish bar was Jemmie Tresize singing and shouting defiantly to every Irishman in earshot. His belly was up to the bar. In one hand was a drink and in the other he heaved the massive ball and chain.

John B. Sweat designed the original 1866 wooden clapboard two-story courthouse. It stands behind a low brick wall on a grassy knoll on Fourth Street, within sight of Lake Superior and near the shoulder of scenic M-26 highway. In 1925 it was expanded and given its present Colonial Revival style. A columned portico, pilasters, and entry details were the principal improvements. The shimmering white exterior paint lies beneath a maroon peaked roof, striking a crisp look when the clear blue sky occupies the background. The years of the birth and transformation of the courthouse appear in opposite corners above the main front entrance. One visit revealed freshly extinguished cigarettes in a handmade wooden ashtray standing just inside the front door.

County offices are on the first floor, and the modest courtroom is on the second floor. The latter features a bright blue carpet, white walls, and a lighter blue tone for trim that hints at a mixture of the color of the carpet and walls. A curved banister separates the public seating from the elevated adjacent tables before the bench for the parties, suggesting close quarters for a community where everyone knows each other. From the perspective of the public, the jury box is to the right of the bench, and glass-paneled bookshelves bearing law books are to the left. The jury room appears rustic, as does the small judge's chamber.

Another favorite local story recounts the hospitality of the area. Peter White was elected the first clerk for Marquette in 1851. He was required on one occasion to go by foot in the dead of winter to Eagle River to get the local county clerk's certificate to a lot of legal documents.

The clerk in Eagle River would have none of it when White said that he would return to Marquette the next day. "We never allow a winter visitor to depart under two weeks, and as you are the first man who has ever come from Marquette or Carp River up here by land, we must give you a good time," said the clerk.

After one night of lively partying, White was whisked to a local store where he was forced to put on an elegant suit. According to White, "for the next eight or ten days I was put through such a round of pleasure and hospitable attentions as never before nor since witnessed by me. I could not have been more civilly feasted and toasted had I been the President. Such was the hospitality of the early settlers of the copper region."

Present-day visitors will also find visiting Keweenaw for fewer than a handful of days difficult, owing to its continued hospitality, natural beauty, and lovely old courthouse on a tranquil green square near the south bank of Lake Superior.

LAKE
COUNTY

BALDWIN—A bloody fight and a devastating fire are two epic events that forever mark the Lake County Courthouse. It stands prominently along the right of way, looking southward down the center of the commercial strip where traveling tourists and rooted residents gather.

The impressive white portico and its four supporting columns make up the face of the courthouse. On the west end of the building through a large arched window one can see the somewhat tattered and charred flag saved from the blaze and presented decades later for the dedication of a new addition. The secure entrance is to the east, proclaiming in large green letters the name and purpose of the building. To the north the building is firmly connected to the jail. North, south, east, and west, the court radiates its presence and its position in the community.

At first the county was named in 1840 for Aischum, a Potawatami chief whose name appeared on every Native American treaty affecting Michigan lands from 1818 until 1836. It was renamed Lake though it is landlocked and does not contain in abundance or size any greater inland lakes than most other counties. The county was formally organized in 1871 and was at different times part of Ottawa, Oceana, Newaygo, Mecosta, Mason, and Osceola counties. An influx of homesteaders who were Civil War veterans catapulted the county toward independence.

In the twentieth century the county gained prominence as home to Idlewild, a summer resort community that attracted African American vacationers from primarily around the Midwest, as well as renowned performers from across the nation. Attendance peaked at around 25,000 during Independence Day Weekend 1959. Civil rights legislation of the 1960s contributed to the decline of the area's

popularity, though efforts are under way to convert Idlewild into a destination for its historical importance.

Lake County's other claim to fame is the hazily recorded Battle of Chase. It was the culmination of a contest for the county seat. Chase, which was named for Salmon P. Chase, a governor of Ohio, was the county seat at the time of organization, and for $100 a year it rented the upper story of a building to hold court. Earlier, it was called Green Dell and, before then, Joiner for an early settler. Meanwhile, Hannibal, a town named for an early settler's surname, grew and was renamed Baldwin City and finally just Baldwin in honor of Michigan's Governor Henry P. Baldwin.

These two communities, along with Nirvana and Yates Township, vied for the county seat. A coalition of towns in August 1874 pledged $5,000 for county buildings if the seat would relocate to Baldwin. The vote carried 355 to 299, but Chase resisted, hoping perhaps to win an injunction in court.

The sheriff and clerk, who were from Chase, refused to do business outside of their hometown. The treasurer, who was from Baldwin, refused to pay any orders not issued from Baldwin. The standoff prompted a committee from Baldwin to approach Chase on April 30, 1875, about moving the safe full of records to Baldwin so that the county could again function. Chase rebuffed the delegation.

Here the record is difficult to resolve. What seems clear is that a larger group from Baldwin returned the same day and came home with the safe after some sort of struggle. It is unclear if they came at night or during the day. It is also unknown if they used a railroad and, if so, whether their return was engine powered or hand driven.

One account claims that the Chaseites buried the safe

beneath the court building and that the Baldwinites razed the building before they made off with the safe. Another version of the story asserts that the whole building was lifted and moved.

The most credible story is that the safe was too large to fit through a door and was housed in a lean-to near or attached to the court building. The Baldwinites secured a group of burly lumbermen to accompany them to Chase. One part of the group dismantled the lean-to and secured the safe while the others stood guard and beat back the Chaseites who were roused by mill whistles. The train blew its whistle when the safe was loaded onto the flatcar and the brawling Baldwinites jumped onto the train as it left. In its wake the battle left about twenty physically injured men requiring care, with a broken collarbone registering as the most serious. Bruised egos were in abundance. The safe would change hands a number of times and eventually ended up sans records back in Chase.

For a time court was held in Baldwin in the village hall and also in J. H. Cobb Hall. In October 1876 the county bought the building of a Mr. Chick for $600. The next year the clerk authorized money for a privy and vault. For $300 a jail was built on the west lot. Luther complicated matters when it offered $6,000 for county buildings if the seat would relocate there. Baldwin increased its offer of $2,000 to $2,500 and held onto the seat. A cornerstone was laid in 1886, and construction was completed in 1888 for $10,000. The grand brick building featured the columns and portico, as well as a distinctive tower above its attic. Most construction materials were purchased locally, with the notable exception of ironworks for the jail that had to be special ordered.

Fire struck on April 3, 1927. It started at the base of a chimney and quickly moved up to the attic and engulfed the tower. Some records and furniture were whisked to safety as crews fought the blaze for over six hours. When the building seemed lost, fire crews turned their hoses to the vaults, keeping them cool and saving the county's records. The Reverend William O. Homer saved the flag, which at the time had only forty-eight stars.

The county spent $50,000 rebuilding the structure in the image of its predecessor, though without the tower. The portico and columns were recreated. Masonry and reinforced concrete with a cornice wrapping around the building formed the exterior of the reborn court. Inside, it was much like it had been before, with the exception of paneled walls, lower ceilings, and carpeting.

In 1998 the county broke ground on a renovation and expansion that ended in 2000. The $6.5 million project, which included financial assistance from the U.S. Department of Agriculture, renovated 11,448 square feet and added 26,852 square feet. Wooden implements from the old circuit court—the bench, jury box, and banisters—were placed within the smaller courtroom, which houses probate and district court. The new circuit court is spacious and modern yet retrospective in design. Like the lobby areas, it employs a motif of white walls, dark green trim, and light-colored wood. In large green letters on its front and back wall it declares, should anyone be wondering, "Lake County Trial Court." Modern voice and video recording devices are unobtrusively deployed throughout the room.

The flag Rev. William Homer saved made its way from his estate back to the county, which had it specially framed and then rededicated on June 16, 2000. Ironically, it looks out over a fire exit through the arched window. It serves as a symbol for and reminder of a natural hazard that brought the county to its knees. As for a hazard that was human in origin, the Battle of Chase lives on in all its versions in the collective memories and recorded recollections of those who make their homes in Lake County.

LAPEER COUNTY

LAPEER—Lapeer prides itself on having Michigan's oldest county courthouse still in use at the county seat and one of the ten oldest such buildings in America. Its counterpart in Berrien is older and is still used, but it is not in the county seat. The improbable survival of Lapeer's most prominent symbol begins with a rivalry between two early settlers.

The territorial government laid out Lapeer in 1822 and organized it as a county on January 20, 1835, attaching it for judicial purposes to Oakland County. Lapeer's name comes from the French words for "the rock," or La Pierre. Early French traders thus referred to how rocky local riverbeds were, particularly the Flint River.

Enoch J. White led the Whigs and the upper part of town, which was once called Whitesville, against Alvin N. Hart and the Democrats in the lower end of town. The first court in lower Lapeer burned during construction, some believe by arson. Chester Hatch began building a modest court building in 1839 for White in the upper part of town. It was used until about 1845 and cost $450.

An early murder trial in the first courthouse lasted two weeks and ended in an acquittal. The defendant avoided a death sentence, which at the time state law authorized. He reportedly became fearful and all but admitted the crime to the sheriff before his trial ended. He became "violently religious, and spent most of his time in his cell in prayer and singing hymns." After his acquittal, he cursed the sheriff and barged into a church during a service. A historical account states that he "gave an exhortation which produced a profound impression upon the audience." The same report contends that nobody doubted his guilt but everyone was reluctant to impose such a harsh punishment based on circumstantial evidence.

Hart in the meanwhile invested a princely $10,000 in a large white Greek Revival courthouse. It was built in 1845–46 by Norman Davidson of native white pine. Hart offered the building for the county to rent for $1 a year. On March 1, 1847, Judge David Freer presided over the first court session there, which he promptly adjourned for lack of business.

The state senate, of which Hart was a member, passed a bill in 1845 that allowed local governments to raise taxes to pay for county buildings. Despite earlier talk of a gift, Hart looked to recoup his investment in the courthouse. Voters in 1851 rejected buying the building for $4,500. The following year the board of supervisors moved court back

to White's building. Hart eventually accepted $3,000 for the building in 1853.

Court moved back there, and White's building became a high school. "Thus good finally resulted from the acrimonious contest," said one source. The school later burned in 1876. Hart's court was moved eighty feet to the south and placed atop a brick foundation. The budget for the move was $900. The local opera house served for a while as the temporary courthouse.

Thus Hart won the contest for the courthouse. It measures ninety by forty-five feet. Four large Doric columns support its massive portico, where the year 1846 is prominently displayed in large shiny gold numbers. Previously, the same spot bore the erroneous date of 1839, which probably referred to the building date of Lapeer's first courthouse. It is believed that this date may have been added at the building's rededication in the late 1930s when it received a new roof and had a new foundation excavated.

The courthouse has a three-tiered dome on the opposite end of the portico, which was unusual for the time period. The tower is square and rises to support a dome shingled with brass and with a diameter of ten feet.

In 1887 the board of supervisors rejected a bid from Imlay City for the county seat, along with $50,000 for a new courthouse. In the late 1890s Lapeer's courthouse was in general disrepair, and the grounds were filthy due to grazing cattle. In 1897 the building was wired for electricity.

A plaque on the porch of the building commemorates a case in which a local judge struck down on constitutional grounds a 1913 state law authorizing the sterilization of mentally impaired individuals who were in public custody. The Michigan Supreme Court upheld the case in 1918.

In July 1920 the courthouse gave shelter in a more literal sense to a mentally impaired fourteen-year-old boy. He lived under the courthouse steps for about a week. He left his state home and stumbled upon a carnival in town. He could hear and watch the fun from his safe haven. At night he left to exercise and to wander among the tents to pet the merry-go-round horses. Town boys befriended him and brought him food. Eventually his attendants found him and took him back into custody.

In the coming decades the building underwent many changes. It received a new heating plant and had the bookshelves in the tower room moved to the courtroom on the second floor. The tower room became a jury room. Fluorescent lights and acoustical ceiling tiles made their appearance.

Complaints about the state of the courthouse and its space constraints came to a head in the late 1960s and

through the 1970s. One judge bemoaned the fact that the building only had "outhouse facilities" for jurors because there was no restroom for them in the building. The debate on construction began in 1969, and only in 1977 did Lapeer decide to locate a new facility downtown.

The modern court building is subdued in design. It is meant to be a backdrop to its predecessor and not to take away from that symbol. Numerous sight lines connect the new building to the old one. Tomblinson, Harburn, Yurk and Associates of Flint designed the 1978 building, which is about 19,000 square feet. It cost $3.5 million and in May 1978 brought the county its first groundbreaking for a new courthouse in over 130 years. It was opened in 1980.

It is believed that in 1978 Michigan's oldest courthouse was hearing Michigan's oldest case at the time, a 1934 armed robbery that was transferred from Genesee County. It was a new trial after appeal, and one of the witnesses was not even born at the time of the alleged crime.

The third floor in the new building was empty at first,

but about twenty years later it too was opened at a cost of approximately $90,000. The county spent nearly $3 million in renovation projects between 1997 and 2005, revamping the interior.

Nor was the old courthouse ignored. The sale of bricks, grant applications, and penny drives helped to cover over $1 million in renovations. A donation of 170 gallons of paint made a difference, too.

Though rarely used, the interior of the courthouse still appears like a public building. Vintage furniture and an elegant configuration fill the second-story courtroom. The walls feature an early painting of the state seal. It dates to at least the early twentieth century because it features a design that the Legislature changed at that time. To celebrate its most recent round of renovations, the old courthouse welcomed the justices of the Michigan Supreme Court, who held oral arguments there on September 14, 2007, before attending an evening gala later that day.

Like its closest historical counterpart in distant Berrien County, Lapeer's old courthouse is a living link to the past. Its proximity to the new building is unique, and the deferential design of that building is well deserved. Between these two buildings, there is no question of seniority.

LEELANAU COUNTY

LELAND/SUTTONS BAY—As the tip of Michigan's little finger, Leelanau County unlike most others is defined geographically by the natural boundaries of Lake Michigan. The thirty-five mile peninsula boasts over one hundred miles of coastline and the forty-fifth parallel, the midpoint between the North Pole and the equator, nearly perfectly bisects it. This land is also home to Michigan's most recent county seat change.

Leelanau's itinerant county seat reaches back to its very origin. When the county was organized on February 27, 1863, the Legislature gave local voters three choices for the county seat: Northport, Leland, or Glen Arbor. Voters selected the relatively remote enclave at Northport. The county's population was 2,158 persons.

The name of the county means "land of delight." Due to a typographical error attributed to Lansing, it was spelled on maps and in records as Leelanaw until officially changed to its current and intended form in 1896.

Judge F. J. Littlejohn presided over the first session of circuit court in Northport in a schoolhouse on a hill on May 5, 1864. In September of the following year the first criminal case was filed, a charge of adultery against Peter Drew. For unexplained reasons the prosecution withdrew the case in June 1866.

The county has record of a suit before organization for recovery for the death of a dog. The plaintiff sought $100 but only recovered $25. By any measure of inflation the dog proved quite an expensive breed for the defendant.

No permanent court was ever constructed in Northport. County offices were housed in rooms above a store. After a fire and a vote of 635 to 517, the county seat moved south along the peninsula to Leland in 1883. The origin of its name is uncertain. It is generally accepted that due to its location on the eastern shore of Lake Michigan where the prevailing westward winds blow it was the "lee land." It is at the mouth of the Carp River.

Well before the move, a letter writer to a local newspaper cautioned against it on March 19, 1875. He argued that Leland only had a furnace, a company store, and a lot of smoke but no hotel, grist mill, or brewery. He recounted the experience of a friend, who sought a hotel or a place to dine there. He was directed to the store, where he had beer and crackers.

From 1883 to 1966, Leland had a wooden courthouse that once belonged to an ironworks enterprise that never quite took root despite its efforts at making pig iron. Many of the coastal towns emerged as fuel stations for passing steamers, selling their hardwood timber for the boats to burn.

The county built a small and sturdy jail in 1901 reportedly from recycled bricks that once made up the chimney of the ironworks. The small structure still stands on the courthouse lawn, having served at various stages as a historical museum, the prosecutor's office, and storage space.

Its neighbor is the now former courthouse, built in 1966. It is a modern one-story, flat-roofed brick building. The architects were Field, Graheck, Bell & Kline of Traverse City, and the general contractor was Arnold & Tezak, Inc. The hallway featured portraits and biographies of the county's many probate judges. Elsewhere one could see a judge's robe hanging on a coatrack in the middle of a public hallway.

The courtroom as it appeared when it was in use at Leelanau County's former courthouse in Leland

The roof of the courtroom was somewhat raised, creating space for rows of windows that let in natural light. The room was somewhat narrow but long. Rows of large bulbous light fixtures lined the room, along with hanging ceiling fans. The public sat in theater-style wooden folding chairs that were connected to each other in rows and bolted to the tile floor. Jurors enjoyed white cushioned swivel chairs that lean backward. The walls were lined with brick, except for the wall behind the bench, which was finished wood that contrasts with the standing flags. With the recent departure of the county government from Leland, it is unclear what will happen to the building and its surrounding grounds.

Now anyone who has official county business to transact will have to travel to Suttons Bay, the new county seat. The town is named for an early settler. It was once called Suttonsburg and Pleasant City. Sixty-two percent of voters chose it for the county seat in August 2004. The new 68,000-square-foot courthouse was built on forty-six acres off M-204, west of Suttons Bay and east of Lake Leelanau. The Sheriff's Office Building preceded it, and the two are connected underground by a tunnel, providing a secure transport route for inmates from jail to the courthouse. The total cost of the courthouse was $10.6 million. DeVere Construction of Alpena designed and built the courthouse. The peaked-roof structure is reminiscent of inns that dot Leelanau and drive its tourist industry. Construction con-

tinued through the end of 2007, and by February 2008 the facility was ready to welcome its new occupants.

Restrictive land use and zoning rules in Leland allegedly played a role in the move, as did the fact that a new jail facility was recently bonded and built outside Suttons Bay. There is also the feeling that Suttons Bay is more commercial and business-oriented than the reputed bedroom community of Leland.

Outside of the new courthouse is a large stone with a plaque commemorating Emelia Schaub, Michigan's first female county prosecutor. The stone previously stood outside of the courthouse in Leland. Schaub was elected to her first of six terms in 1936. She gained notoriety earlier in her career in 1926 as reportedly the first female attorney in America ever to successfully defend a murder case. As prosecutor she worked to return lands to Native Americans, who were pushed up the Leelanau Peninsula and eventually expelled as settlement expanded throughout the Lower Peninsula. Michigan returned lands and created a de facto reservation, which achieved federal recognition in 1980. The Grand Traverse Band of Ottawa and Chippewa Native Americans owns about 680 acres in Leelanau.

Those who visit Leelanau come with a purpose, for it is not on the road to anyplace else. Residents and visitors alike will decide if the new courthouse will add to the natural beauty of its county's setting as the picturesque little finger jutting into the water and coaxing the rest of the mitten to experience the lake that is author to Leelanau's shape.

LENAWEE COUNTY

ADRIAN—There is hardly a spot in Lenawee County one cannot see from the tower atop its historic courthouse. Capping the 132-foot tower is a 21-foot pole prominently displaying the American flag all day and night.

The flag always flies because getting it up the pole involves a herculean effort featuring at least one trapdoor resembling a box top and several staircases—wooden, spiral, and aluminum. If by chance one of the fastens goes loose and the flag flies improperly, concerned citizens intent on not desecrating Old Glory lobby local leaders to rent a crane and correct the situation. On at least one occasion, it was the dead of winter, and the job had to wait until a warm day made the task feasible. During times of mourning, no flag flies atop the tower because it is not equipped to fly the flag at half-mast. Instead, a different flag pole on the eastern grounds of the building flies half-staff.

Pride in the flag is but one example of how Lenawee spared no expense on its shining symbol on a hill. Lenawee County was first settled in 1824. A group of about twenty people almost exclusively from Jefferson County in upstate New York founded Tecumseh. One of their leaders, General Joseph W. Brown, met with Lewis Cass, the territorial gov-ernor. According to one account, Cass chose the name Lenawee, which came from the Shawnee word for "men" or "the people." When asked later by someone where Tecumseh was, Brown replied, "thirty miles from Monroe and forty miles beyond God's blessing." Brown's wanderlust later led him to Texas, where one of his sons fought at the Alamo.

The departure of Brown, who had some political clout, along with the central location of Adrian and the arrival of a railroad line there, convinced Michigan's first Legislature, heeding a strong lobbying effort from Adrian, to make Adrian the seat of Lenawee County. Adrian's first court-house was built in 1837.

It had a short life, burning down early in the morning on Sunday, March 14, 1852. The fire happened during the trial of a man accused of murdering his wife. Local lore attributed the fire to the man's brother. According to one account, the building "burned up about 4:00 a.m. by some unhung scoundrel." No photograph, drawing, or detailed verbal description of the two-story building is known to exist.

For the next thirty-three years, Lenawee County had no permanent courthouse. Millage proposals failed

because voters outside of Adrian had little interest in subsidizing what they considered a proposal to benefit Adrian. Finally, the city of Adrian offered an additional $15,000 if the county would contribute $50,000. The additional funds from Adrian paid for much of the decorative and ornamental elements of the building. The difference is apparent if one compares the courthouse with its twin in northwest Ohio's Paulding County. Edward Oscar Fallis of Toledo designed both structures in the Romanesque style, beginning and completing the one in Ohio shortly after construction in Adrian ended in 1885. But the courthouse in Adrian was completed with an eye toward both form and function. Better yet, it came in just under budget.

A line of Michigan sandstone covers the foundation. The bulk of the exterior is dark brick. A strip of glazed blue tiles wraps like a ribbon around the lower part of the building. Granite columns support the large archways. Terracotta friezes appear liberally, depicting a flaming torch (justice), an upraised hand (mercy), the American eagle, Chief Tecumseh, and the Goddess of Agriculture, among other things. The last item has continued relevance, as Lenawee County is heavily farmed. Predominant crops include wheat, corn, and beans. Indeed, the county flag's principal symbol is three shafts of wheat.

Other than recent renovation of the steps, the outside of the courthouse is virtually unchanged since it was dedicated. The interior, however, has evolved dramatically. The grand staircases and some of the decorative plaster and paint on the walls are substantially the same. But elsewhere new walls and ceilings were added to create necessary office space. Fire regulations required the elimination of large open spaces, obscuring the once visible tower interior from the lower parts of the courthouse. Extensive heating and

air conditioning machinery are tucked along with storage items in the large attic area. An elevator was added.

One of the courtrooms was converted into office space. The other courtroom is now the meeting location of the county commissioners. The chairperson sits at the old bench, and seating for the public is still in a gallery behind a barrier. Behind the old bench is a mural depicting a stream lined with trees. The artwork was discovered after someone explored behind a velvet curtain obscuring it. The jury box was removed. If the need arises, this room may still be used as a courtroom. Though the old courthouse no longer holds court, it still serves citizens every day who visit to do business in the many county offices located inside. Since its construction, the old courthouse has continually served its constituency, which now stands at approximately 100,000.

The Rex B Martin Judicial Building across the street presently houses most of the court functions, including the circuit, district, and probate courts. It is named for one of Lenawee County's most respected circuit judges, who presided for many years in the old courthouse. Federal funding helped to cover its $4.3 million price tag when it was dedicated on May 26, 1980.

The dedication of the old courthouse nearly one hundred years earlier was quite an event. The featured speaker was Thomas M. Cooley, chief justice of the Michigan Supreme Court and one of the founding faculty members of the University of Michigan Law School with a national reputation for his scholarly work. As a young attorney, he established his first law practice in Adrian, a fact that a plaque from the State Bar of Michigan and the Lenawee County Bar Association commemorates on nearby Maumee Street.

The cornerstone of the old courthouse was opened

on its hundredth anniversary. Much to the astonishment of the professionals who unsealed it and said that "soup" is what they expected to find, the materials inside the lead box within the cornerstone were intact. The integrity of the materials was attributed to the four feet between the cornerstone and the ground. Local newspapers from the time, a court calendar, and other interesting artifacts were retrieved and are on display in the Lenawee County Historical Museum a few blocks away. Owing to the thrift or perhaps the parsimony of the county officials back then, they also included wax impressions of contemporary coins. Community leaders resealed the cornerstone after filling it with artifacts of their own, to be retrieved sometime in 2085.

With any luck and the continued determination of Lenawee County to preserve its gem of an old courthouse, future residents will live to see that day in 2085. And the flag atop the tower will still proudly wave above the Irish Hills of Lenawee.

LIVINGSTON COUNTY

HOWELL—Though only rarely still used for court functions, the 1890 court in the heart of Howell is a symbol of law and order for Livingston County. Its tower rises above town and is painted on signs throughout the county's West Complex a few miles down Grand River where circuit court presently resides.

The county is named for Edward Livingston, secretary of state under President Andrew Jackson. Howell, which was originally called Livingston Centre, is named for a friend of an early settler. The settler honored Thomas Howell, son of Judge Howell of Canindagua, New York, though some say that the pretty sister of Thomas is the true namesake.

The Legislature laid out Livingston on March 21, 1833. It was for a time divided north-south between unorganized Shiawassee and Washtenaw Counties, respectively. For judicial purposes, the split was the same, except Oakland had jurisdiction over the north end. After organization, which happened on March 24, 1836, court first met in Howell at a schoolhouse on November 8, 1837. The county transported prisoners to Ann Arbor while voters rejected proposals to build county facilities in 1837 and 1838.

Livingston rented the ballroom of the residence of Benjamin J. Spring as a court in 1842 for $15, which included the wood that Spring furnished. The court then moved to the meetinghouse of the Presbyterian Society. For about three years the county paid $40 in annual rent.

Brighton agitated for the county seat and therefore opposed building anything permanent in Howell. Brighton attempted to gain territory from Oakland County, which would have shifted it from the eastern edge to nearer the geographical center of the county.

Ultimately Howell prevailed, and Enos B. Taylor completed a courthouse in 1847 for $5,600. The plans of Justin Lawyer called for three-foot-thick foundation walls rising three feet above the ground with a brick wall making up the two stories, which were capped with a belfry. An additional $328 paid for the stucco exterior of the simple Greek Revival building in 1848.

Livingston allowed religious groups without their own meetinghouse to use the courthouse for worship. Methodists, Baptists, Congregationalists, and Episcopalians took advantage, displaying a lack of concern about separation of church and state, at least by today's standards.

In the winter of 1889 a building commission condemned the court. In the meanwhile court met at an opera

house, which cost $15 per day. The county in the same year approved $30,000 for a new courthouse by a vote of 1,470 to 1,059.

Dignitaries laid the cornerstone before a crowd of about 8,000 on August 10, 1889. Judge Josiah Turner remarked that no attorney who practiced with him back in 1857 survived. Material from the razed old courthouse was incorporated into the new Richardsonian Romanesque building.

Albert French of Detroit designed the structure, and Waterbury and Wright of Ionia built it. Its older sibling in Allegan County met the wrecking ball in 1960, while its younger counterpart remains in Barry County.

The bulk of the exterior is red brick, with Ohio bluestone trim. Its total cost was about $49,000. It was opened on April 17, 1890. Howell paid about $1,000 for the clock in the tower, which originally had a black face and gold lettering. Now the face is white with black detail. Its diameter, minute hand, hour hand, letters, and minute marks measure, respectively, eight feet, three feet, two feet, nine inches, and three inches. The clock came from E. Howard Watch and Clock Company, and the 1,200-pound bell from MacShane Bell Foundry of Baltimore. The clock was electrified in 1944, obviating the need for continued winding.

A March 15, 1890, invoice records $50 for a gilded copper weathervane consisting of a bird, balls, arrows, and letters. Many assume it is in the shape of an eagle, but it is actually a waterfowl resembling a duck or a goose. The county at one point believed it was missing a wing but later found that it had simply bent backward and obscured itself.

The interior of the courthouse is ornate and full of color, much more so than its twin in Barry, which bears greater resemblance in exterior look. Red oak woodwork, intricate blinds, a black-and-white marble floor, adamant plaster, and ample stenciling of interior walls adorn the building. The frescoes are by John Rogers Burdick and Matthew Dowling. Restoration efforts began in earnest in 1976. Voters narrowly approved a $1.1 million bond by only about one hundred votes. Grants paid for some work, too.

Architect William Kessler and Associates of Detroit worked amid the confines of the building's status as a historic landmark and the prospect of losing the square if, according to original deeds, it was no longer used by the county for public purposes. Reconstruction by Elgin Builders of Southfield began on February 22, 1977. Attic space became office space, with creative use of the existing support beams. An employee lounge is suspended in open air above the highest office space. A skylight connects views of the tower and weathervane for those who use the lounge.

The courtroom is large and full of vibrant color. Before restoration, the moving of a wall clock revealed a stenciled

seashell. The lonely shell now has numerous counterparts all about the room, which occasionally accommodates visiting judges or ceremonial functions such as the investiture of a new judge. Restoration was complete in 1979.

Livingston also embarked on building county facilities on the outskirts of town. The Law Center, which now houses the prosecutor's office and the friend of the court, was built in 1975 and renovated in 1986. For a time it housed the circuit court. Next door to the old courthouse is the Administrative Building Annex, which was finished in 1988 and contains offices such as the board of commissioners. The brick wall facing the old courthouse has a reflective window that traces the silhouette of the old building.

In July 2000 a new judicial center in the West Complex went into service. It is the current home of the circuit court. Near it runs a train line, and one can hear the faint rumble of the cars and the muted sound of the horn, though at least one court reporter remarked that by now she tunes out the trains. The new court is beyond the range of the bell in the tower of the 1890 courthouse. Yet anyone entering the parking lot of the new facility with its signs depicting the old tower can sense the ripple of another kind of echo born of a community aware of its history and intent on preserving it.

LUCE COUNTY

NEWBERRY—Concerned citizens stepped in when Luce County threatened in 1974 to tear down its two historic landmarks: the courthouse and the sheriff's residence and jail. They formed into the Luce County Historical Society and turned the latter structure into a museum, which has operated since 1975. But the courthouse's date with the wrecking ball could not be averted, making way for a modern brown building still in use today.

Luce County's first courthouse building was completed in 1890, following closely on the heels of the organization of the county in 1887 when it was separated from Chippewa County. It was Victorian in design, featuring local sandstone and a cone-shaped tower. The namesake of the county is Cyrus G. Luce, who was governor of Michigan at the time of the county's birth. The sheriff's residence and jail was built in 1894.

Newberry has always been the county seat. It was founded in 1882 and was the only sizeable settlement when the county organized. First named Grant's Corner, it was later renamed for Detroit industrialist Truman H. Newberry. Newberry helped to bring the railroad from Marquette to St. Ignace, which put Newberry on the map literally and figuratively. Other spots in Luce County were named for railroad shareholders who never lived in the area.

The surrounding area is called Tahquamenon, a native word for "dark waters" describing the runoff from swamps and marshes that stains area rivers and the often visited Tahquamenon Falls anywhere from a bright yellow to a dark brown. The regional school district by the same name is 1,200 square miles and geographically is the largest such district east of the Mississippi River. The county itself is dwarfed in comparison at 908 square miles, of which the State of Michigan owns 40 percent.

Though the old courthouse is but a memory, vestiges of it remain in Luce County. The new circuit courtroom contains much of the original furniture, including benches for the public and chairs for the judge, jury, parties, and attorneys. Unlike in most courtrooms, the bench does not dominate, for it is set to one side and balanced by the jury panel, which is set to the other side. The layout of the room suggests a harmony and a shared responsibility between judge and jury.

The original bench, along with several other artifacts from the courthouse, is next door in the museum. The bench had to be shortened to fit in its new space with the witness chair. The wooden mantle from a fireplace in the

old courthouse was moved to the museum too. A black judge's robe hangs on one of the doors.

Luce County had its share of distinguished judges, none more accomplished than Louis H. Fead. He came to Newberry after earning his law degree at the University of Michigan in 1900. In the fall of that year, he was elected prosecuting attorney, serving from 1901 until 1913, when he became circuit judge. He was later appointed chief justice of the Michigan Supreme Court, serving from 1928 until 1937, when he lost his election campaign. He engaged in private practice in Detroit until his death in 1943.

Before Judge Fead came to Newberry, Luce County had some interesting law and order reports in the *Newberry News*. A local historian compiled the following snippets from issues dating from the first issue of June 10, 1886, until 1900.

Sneak thieves raided the editor's clothes line last night.
There is a cow in town that is accused of nearly everything from picking locks to pulling up window shades.
People who are wise will not let their clothes hang on the line overnight unless they stand guard with a double barrel shotgun. We need a village lockup.

Animals still continue to perambulate at large—in spite of ordinance.
It was decided to give Alderman McLeod's pigs one more chance.

Other materials from the court that are now in the old jail include law books, court dockets, and other records, many of which are the sole inhabitants of the old cell blocks constructed by Champion Iron Co. of Kenton, Ohio. There is a small barred window between one cell block and the large kitchen where the sheriff's wife is said to have cooked for those in custody. She would slide food through a small slit below the bars.

Local oral tradition contends that she installed a small table on the other side of the window for her diners and that she insisted on proper manners. She was reportedly particularly kind to one man on trial for murder based solely on circumstantial evidence. She was convinced of his innocence, but he was eventually convicted.

Were it not for the determination of a few motivated individuals, the place that was home to the hospitality and faith of the sheriff's wife would, like the courthouse in which her friend was condemned, be present only in the annals of history and the few remaining artifacts that manage to get saved.

MACKINAC COUNTY

ST. IGNACE—Mackinac County's art deco courthouse of 1936 inherited a rich tradition. The story begins with the name of the county. The French changed the original Native American word "Mishinnimakinong" to "Michilimackinac"—which was later shortened to Mackinac. Literally translated, the native name means "the land of the great fault." There are a number of rock crevices in the area, and the name probably refers to them. Historians have discredited a different theory concluding that the inhabitants actually meant "Island of the Tortoise" for nearby Mackinac Island.

Mackinac was a strategic fort and center of trading that went from French to British to American control. Britain held the island in violation of the treaty ending the American Revolution and, after finally handing it over, soon found opportunity to regain control during the War of 1812. Only after that war did America finally acquire lasting control.

The island held the county seat at first. Its current city hall was constructed in 1839 as the Mackinac County Court House. In 1859 Mackinac County heard the famous murder case of *People v. Pond.* The case became an important common law precedent for the right of a dweller in his home to defend against an assailant, even by deadly force if necessary, against an assault on an outbuilding—a net house in this case. The trial judge refused to instruct the jury on this right of the defendant, who was convicted. The Michigan Supreme Court ordered a retrial, which never happened because Pond died first. But the precedent stood.

Around the same time the county was dealing with a mini–civil war waged against King James Jesse Strang and his camp of Mormon followers. Much of the drama played itself out in court. Strang, a follower of Joseph Smith, claimed in 1844 that he had a letter from Smith in which Smith said that he knew he would be a martyr and designated Strang as his successor.

Most Mormons rejected the letter as a fake, but a sizeable minority followed Strang to Beaver Island in Lake Michigan off the northwest coast of the Lower Peninsula, which at the time was under the jurisdiction of the court in Mackinac. Brigham Young himself viewed Strang as his most dangerous rival.

Strang and his flock of 2,500 or so quickly established themselves by about 1849 and threatened the economic and political power of Mackinac Island and other surrounding areas. Local loggers and fisherman saw Beaver Island as the logical new center of commerce in the Straits of Mackinac. Fear and hatred of the Mormons made a tense situation worse. The fact that Strang ruled as an absolute monarch, instituted polygamy, and ordered all women to wear short skirts and bloomers did not help matters.

Strang served for a while as a state legislator, and his end came at the hands of some angry constituents who were fellow Mormons. On June 16, 1856, they lured him onto the U.S.S. *Michigan,* where, in broad daylight before scores of witnesses, assassins in hiding shot him twice in the head plus once in the back and then beat him with their pistols. The captain refused the local Mormon sheriff's request to turn over the culprits.

They were taken to the sheriff on Mackinac Island, where they were promptly released and hailed as heroes. None was ever convicted of a crime. Strang died of his wounds on July 9, refusing all the while to name a successor for his panic-stricken people. A few days earlier, according to one account, a mob led by the county sheriff "descended on Beaver Island, ravaged the Mormons' property and drove the people, like so many frightened sheep, from the island."

A less brutal battle over the location of the county seat happened in the early 1880s. St. Ignace, named by Jesuit missionaries for St. Ignatius Loyola, the founder of the Jesuits, won the bitter fight by a vote of 479 to 128 on April 3, 1882, and built a courthouse on the southeastern edge of the Upper Peninsula. It was completed in the same year by architect Julius Hess at a cost of $25,000.

It was a three-story square brick structure with a jail in the basement. Offices were on the first floor, while the court, judge's chambers, and two jury rooms were on the second floor. The top floor was the residence of the sheriff, who was also custodian of the building and the grounds. Half embedded in the top floor was a large clock tower. The original cornerstone, which once contained records, documents, newspapers, and coins, stands as a small monument outside of the present courthouse.

The current structure was completed in 1936 as a Works Progress Administration project for about $75,000. The WPA first awarded a grant of about $31,000 to repair and expand the existing courthouse. But local officials reportedly wanted a new building, so they tore down three walls of the structure. They then convinced Washington to allocate more funding for the new courthouse. It lies with its one-story jail on the outskirts of town near I-75, the road that forever changed things when the massive Mackinac Bridge was completed in 1958. The car ferry service between St. Ignace and the Lower Peninsula was immediately obsolete, though pictures of various ferries, icebreakers, and other ships are on display throughout the courthouse hallways.

The circuit courtroom on the third and top floor of the

building is perhaps the finest example of Art Deco styling in the building. It features a low vaulted ceiling, wooden furnishings, and throwback theater seating for the public, which might expect to find similar seats in an old movie theater.

Anyone sitting in those seats and aware of the history behind Mackinac County and its courthouse may indeed figure that it is Hollywood material.

MACOMB COUNTY

MT. CLEMENS—High atop the Clinton River on parcels of choice land stand the triad of buildings that are the seat of the government of Macomb County. Their predecessors stood upon the same land, selected by and named for Christian Clemens, an early settler.

The seat was chosen a few months after Macomb County was established by proclamation of the governor on January 15, 1818. The namesake was General Alexander Macomb, born in Detroit in 1782 and later commander of the fort there. He was a friend of Governor Lewis Cass, who appointed Clemens, a nonlawyer, circuit judge for the county. Clemens convened the first session of court in his home. He would serve fourteen years. Mt. Clemens would later gain national distinction for its mineral baths, earning the nickname "Bath City." It was also known for a while as a rose capital, until imports from South America outstripped local production.

With $400 from the Legislature, the county built a simple two-story log structure as the first courthouse. It contained a jail in a small tower, and it also provided space for school, church, and town meetings. It burned down in 1835. Its two-story successor was built in May 1840 by T. P. Castle, with William Phelps completing the masonry work

for the approximately 200,000 bricks used. The building featured four front pillars and a colonial design. Around this time, there was a failed effort in the Legislature to move the county seat, a proposition believed advanced by those who favored Utica.

Another effort to move the county seat came in 1879, when Romeo offered $30,000 for construction of a new courthouse. The effort stalled with a tie vote in the board of supervisors. Mt. Clemens, for its part, counteroffered $20,000 in bonds and $5,000 in private subscriptions. Mt. Clemens won, and Mayor George M. Crocker spoke at the laying of the cornerstone on October 21, 1880. "My friends—all roads lead to the courthouse," he declared. Indeed, one argument aired against Romeo's effort was that the network of roads and the location of the Grand Trunk Railroad advised against moving the seat from Mt. Clemens. Crocker also recalled the early leaders of the county, who "have crossed the dark and silent river."

The new grand Gothic monolith dominated the skyline of Mt. Clemens when it was opened in November 1882 at a cost of about $52,000. Architect N. J. Biggs designed the courthouse, which measured about seventy-nine feet on each side. Its large clock tower was imposing, stretching 148 feet high in the southwest corner of the building with a statue of justice at its apex. Cast iron Corinthian columns supported the belfry. The main entrance was framed by symmetrical curved stairways that beckoned the public's ingress. Outside the building were two 8,450-pound Civil War cannons that had defended a fort outside of Philadelphia from the advance of General Robert E. Lee. They were donated to the World War II effort, leaving one troughlike pedestal on the grounds to the present day. There is talk of someday finding guns from the War of 1812 to honor General Macomb.

The county did not install a clock in the tower until April 15, 1889. One source claims it disappeared in 1930 after it was carefully dismantled and placed near the construction site of the next courthouse. Another states that the clock went to the World War II effort after local leaders were fed up with the inaccuracy of the four-dial clock and its tendency to strike the bell the wrong number of times. Pranksters, further, made a habit of causing the bell to strike ten to twelve times late at night.

The building itself could not keep up with the growth of the county. The courtroom on the third floor, which measured thirty-eight by seventy-six feet and had a ceiling of twenty-four feet, had to be divided to make way for a second circuit court judge. Only fifty years after this courthouse opened, Macomb County began work on the "Million Dollar" replacement: a towering art deco edifice that continues to serve the county.

George J. Haas of St. Clair Shores designed the 1931 building, and general contractor Otto Misch Co. built it. The thirteen-story steel frame structure is lined with gray limestone. Built during the Depression, only five of its floors were furnished and ready for use at its unveiling in 1933. The 1880 courthouse was razed, although its cornerstone was kept and stored but not placed on public display. Subsequent piecemeal projects had the art deco building substantially complete by 1944. The road commission, for example, paid the cost of completing the eleventh floor so that it could occupy the space. Federal relief and local debt restructuring assisted the county in covering the $662,000 cost. Detractors cried that the white elephant or "county silo" would never be filled. Others described it more favorably as the Mt. Rushmore of Mt. Clemens.

The last description notes the granite sculptures appearing at the crown of the building. They measure thirteen-and-a-half by five feet, depicting military figures: soldier, sailor, marine, airman, Native American warrior, and minuteman. The airman can be viewed as homage to

nearby Selfridge air base, which staged a flyover above the skeleton of the building during the laying of the cornerstone on July 1, 1931. There once were terra-cotta flowers near the figures, but they began to crumble and fall. In 1964 the county had a contractor replace the flowers with smooth slabs. The upper stories are set back from the main wall plane, giving the street-level viewer the impression that the building thrusts skyward.

Inside, there are subtle indications that the building once housed the circuit court. For juries, there is a dolly that would make round trips down and up several stories to and from the café. One senses a time warp as several floors are visited, for they were finished at different times. At the entrances, bronze plaques of a sower, surveyor, seaman, and farmer symbolize early Macomb industry.

Macomb again felt a space crunch, as its population tripled between 1946 and 1960. The art deco silo was bursting at the seams, as entries and hallways became working areas for new personnel. Macomb created a building authority in 1967, which oversaw construction of a 189,000-square-foot building measuring 100 by 280 feet. It stands next to the art deco building, slightly shorter but much wider. Reinforced

concrete slabs and columns with a precast panel covering make up the bulk of the building's exterior. Ellis/Naeyaert Associates, Inc., were the architects and engineers. The general contractor for the $8 million project was Utley-James, Inc. Occupied in October 1970, the building was not officially dedicated until September 9, 1972. Court moved to this structure, with administrative offices remaining in part in the art deco building. Outside the entrance to the 1970

building stands a statue of General Macomb, sculpted by Frank C. Varga and dedicated on July 1, 1977.

The triad was complete in October 1998, when the county dedicated its newest, multimillion-dollar administration building. It measures 188,000 square feet and cost over $16 million. Tunnels connect the three buildings.

Since 1880, "The Old Crowd" gathers near the county buildings for a day of fun and camaraderie on every third Thursday in August. Festivities include a parade with a booming drum and, invariably, fishing and eating on the lake and its shore. The idea was conceived to invite back all the men who had departed Mt. Clemens before the Civil War. A plaque depicting a fisherman was unveiled in 2005 for the Old Crowd Quasquicentennial. One source claims that membership "is by election and qualifications are to be at least forty years of age and to have lived in Mount Clemens for a minimum of twenty-five years or, the son of such a resident."

By that standard (and to the extent that architecture and genealogy can intersect), every county building in Macomb's history belongs to the Old Crowd. They belong, in turn, to the community, overlooking the Clinton River from the spot Clemens ordained.

MANISTEE COUNTY

MANISTEE—The predecessor to Manistee County's current courthouse must have been much beloved, for its cornerstone was saved after a ruinous fire and permanently affixed to the lobby of the new building. Even more telling, when the sheriff rushed in during the fire to release the eight prisoners, he told them to go home, but they remained to help fight the blaze.

Some claim that Manistee means spirit of the woods, for the sound of wind blowing through the forest. Others claim that it denotes a river at whose mouth are islands. Whatever the name's beginnings, the county started by act of the Legislature in 1855. Earlier, it was part of Mackinac, Ottawa, Oceana, and Grand Traverse Counties. Its population in 1854 was 394. By 1870, it was 6,074.

In 1856 it bought some land and contracted for construction of a jail, courthouse, and sheriff's residence for $3,000. William Magill built the jail, but then the county withdrew from the contract. He reached a settlement with it in October 1858. The jail later burned.

Sheriff Sam Potter reportedly received prisoners and asked them if they wanted to escape. When he heard no, he showed them the key, told them to be inside each night of their sentence, and said that he'd break every bone in their bodies if they tried to escape. During the day they pursued fishing or some other amusement while carrying the key, and they faithfully returned by night.

Thomas J. Ramsdell arrived as the first attorney. He was clerk of the Michigan Supreme Court in 1859 and came on the advice of Chief Justice Martin, who also selected the law books that Ramsdell should pack. He came from and was educated in New York, arriving in Manistee at about the age of twenty-seven on a one-horse sleigh with an old gray horse pulling him and his law books. He traded the horse and sleigh for forty acres and got to work, drawing up the first legal papers in the county records. He had a long and distinguished career as a leading citizen who served many roles, including judge, state legislator, county treasurer, and prosecutor.

In 1867 circuit court was held in a small room called Burpee's Hall over a billiard saloon. One writer described the setting as follows. "The click of the billiard balls chimed in sweet harmony with the forensic eloquence inspired by Coke and Blackstone, while the inspiration below would sometimes become so high that the court would dispatch the sheriff to put them down." The clerk was in a small corner room south of the bridge and the treasurer was nearby in Canfield's store "with the funds in a safe so unsafe, that some scamp, with the aid of a knife or a similar instrument, cut his way in and scooped the deposits."

The next circuit court was at Eliss's Hall, then at Thurber's Hall "where the winds whistled at the court and helped the counsel howl at the jury, while the witnesses had the truth froze out of them around the stove." Court then moved back to Eliss's Hall before trying its hand in a congregational church. It then "slid back" to Eliss's Hall, followed by City Hall, where it "tarried long enough to take breath, and then the circuit court was hustled up to the Temperance Hall," where it was "sandwiched" between temperance lectures, prayers, shows, and dances.

Matters improved by the late 1870s. The county began building a Victorian style court in 1876 for about $40,000. It was made of Illinois sandstone and red-faced brick from the kiln of a brickyard in Eastlake, Michigan. Watkins & Hidden of Bay City were the architects, while Fry & Washer of Grand Rapids were the general contractor. When the courthouse was completed in January 1878, it stood on a hill of heavy clay soil at the center of the city. It measured seventy-two by eighty-eight feet, and from the ground to the top of the spire was about one hundred thirty-two feet. A furnace, the holding cells, and the sheriff's residence were in the basement. The second story housed county offices. On the third floor was the courtroom, which measured forty-six by seventy feet with a thirty-eight-foot ceiling. Groomed grounds contained by an iron fence surrounded the building.

The cornerstone contained the clerk's seal, a copy of the *Manistee City Times,* and four coins—an 1876 half-dollar, an 1866 three-cent piece, an 1865 two-cent piece, and an 1865 penny. These items were recovered after the court burned down on the night of February 23, 1950. The lobby of the new building features photographs of the fire and its aftermath, including firefighters streaming water in through a window as they stand on icicle-covered steps, and local leaders displaying the old box from inside the cornerstone.

That cornerstone now appears in the lobby of the new court building. The inscription "Manistee County 1876" is joined by "destroyed by fire February 23, 1950." Court moved for the time being to a former school building at the corner of First and Hancock that was owned by a local garment company. For a while the clerk and treasurer used the new vaults of the old court as offices. A stove, lights, and phones were installed, and all records were in good shape. The county estimated that cost overruns due to temporary facilities and transporting prisoners would cost over $10,000 annually. On the night of the fire, prisoners who

had been released and instructed to go home insisted on staying behind to fight the blaze.

The cornerstone for the new building was laid August 11, 1951. The architect was J. & G. Daverman Company of Grand Rapids. The builder was Elzinka & Volkers, Inc., of Holland, Michigan. Voters approved a $300,000 millage on November 7, 1950, for the $370,000 project. The balance came from insurance proceeds from the old building.

When completed, the courthouse hosted an open house on June 28, 1952. Its fireproof construction consists of reinforced concrete in the foundation walls and footing with brick and cinder block for the superstructure outside walls. Exposed cinder blocks form the interior partitions. The exterior walls are brick with Indiana limestone trim. The interior floors are mainly asphalt tile, with terrazzo appearing elsewhere.

The circuit court on the third floor is natural birch wood and light in color. Jurors sit in swivel chairs bolted to the ground while the public is provided benches. A light blue carpet covers the floor. A striking departure from the wooden interior is the black marble wall directly behind the judge's bench. It holds up the state seal and contrasts sharply with the white leather chair for the judge.

In 2002 a one-story brick addition housing county offices was attached to the courthouse. Kendra C. Thompson Architects, P.C., designed the structure, while Structural Specialties, Incorporated, erected it. Both enterprises are local. The complex is now called the Manistee County Courthouse & Governmental Center. One dreads the day that fire should ever strike this building but does not doubt that the people of Manistee would rally like they did in the 1950s when facing just such a challenge.

MANISTEE COUNTY

MARQUETTE COUNTY

MARQUETTE—Hollywood came to the Marquette County Courthouse in 1959. Director Otto Preminger captivated the area with an all-star cast—Jimmy Stewart, Ben Gazzara, George C. Scott, and Lee Remick—to film scenes for *Anatomy of a Murder*. The film was later nominated for the Oscar for best picture. The screenplay was based on a novel by John D. Voelker, noted author and former prosecutor from nearby Ishpeming who also served on the Michigan Supreme Court.

The ground floor of the courthouse contains an extensive display about the filming, including photographs and artifacts. Some of the marble stairs by the display are chipped, reportedly because Preminger dropped some equipment on them during the filming. A more official commemoration occurred on August 17, 2007, when

Marquette hosted the debut of a postage stamp honoring Jimmy Stewart. An image of the courthouse was used to cancel first-day covers of the stamp.

Marquette spared no expense on its second courthouse, lining the interior with the Italian marble that Preminger modified. The first courthouse in this county named for the Jesuit missionary was built on the same site in 1858 for about $4,300. As the county prospered and its population grew past 40,000, the county decided to spend a princely $210,000 on a bigger and better facility. To make way, the old courthouse was moved to the northwest corner of the square. Later expansion in the form of a modern-inspired annex was delicately built around the second courthouse.

Local architects Demitrius F. Charlton and R. William Gilbert designed the neoclassical revivalist structure.

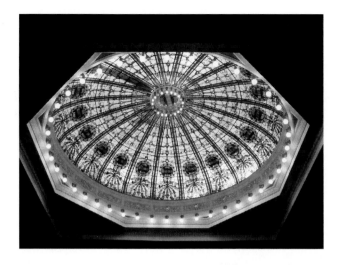

Northern Construction Company of Milwaukee built it, completing it in 1904. Native red sandstone lines much of the exterior. The twenty-three-foot solid granite Doric columns were specially ordered from Maine. Some boast that the relative absence of wood in the structure makes it virtually fireproof. Local copper lines much of the top of the courthouse, including the portico above the columns. The interior features intricate details—mosaic tile floors in one corridor, wool carpeting elsewhere, artfully crafted radiators, and stained glass, to name but a few.

But from inside and out, the grandest feature of the courthouse is its copper dome. Viewed from outdoors, it appears as a gossamer crown capping an already magnificent building and sheathing the delicate glasswork below. From the inside of the massive courtroom, it is a kaleidoscope of stained glass. Fans of *Anatomy of a Murder* will recall that this large courtroom figured prominently in the film. The building has a smaller courtroom that has the advantage of better technology, including audio and visual service and a more intimate environment.

The courthouse also contains some impressive vaults, the largest consisting of three mini-stories. A sixty-year-old woman by the name of Alice was researching genealogy in one of the vaults in 1968 when she fell down some stairs. She later died from her injuries, and current employees speak of her continued paranormal presence in the form of slamming doors, flying records, and, on occasion, images of a gentle little old lady in a red dress.

Another figure who is no ghost but who still left his mark on the courthouse is Theodore Roosevelt. While campaigning for president as a third-party candidate in 1912, Roosevelt spent a good deal of time campaigning in Michigan, which he carried in the general election. George A. Newett, publisher of Ishpeming's *Iron Ore,* reported that Roosevelt was a profane drunk. Roosevelt brought suit for libel in a weeklong trial at the court in 1913. After a parade of character witnesses refuted Newett's defense that the report was truthful, Newett relented and admitted that the report was erroneous. Roosevelt withdrew his claim for damages and asked only that the jury award a nominal sum. The judge and jury obliged, awarding six cents, or enough to buy a good newspaper.

The newspaper headline in 1984 was that Marquette County completed renovation work at a cost of $1,784,648. Someone must have taken note of the words that Judge J. W. Stone spoke at the dedication of the courthouse on September 17, 1904.

> This beautiful structure, this temple of justice, is to stand here as a monument to government, to law and order. . . . Its presence here cannot fail to have a salutary influence upon the people old and young, rich and poor. And, if a thing of beauty is a joy forever, its appeal to our sensibilities will ever make us glad.

Whether on the silver screen or in the shadow of its grand copper dome, the Marquette County Courthouse, ever ready for a close-up or a wide shot, never fails to please.

MASON
COUNTY

LUDINGTON—The boy governor who led Michigan against Ohio in the Toledo War would probably approve of the red brick courthouse in the county named for him. It is formidable, perhaps even fortlike at first blush. From it, Mason could have defended any Buckeye incursion, though it is doubtful he would draw a line in the sand that far north, given what happened at the mouth of the Maumee near Toledo.

The county was organized January 3, 1855, and detached from Ottawa County. From 1840 to 1843, the unsettled territory of Mason was called Notipekago. Burr Caswell built the first courthouse as his residence in 1849, a Greek Revival frame structure located in Pere Marquette Township. The county moved in the year following organization and stayed until 1861 when the seat moved to Lincoln. It had a tiny jail in the basement with a dirt floor and stone walls. Meals were lowered to prisoners by a mechanism resembling a dumbwaiter. This structure was preserved and moved decades later by the local historical society to the White Pine Village in Ludington. The first recorded business in Mason's circuit court was paying a justice of the peace "$15.37 for the expense of disposing of a dead stranger."

Lincoln earlier was known as Black Creek and then as Little Sauble. It became a ghost town when the lumber industry departed. Here court met in the second floor of a store owned by Charles Mears. It remained here until the seat was moved to Ludington by a vote of 860 to 164 on April 1, 1873.

Ludington, which was first called Pere Marquette for the missionary Jesuit priest who died and was buried nearby, was named for Milwaukee lumber magnate James

Ludington. The port town was the center of the lumber trade on Michigan's west coast.

For a time the county rented local bank vaults for county records. Ludington and a few other prominent individuals donated $5,000 for a building fund. Ludington's first court was a one-story brick structure at the northwest corner of Pere Marquette and Lavinia Streets. A second story was added in 1883, but space constraints were still an issue.

On April 4, 1892, voters passed a $50,000 bond issue for a new larger courthouse. The smaller courthouse was destined to be the Ludington Business College from 1895 to 1912. It was demolished in 1920.

Sidney J. Osgood of Grand Rapids designed the large red brick courthouse in the Richardsonian Romanesque style. The county accepted the $39,150 bid of general contractor Charles T. Gatke. The total cost of the building and furniture, which came from Grand Rapids, was $48,107.81. The county had to spend $11,000 to acquire the land on the eastern end of downtown facing Ludington Avenue, the main east-west artery.

Dark red Milwaukee pressed bricks make up the bulk of the exterior. Red Jacobsville Formation sandstone quarried near Houghton in the Upper Peninsula constitutes most of the remaining exterior. This sandstone was used for the raised basement walls, beltcourse, window sills, lintels, and other outside trimmings. J. B. Goodell & Co. of Muskegon did the cut stone work. The structure features a combination hip-and-gable roof with a pyramid-roof clock tower.

J. C. Albright of Saginaw installed the original slate roof, along with all of the ironwork. In 1954 asphalt shingles were installed. Extensive scaffolding was used for additional roofing work in the summer of 1992. Weatherly and Pulle of Grand Rapids did the plumbing and heating work. The vault and gas and electric fixtures were from Chicago.

Construction commenced in 1893, as the cornerstone, which was laid July 4, and the peak of the triangle facade below the clock tower facing Ludington Avenue attest. The clock was not installed until the early twentieth century. Sources disagree as to whether the year was 1902 or 1907.

There is a cylindrical tower in the southwest corner of the building. It contains a circular staircase once used to bring prisoners from the basement up to the courtroom. The jail is no longer in the basement, nor is the custodian's residence, which at one time included a garage. Now offices fill the available space.

A defendant who sailed through Mason County's judicial system in 1939 probably used the staircase. He was a

jilted lover who shot and killed his former lover in the presence of a deputy. In the span of forty-eight hours he committed the crime, surrendered immediately, was charged, convicted, and sent on his way to serve a life sentence. About twenty years later he gained release in an appeal that reduced the charge to manslaughter and credited him for time served. He also questioned the fairness of his trial. His court-appointed attorney allegedly decided that the defendant was guilty, saying that he did not require an attorney but merely needed to confess.

Since then, criminal procedure underwent tremendous change, usually at the behest of U.S. Supreme Court rulings familiar today to lawyers and the general public alike. Similarly, the courthouse changed dramatically. The decorative tin ceilings and the arched entrance with etched glass to the courtroom remain intact.

Partitioning of the original courtroom and board of supervisors meeting space gave birth to new office space. The Ludington Street entrance was sealed off to make more offices. An elevator was installed in the southeast corner of the building. A new heating plant and replacement windows and window casings were acquired. The old cannons on the courthouse grounds from the Spanish-American War were scrapped in 1942.

But the problem of bat encounters remains, at least according to a local article published in 2002 claiming that just about every employee has a story about an encounter with a fuzzy flying mouse.

What also endures with Mason County's fourth courthouse despite its changing form is its function: serving the people in the name of the fighting boy governor, even without the cannons.

MECOSTA COUNTY

BIG RAPIDS—The mighty Muskegon River is the lifeblood of Mecosta County. It carried the first wave of settlers in the 1850s. In the coming decades it brought with it the lumbering industry. The lumbermen named the county seat Big Rapids for its location near the largest of the many rapids on the river. Between 1860 and 1870, the county's population swelled with the ebb and flow of the river from 671 to 5,642.

Mecosta County was organized on February 11, 1859. It was named for a Potawatami chief whose name means "big bear." For several months the seat was originally named Leonard, for Dr. F. B. Leonard, an early settler and large landholder.

The first attorney recorded in the county arrived in the fall of 1859. According to one account, "he found but little to do, and did that little so unpopularly that he eked out a very

meager living." He left on the eve of winter, still wearing his summer clothes. In April 1860 Judge F. J. Littlejohn presided over the first court session. Mecosta was first attached to Newaygo for judicial purposes.

The location of Big Rapids on the western edge of the county inhibited its early efforts to raise money to build county buildings. In the early 1860s county officers rented a building at 117 South Michigan. In the early 1880s two downtown buildings at the corner of Elm and Michigan housed rented county offices.

Only in April 1884 did voters approve $30,000 over two years to fund construction of a courthouse. Construction began in 1885 and was completed in 1886. Crocker & Hudnutt of Big Rapids was the general contractor. County leaders credit Messrs. Warren and Ives, two early developers, with reserving four blocks for county and church buildings.

The building was on a hill, and its main entrance faced north. The color scheme of its stone exterior is similar to that of the existing historic courthouse in Houghton County: yellow, orange, and green. Up to the first level, the exterior consisted of split fieldstone. Brick facing continued to the eaves, and sandstone caps arched over the doorway and windows. The high-peaked roof was slate. A large off-center clock tower in the northwest corner dominated the upper half of the structure. It towered above a statue holding the scales of justice atop the utmost portion of the center of the building. A photograph of the imposing building adorns a wall near the main staircase of its successor. For safety reasons, the clock tower was dismantled and the statue removed in the 1940s. The interior featured high ceilings and carved woodwork, particularly in the courtroom.

A large photograph of the 1886 courthouse hangs above the main staircase of the 1970 courthouse.

Earlier, Mecosta erected a jail in 1868 for about $2,500. It and another jail predated the 1893 jail, which still stands across the street from the court. Its turrets and hip-and-gable roofs typify its Queen Anne architectural roots. It cost $25,000 and was used as a jail and sheriff's residence until 1965. For $270,000 its modern counterpart adjacent to the courthouse replaced it that year. It has since undergone some renovations of its own. The grounds of the old jail serve as a park and concert venue.

On October 4, 1893, the courthouse grounds welcomed and dedicated a Civil War memorial. The women of Mecosta County raised $3,000 for the project and commissioned it from Smith Granite Co. Three slabs commemorating persons from Mecosta who died in subsequent wars were added on V-J Day 1954, as was another slab within the last few years.

As Mecosta grew, it welcomed Woodbridge N. Ferris, who would later serve as governor and as U.S. senator. He and his wife founded the Ferris Industrial School, which over the years had several other names until a fire in 1950 threatened to close the institution. The state stepped in, and Ferris State University as it is now known is a major employer and attraction in the county as it continues its tradition of open enrollment.

Two Ferris students spotted a fire in the courthouse on the morning of April 5, 1957. A basement stock and furnace room caught fire, and flames were shooting six feet into the air from southwest windows. The fire department doused the flames, with the chief estimating that another fifteen minutes would have doomed the building. Court went on as usual that day, but with open doors and windows due to the odor of burnt wood. Workers huddled in coats due to the exposure and the fact that the furnace remained off until 11:00 a.m.

But the days of the courthouse were numbered. Growth of the county and its services, as well as dilapidation of the building, forced the county to rent more space in various other buildings. By 1970 it became a parking lot, and its successor bore a new moniker: Mecosta County Building. The ghosts of the old building for a time remained in the neighborhood in the form of a displaced bat colony.

Stephen T. Gerganoff of Ypsilanti designed the modern-inspired two-story building, and Gust Construction Co. built it. The county paid $1,233,857 for the 34,600-square-foot building, which was dedicated November 7, 1970. In total, the building cost about $35.20 per square foot.

There it stands, welcoming those who visit, whatever their business. The nearby river no longer floats timber to sawmills. Its most frequent passengers now are pleasure seekers, plying the eighteen miles between Rogers and Hardy Dams.

MENOMINEE COUNTY

MENOMINEE—Some call the cupola atop the Menominee Courthouse and the spire of the nearby Holy Spirit Church the "gateway to northern Michigan." The cupola is certainly hard to miss, presiding over the Michigan side of the Menominee River since the building was completed in 1875 for $32,000. One dollar of that total was the price Ludington Co. accepted for the land at the intersection of 10th Avenue and 10th Street.

Gordon Randall, the architect, boldly made the cupola out of wood supported by latticework trestles spanning the short dimension of the courtroom on the third floor. A more conservative approach would have been a masonry structure rising directly from the ground-supported foundations. As was common at the time, the wooden cupola was painted beige to make it look like stone. None of the original construction of any part of the building depended on machinery. Animals, pulleys, and simple human labor did the job.

The exterior walls are masonry-bearing walls, and the floors and roof framing are predominantly wood. Subsequent renovations, however, have added steel beams and concrete slabs in scattered locations.

Randall was a student of the Greek Revivalist architect Asher Benjamin. The style of the building's architecture is called High Victorian Italianate. Strong characteristics of the style include the widespread use of flat, segmented, and round arch windows, round arches above segmented arches, and a conscious attempt to verticalize classical features.

The architecture would no doubt be new to Chappee, a French Canadian who is the first recorded settler of Menominee. He arrived in 1796 to establish a post for the American Fur Company. The name Menominee comes from a Native American word for rice, which grows in the marshy lands near the mouth of the Menominee River.

But Menominee County might have been called Bleeker County. Anson Bangs, an early settler, persuaded the Legislature to create the county in the name of an old family from Albany, New York, a family into which he would later marry.

Many residents found parts of the act repugnant and convinced E. S. Ingalls, another early settler and a future judge who would write a book on Menominee's history, to lobby Lansing to organize a county. He went to the January 1863 session of the Legislature, prepared an act, and had Representative James S. Pendall of Marquette present it. The act passed, and Menominee County was born for its 496 residents. The future creation of Iron and Dickinson Counties reduced the territory of Menominee County.

In a little over a decade, Menominee's first and only courthouse stood. Connected to it were a jail and a sheriff's residence. In 1909, a sixteen-by-twenty-foot entry was added to the original forty-eight-by-sixty-foot structure. A significantly larger brick addition was added in 1938, though it blends well and is difficult to discern from the front end of the building.

A few decades later, the jail and sheriff's building were demolished to make way for new structures. Dissatisfied with how the modern architecture appeared next to the old courthouse, some residents forcefully opposed demolishing the court for a new one. At least one person threatened to chain herself to the building to prevent demolition.

Efforts then turned toward renovating the building.

Nearly $2 million was spent on the interior and exterior. At the rededication ceremony in September 1984, the cornerstone refused to budge, perhaps communicating that it and the building meant to stay forever.

Menominee County is considering plans for expanding its courthouse yet again, by perhaps fanning out new wings for the 1938 structure. The historic status of the courthouse and its place on the Michigan and the National Registers of Historic Places complicate matters, but local officials are hopeful that an appropriate plan will materialize for preserving the beauty of the complex.

There is an ugly incident that blemishes the otherwise beautiful Menominee Courthouse. What culminated in a lynching on the evening of September 27, 1881, began many months before. Frank C. and John McDonald were loggers and cousins from Nova Scotia working in Menominee. They had a reputation for drunk and disorderly conduct and were confined at the state penitentiary in Jackson for an incident in which Frank beat the county sheriff unconscious. The sheriff returned from the beating and deputized George Kittson, whose family was one of the first to settle the area. The burly 200-pound Kittson had little trouble apprehending the McDonalds.

After their sentences were served, the McDonalds returned with a score to settle. Before they could encounter George Kittson, they brawled at the Leon Cota saloon in Frenchtown with his brothers William, who was fatally stabbed, and Norman, who was stabbed but survived. An explosive mixture of alcohol, knives, and jealousy over women helped to spark the fight.

The McDonalds were whisked to the jail, where they remained for about a day. Thinking that passions had cooled in town, the sheriff left them in the custody of a few deputies. But all day word spread of the alleged murder as lumberjacks and miners gathered in town to discuss the matter as they imbibed alcohol. There was a general foul mood in the air to begin with, for President Garfield had succumbed to his assassin's bullet only about a week before. The McDonalds were comparative strangers, and local sympathies were against them. Soon, an unruly mob descended upon and broke into the jail, using a telegraph pole as a battering ram. The McDonalds were seized and dragged by rope through the streets. Their corpses were hung from a tree on Bellevue Street. At least one account maintains that they were brutally killed long before they reached the tree.

Before he died, one of the McDonalds requested a priest. The priest pleaded with the crowd, who knocked him down and spat on him. The priest cursed them and said that they would die with their boots on. Indeed, it is believed that none of the ten men who reportedly led the mob died a peaceful, natural death. Their deaths were violent—a snake bite, a drowning, and a sawmill accident slicing one man in half, to name a few. None was ever convicted of any crime.

One account captured the thought of Menominee's more level-headed inhabitants. "That they richly deserved their fate is probably true, but this is supposed to be a government of law and order and such scenes as this are a burning shame and disgrace."

There is a lumber camp ballad about the McDonalds. It ends with the following: "Shun whisky and bad company / or you'll shed bitter tears."

There is no authoritative pronouncement declaring that the good people of Menominee have renounced alcohol and bad company. But there has been no more lynching, and the courthouse stands steadfast as a symbol for law and order in Menominee County.

MIDLAND COUNTY

MIDLAND—At the confluence of the Chippewa and Tittabawassee Rivers, many a fine thing bubbles up from the bygone-era brine below Midland County. Among them is the distinctively designed Midland County Courthouse.

Native Americans called this land and its rivers "Little Forks." The county seal depicts a pine tree, a brine well, and a horn of plenty, symbols that encapsulate lasting features of Midland County.

Midland County was first organized on March 29, 1850. Its officers met initially at the house of John Larkin. In 1856, the county authorized $6,000 in bonds for construction of a courthouse on land donated by Dr. Daniel H. Fitzhugh. Timothy Jerome erected the building the following year. He had to make a number of unrecorded alterations before the county would accept it. Circuit court first occurred at a schoolhouse on the corner of Ashman and Ellsworth. The two-story white frame colonial courthouse had four exterior columns supporting a simple triangular portico. A jail and sheriff's residence, the first brick building in the county, was completed in 1865. Inmates reportedly assisted the sheriff's wife around the building while her husband tended to his lumbering business.

In a notable early case, a suit for nonpayment on an account rested on evidence in the form of one sheet of paper. The plaintiff kept every local reputable attorney in his employ, intending that his opponent retain no more than a shyster. Local lore contends that the defendant's attorney spotted this evidence on a table during an unspecified meeting. He took hold of it, calmly chewing and swallowing portions of it while everyone else present was otherwise engaged. The case was dismissed for lack of evidence.

An assault and battery case resulted in a sentence of a three-dollar fine and "whisky for the crowd." Court adjourned to the Red Keg to collect the fine and costs, where it was decided to convert the three-dollar fine to more drinks.

The first courthouse was retired in 1926. Three years later, it was auctioned for $245 to Hiram A. Crane and razed. Its successor was born of the chemical industry that took root several years earlier with the arrival of Herbert H. Dow. In 1890, he brought to Midland his electrolytic process for extracting chemicals from the ancient sea brine underneath the surrounding flatlands. He rented a barn, connected a homemade rope drive from a flour mill's steam engine, reactivated a nearby brine well, and proved that his process worked. In time, Dow Chemical Company would grow into a world player and the centerpiece of the local economy. Dow—the man and the company—played a pivotal role in designing and building the new courthouse, beginning with local authorities' proposal in 1919 of $225,000 in local bonds for the new building. Dow pledged additional funds and technical expertise as a gift if he could influence what shape the building would take. A countywide vote in 1920 was favorable, due in part, some said, to plans for a memorial room dedicated to the 675 local men who served during World War I.

The building's rustic Tudor Revival style was the brainchild of Detroit architect Bloodgood Tuttle. He heeded Dow's call for local flavor that eschewed the mold of other public buildings in the state and, indeed, the nation. That flavor finds its expression in the exclusive use of local materials for the external construction, a rarity in the construc-

tion industry. Dow insisted on collecting local fieldstone, and it is believed that few local farmers failed to contribute stone from their land. When the 1950s addition was built, a sign on the courthouse lawn invited everyone to "Place Stone Here For Your New Court House Addition."

The stone walls of the two- and three-story structure are half-timbered with stuccoed gable ends and hipped roofs covered in orange, red, and tan clay tiles. Dormer windows breaking the cornice line are also featured. For the exterior of this courthouse, Tuttle emphasized the latter part of the word, as the building has a distinctively residential look and feel.

The sparkling murals are a unique component of the building. Dow developed a new material for the murals: finely ground colored glass mixed with magnesite cement. He hired Paul Honore, a Detroit artist, to mix and apply this magnesite stucco throughout the interior and exterior of the building, depicting scenes of local history and industry—Native Americans, pine trees, trapping, logging, farm-

ing, and chemical manufacturing. Dow's technical innovation was designed to produce murals that would not crack or fade over time. As Honore told *Popular Mechanics* in 1926, "The color in my murals is imprisoned, so to speak, in sunproof grains of glass." The original courtroom has a curved ceiling that frames the bench, above which is Honore's interpretation of a Native American Council. Engraved in the walnut wood below the mural are the seal of Michigan and the unpunctuated words, "Justice and Mercy the Alpha and Omega of human attainment."

Herbert Dow used a magnesium shovel at the ceremonial groundbreaking on November 3, 1924, and he laid the cornerstone for the H-shaped building on March 29, 1925. Spence Brothers of Saginaw won the building contract. The courthouse was occupied and opened to the public on January 1, 1926. On Sunday afternoons, Boy Scouts would guide visitors through the building. In three months in the summer of 1926, a register of visitors' signatures collected 6,487 names, which was claimed only to account for about a third of visitors from outside Midland County.

In total, $202,000 in public funds paid for the courthouse. Dow did not record or release in any detail the amount of money and other resources that he and his company contributed to the project. The county has since blended two additions to the original structure. The first was an addition to the southeastern section along thirty-five feet of exterior wall, which was completed in 1958. The county spent about $750,000 on the fifty-two-person jail, sheriff's quarters, additional offices, and auditorium.

With the Legislature's approval in 1976 of a second circuit judgeship for Midland, the county retained Robert E. Schwartz and Associates as architects to design a major addition. Apart from another courtroom, the new space would house the prosecutor's office, district court, a personnel office, law library, elevators, and barrier-free entrances. For about $1 million, Helger Construction Company completed work in 1979.

The newer circuit courtroom benefits from the now-interior murals of Honore, which are partially visible in the rear of the courtroom through windows that were incorporated into the new walls. In 2002, with the support of the Dow Foundation, the acrylic-monoprinted mural of artist C. L. Coates was unveiled in the courtroom. Its digitized images were printed on special wallpaper-like canvases. The mural bears the message "Justicia Absit Praiudicium," which, according to a nearby plaque, "is a tribute to our belief in true and equal justice based on the precepts of our Constitution and Bill of Rights."

In 2006, the older courtroom underwent artistic reno-

and a local bar association contributed to the cost of the project.

Elsewhere in the courthouse, Biron Roger, a prominent Detroit artist, painted murals along two walls in the large public lobby. Like Honore's works, they also tell the story of Midland County through scenes of Native Americans, early European settlers, logging, and farming. In another panel, Herbert Dow makes his only direct appearance in the building. Roger depicts Dow allegorically as a gray-haired "Johnny Appleseed" streaking across the industrial landscape of Midland. Instead of seeds, Dow's bag contains small packages labeled magnesium, bromide, and chloride. Rogers left the final panel blank, except for the statement, "The Artist has depicted the past. Your deeds will determine 'the future.'"

Wherever its future leads, Midland County is firmly rooted in a past that is both prologue to and manifest in the magnesium stucco murals of its one-of-a-kind courthouse. Inside and out, the walls of the Midland County Courthouse sparkle as they speak.

vation and technological upgrading. The jury box was made wheelchair accessible. New gold leaf was added to parts of the interior, and chandeliers were refurbished. Community foundations, the county's courthouse preservation fund,

MISSAUKEE COUNTY

LAKE CITY—What turns from a foul mouth to a muskrat? The answer is the county seat of Missaukee County, if one employs playful manipulation of location names in deciphering the riddle.

Missaukee County was organized in 1871 and separated from Wexford and, earlier, Manistee Counties. Some attribute the name to a Native American chief whose moniker means "at the mouth of the big waters." Others point to a heroine not remembered for her deeds but for her name, Miss Aukee. Missaukee Lake near the present county seat was once called Muskrat Lake, as well as Round Lake.

The designated temporary county seat until an election in June 1873 was Falmouth, which reportedly due to the rough language of its men was known earlier as Foul Mouth. Its original name was Pinhook for the pins lumbermen wore in their shoes and for the peavey hooks they used to roll logs.

Perley, Palmer & Company built a twelve-by-sixteen-foot building with offices on the first floor and a courtroom upstairs. The county rented the building for $115 a year. When the vote came for the permanent county seat location, Lake City won, either by a margin of one vote, or a margin of 131 to 95. Sources disagree on the tally. Unlike other counties, Missaukee did not experience, despite some hard feelings and allegations of "colonizing votes," a protracted county seat fight because Lake City has held the designation ever since. An early family that settled the city called it Reederville and then Reeder before Lake City stuck. It was incorporated as a village in 1889 and as a city in 1932.

One source recounts the story of an unidentified man who visited a lumber camp on the day of the election bearing cigars and jugs of alcohol. He occupied the fifty men and their votes for Falmouth with merriment and story after story, keeping them away from the polls.

Lake City built a near duplicate of Falmouth's court. It was two stories, measuring sixteen by twenty-six feet, and built near the present site of the county courthouse. Offices were on the first floor, and the courtroom was upstairs.

The county planned a $500 jail in January 1876. In April it decided to include a second story for the sheriff. The $897 building was completed in the summer, but it burned just two years later. Its thick wooden planks burned so intensely that firemen had no hope of extinguishing it. They instead doused the courthouse, which was hardly twenty feet away and survived, but with a scorched rear. A fortuitous westerly breeze assisted efforts to save the courthouse.

In 1881 a drive for a new court facility gathered steam. A $7,000 bond passed on June 19, 1882, by a vote of 187 to 137. George Nelson of Norwich Township designed the structure, while John G. Mosser of Cadillac erected it. The total cost was $10,014.88. The county spent $279.18 for the stone for the walls. A new jail went up in 1886 for $7,000. It was a white wooden structure with a dark roof and matching trim around its many windows. Photographs indicate that its steeple was removed sometime before the courthouse ultimately burned in 1944.

Missaukee County apparently did not have a prisoner for its jail until 1877. That distinction went to Calvin French, a ninety-pound man who allegedly assaulted and battered his wife and stepdaughter, who were "both heavier and more active." The jury must have believed in convicting him that he threatened the women with an axe. He served four months in jail.

In July 1889 two inmates confined for some sort of misdemeanors pulled a prank escape. The sheriff was a horse enthusiast and was away at the races. A worker was repairing plumbing when he left the keys near the holding cells. The inmates used a wire to get the keys and release themselves. They snuck into the races and presented themselves to the sheriff after the last race just when he learned that they were missing. They presented him with the keys and said that they were ready to return.

There was some controversy over the court's stoves, which a heating plant finally replaced in April 1913 for $1,600. It is believed, however, that the heaters may have caused the fire that destroyed the court on February 17, 1944. The intensity of the heat reportedly curled and distorted the iron picket railing that was along two sides of the building. For over a decade, court was located in a facility one hesitates to call temporary. It later became the residence of a family called Kalis. Like the current facility, it has an address on South Canal Street.

Construction began in September 1953. The new county building and court were dedicated on May 21, 1955. The building cost $162,000 plus $7,500 for furnishings. The county used a bond issue, the sale of county property, insurance proceeds, and other sources to foot the bill. Gordon Cornwall of Traverse City designed the flat-roofed and modern-inspired building. John Saul of the same city was the general contractor. L. J. Deming Company and Michigan Electric Company, both of Cadillac, did the plumbing and heating and electrical work, respectively.

The courtroom is large but with a ceiling of normal height and modest furnishings. Most of the items in the room are functional, lacking any decorative element. The public sits in simple stacking blue chairs. The wooden chairs with blue upholstery for the jury, witnesses, attorneys, and parties are fancier. The tables, bench, and barrier are utilitarian, as are the doors, gray carpeting, and white walls.

A property tax paid for the $83,716.00 jail dedicated August 15, 1959. Architect St. Clair Pardee connected it to the courthouse, and contractor Peter Schierbeek Construction Company built it.

In the late 1970s the county considered plans for a $300,000 addition. Extensive renovation in 1980 added a jury room, law library, conference rooms, and offices. Foul or fair, muskrat or mink, this building is a Michigan courthouse, whatever an uninitiated observer might think.

MONROE
COUNTY

MONROE—Michigan's second oldest county has its share of humorous and dramatic stories connected to its courthouse, from early examples of street justice to a recent unsolved arson within the building.

Territorial governor Lewis Cass created Monroe County by proclamation on July 14, 1817. He named it in anticipation of the August visit of President James Monroe. Monroe was named the county seat that September. The territory included parts of present-day Wayne and Washtenaw Counties, as well as a strip of land that became part of Ohio after resolution of the Toledo War in the 1830s.

In 1822 Cass decreed that Monroe's court would be someplace within two miles of the residence of Francois Lascelles, an early settler along the River Raisin. The first court building was a two-story log structure that, according to an old citizen, was "of a dingy yellow color." The court was on the upper floor, while the east end of the first floor housed the jailer's residence. The west end was the jail. A small space in the rear surrounded by a stockade served as the prison yard. Some miscreants found punishment in the form of lashes and public shaming outside at the whip-

ping post, which was not a common item in the Midwest, according to a historical marker.

The building served its function until the 1830s. It was for about fifteen years the only public building for religious, political, and secular gatherings. It may have been near this structure that a little street justice was witnessed. The dispute was over a bag of flour. The man in pursuit chased and caught the fleeing man, holding him by the collar with one hand and dumping the flour over his head with the other. The recipient reportedly "emerged from that shower a whiter and a sadder man."

History has not recorded the second courthouse very well. It stood until fire destroyed it on February 27, 1879. Decades earlier, residents in a remote part of the county had no use for the building, instead posting on July 2, 1855, a rather incomprehensible legal "notis" written in "wonderful hieroglyphics on a rough unpainted board and nailed to a roadside tree." It read as follows. "We the ondersined has kild an old misheveous brown stra Kreetur, purportin to be Long to some non-resanented inhabitant of this township, which we judged the same to be a newsence! all persons consarned in said Kreetur or otherwise, is hereby Notified to govern themselves Ackordingly."

Monroe's current courthouse was first dedicated on November 17, 1880. It cost about $25,000. Edward O. Fallis of Toledo designed it. It is two stories with a limestone facade. Its most prominent feature is its mansard-roofed corner tower, which contains an 1881 bell from Henry McShane & Co. in Baltimore. It housed special communications and sharpshooters when former president Bill Clinton spoke below at Loranger Square, which is named for the man who donated the land and $1,000 for the first courthouse. After the assassination of President William McKinley, a banner draped on the courthouse read, "It is God's way. His will be done."

The courthouse was completed just four years after General George A. Custer, Monroe's most famous son, had his last stand at Little Big Horn. A nearby monument is dedicated to the blond military leader.

Schuyler County, Illinois, built a twin courthouse in Rushville. A delegation from there visited and inspected Monroe's building and hired the same superintendent of construction.

In 1918 lighting problems inside the courtroom at the arraignment of thirteen liquor violators meant that the court and spectators could hardly identify the accused. A reporter surmised that under the circumstances guards would be needed at every door and window if a more serious escape threat were before the court. A janitor located an old farmer's lantern and placed it on the judge's bench. It was then clear that four of the violators were female.

Decades later the sound of the cries of bald eagles disrupted proceedings. A local man kept them in his nearby home. Around the same time a defendant in a case involving drinking had stark rebuttal testimony for the allegation that his speech was slurred and his eyes bloodshot. Amid the guffaws of those gathered in court, when it was his turn to testify, he popped out his glass eye. He prevailed.

A number of additions give two sides of the courthouse an eclectic look. In 1954 a four-story addition measuring forty-eight by one hundred four feet and costing about $270,000 extended the rear of the building to the south. For about $400,000 the county added another four-story structure, which measures fifty-six by eighty-two feet, to the building in 1966. It runs east toward City Hall, where court temporarily relocated after the 1879 fire.

TMP Associates of Bloomfield Hills designed a 1986 addition that integrates the many faces of the building and bridges physical and stylistic gaps. A large atrium connects the disparate parts, enveloping part of original exterior walls of the 1880 building. A secure entrance and a large American flag welcome employees and visitors alike. The addition cost about $4 million and measures 46,700 square feet.

Inside, the court features two modern circuit courtrooms and a historic courtroom in the old section of the complex that is still in use. Large windows behind columns supporting a stripped-down balcony illuminate the large and dignified room, along with hanging light fixtures. The ceiling is pressed tin painted white.

The complex nearly fell victim to arson on April 13, 1992. Fires set in four locations caused nearly $1 million in damage and a ten-month repair and restoration period. Despite a reward offer of $50,000, no one was ever brought to justice. Two of the fires extinguished themselves.

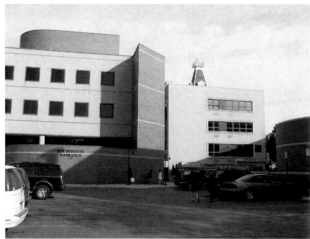

Investigators viewed the arson as amateurish because those two fires used paper soaked with a nonflammable cleaning fluid. The two other fires gutted an office and a ladies' bathroom, where heated pipes burst and caused extensive flooding damage.

Had the county brought anyone to account for the arson, there might have been a powerful movement to reinstitute, if only temporarily, the whipping post that once faced the fire-scorched court.

MONTCALM
COUNTY

STANTON—Most counties in Michigan by their names honor homegrown figures, be they Native American or Anglo-Saxon in origin. Montcalm County instead commemorates a French figure who died defending French interests in the French and Indian War.

Louis Joseph, Marquis de Montcalm de Saint Veran, was a distinguished French military officer. He held the seemingly impenetrable fortress at Quebec. He erred when he brought his men outside its confines to the Plains of Abraham to confront the approaching British. The battle happened on September 13, 1759, and it marked the end of New France as well as the life of Montcalm, who died the next morning. "So much the better," he said when told of his grave condition, "I shall not live to see the surrender of Quebec." At least one historian concluded that nearly a century later Michigan honored this French figure because of the loyalty of local Native Americans to their former ally.

The Legislature formed Montcalm in 1831 and nominally attached it to St. Joseph, Kalamazoo, Kent, and Ionia Counties until it was organized in its own right on March 20, 1850. Greenville was the most sizeable settlement, and court was first held there at the house of Morton Shearer on June 11, 1850.

The Legislature temporarily made Greenville the county seat and called on the county to decide whether to keep it there permanently or to move it elsewhere. Only then could the county legally tax for the purpose of raising money for construction of county buildings.

To aid its campaign for the county seat, Greenville saw to it that the northwest territory that had previously been part of Mecosta County was incorporated into townships

and added to Montcalm County. But the effort was in vain, for a vote of 504 to 374 sent the county seat to an unsettled central portion of the county. It was in the middle of a pine forest four miles from the nearest settler. Fred Hall of Ionia sold the land to the county for $50 and in gratitude the county named its seat Fred.

The name changed by the hand of the namesake. He was sent the application papers for establishing a post office at the county seat. The space for its name was left blank, and he was encouraged to fill the blank with the name of his choosing. He chose Stanton, as he was an admirer of Lincoln's secretary of war. The Legislature approved the name change on February 23, 1863.

At first, county supervisors slept on the floor of the modest meeting place they had at the county seat. A large man named Westbrook Divine is remembered for what he called equalizing the roll when he "rolled himself over the entire line of prostrate and half-sleeping forms."

In October 1861 the county approved $500 to clear the grounds and $800 for a courthouse. Joseph P. Shoemaker completed the frame structure that same fall and was paid $765. Nearby land was given away or sold for a pittance to settlers.

A fireproof building was erected in 1870 by Seth Sprague for about $1,500. It was two stories with external stairs for its second story. In addition to the court and sheriff's residence, space was made for a jail for "malefactors" who earlier had been sent to Ionia. There is a record in October 1852 of holding men in the upper floor of Abel French's store. On the northeast corner of the square was built a brick building for county records.

The new jail suffered the sting of a successful escape one early winter. The daughter of the undersheriff was left to feed the four inmates while she cared for her ill mother, and her father was gone chasing a wanted man. She passed food and utensils through the "diamond hole" of the old wooden jail. She returned for the dishes and a knife was missing. She questioned the inmates about it, they told her she was mistaken, and there was nothing for her to do but wait to tell her father about the situation.

But by the time he returned it was too late, for one prisoner had escaped. He filed the knife into a saw and opened a hole under the window. He made off into the night and, much to the chagrin of local law enforcement, spent the entire winter within seven miles of the jail despite efforts to locate him.

By 1879 Stanton offered $10,000 if the county would match it to build a larger and more elaborate courthouse. The vote passed 2,482 to 1,316, and Jacob V. Consaul of Grand Haven served as the contractor. The imposing brick-and-stone structure with a distinctive spire was completed in the summer of 1881 for $23,000.

Readers of a local newspaper were assured before the dedication that Hon. John Lewis of Greenville in his address would not touch on local politics. The notice read, "our readers may rest assured that there will be nothing that will grate harshly on the most sensitive ears."

Luckily, the court featured fire-resistant vaults, which saved the irreplaceable county records when a conflagration of unknown origin destroyed the courthouse around 10:00 a.m. on February 16, 1905. The building was gutted as frantic denizens salvaged records and furniture before the inferno was overwhelming. Large portions of the brick walls

remained and stood as a grim reminder while the county fought over bond proposals for building a replacement.

Voters repeatedly rejected financing new construction until finally a slim margin of thirty-one votes carried the day in April 1910. Stanton celebrated vociferously. A newspaper account recalled that a band played, dynamite was set off, and "the fire whistle blew so long and loud that it woke up the dead at Greenville." Other towns that allied with Stanton joined the chorus, while towns voting no turned out their lights and went to bed. The same newspaper surmised that the editor of a rival newspaper "quietly slid his stereotyped court house editorial into the 'hell box' and crawled under the bed covers." It opined that his devil would publish his newspaper for the following week.

The new court, jail, and sheriff's residence were completed for $58,280.68. Edwyn A. Bowd was the architect, and the contractors were Wright & Prall. The buff brick edifice trimmed with stone stands authoritatively atop a hill. Its front facade is most imposing, featuring a large frieze and four sizeable columns.

The interior has striking tile floors and stone columns. The dignified courtroom now solely houses county supervisor meetings. The clerk, treasurer, and some other county offices occupy the rest of the space. The southeast corner of the building connects to a Michigan State University extension center.

On September 9, 2002, a new county complex was unveiled less than a mile away from the 1910 building. This one-story building is brick and modern in its interior and exterior design. Together with its remaining predecessor, the two stand like and unlike Montcalm did in defense of Quebec—proudly and openly, but not ephemerally or in vain, respectively.

MONTMORENCY COUNTY

The courthouse in Atlanta before its recent renovation

ATLANTA—The ravage of fire has on more than one occasion fallen upon Montmorency County. It dodged the promethean scourge once in 1942 when records were hastily removed from the burning courthouse only to see virtually all of them lost the following April when the temporary facilities burned down.

Times were not always so rough for this county, which was in 1840 first called Cheonoquet for an Ojibwa chief whose name means "Big Cloud." In 1843 the name was changed to its current form, though some sources ended it with an "i" instead of "y" as it appears now. There are at least two possible namesakes. The Duke of Montmorency, High Admiral of France, in 1620 bought the lieutenant generalship of Canada and soon thereafter sold it without ever setting foot in North America. The other figure was

The courtroom as it appeared in 2005

Montmorency-Laval, the first Roman Catholic bishop of Canada, serving from 1658 to 1684.

As a part of Michigan, the territory was attached to Cheboygan and then Alpena County. The Legislature organized Montmorency on May 21, 1881. Brush Creek, which later became Hillman, was the county seat. It is on the eastern edge of the county toward Alpena and Lake Huron, where sizeable settlement first took root in the county.

Meanwhile, Lewiston in the west and Atlanta in the middle of the county wanted to wrest the seat from outlying Hillman. A Civil War veteran who saw similarity between this Michigan terrain and the valley in Georgia named Atlanta for its Southern counterpart.

A vote to move the county seat was defeated in 1887. With the help of Lewiston, Atlanta tried again and prevailed in 1893. Lewiston's support was strategic, however, for it viewed Atlanta as a stop along the way for the march of the county seat from Hillman to Lewiston. Waiting only a year, it apparently won a vote in 1894 while Atlanta was constructing a courthouse. But fraud was uncovered, the vote of Albert Township was thrown out, and Atlanta narrowly hung on to the county seat, where it has remained ever since.

The brick courthouse, which featured a small clock tower, was completed, and it served its function without incident until a cold, windy, and wintry day in 1942. On January 15 at about 5:30 p.m. a fire started in the belfry and began to work its way down the building. A newspaper account surmised that burning soot ignited the dry birds' nests and rotten wood up there.

The building burned as a crowd gathered and the able-bodied frantically evacuated the structure of its contents. They did a remarkable job, saving most of the vital records. Some furniture was smashed in the effort. A strong wind caught some loose papers and sent them like large snowflakes across the street east of the conflagration. Trucks pulled up and whisked what was salvaged to various safe locations about town.

The county was left to gather what it could from the safes in the smoldering ashes and to marshal together its dispersed property in some temporary facility. The tunnel underneath the community center, which also housed the local schools, was selected, and the choice proved fateful.

In April 1943 the community center burned down too. This time the records could not be saved. Several weeks earlier in January the records of the local newspaper were lost in a separate fire. Montmorency was left reeling. The fact that many if not most able-bodied men were away for the war effort contributed to the poor timing of each of the fires. Later, purchasing materials for building anew also proved difficult in war time. Interior doors were particularly difficult to acquire.

A bond issue passed by a vote of 408 to 351 in April 1942 for funds for a new courthouse. Insurance proceeds and a number of loans meant that no outside help was needed. The township hall served as the temporary court, and a vault was constructed to house records. County leaders selected a portion of the exposed foundation of the ruined community center as the site of the new court. It was completed in 1946 by contractor Grant McReady.

The brick structure boasts a symmetrical front facade facing north onto M-32, the principal east-west road. A wooden sign with a large county seal bearing the names of the three locales that vied for the seat stands on the grounds, along with a flagpole.

The rear of the building attaches to a large judicial annex and health department facility. The 12,000-square-foot addition was built in 2000 for just under $1 million. In 2007, Montmorency accelerated by fourteen years its purchase of the annex from the health department. The purchase was part of a $1.4 million project that included vari-

ous major upgrades to the 1946 building. Todd Seidell, the architect, drew up plans for a new peaked roof to replace the aging and leaky flat roof and to match the profile of the annex. Integrity Construction of Gaylord did the work. Other infrastructure was added or improved: wiring, data storage, heating, insulation, windows, and so on. The courtroom and boardroom were redesigned. Some offices were moved. The entrance was reworked, with a large stuffed elk hanging prominently in the front lobby and visible outside through large windows. Montmorency is one of a handful of counties that are home to Michigan's elk herds. Atlanta prides itself as the elk capital of Michigan.

Apart from the entrance and the roof, the exterior profile gained two striking white columns beneath the new portico. Together, these elements combine to give the courthouse a new and understated grandeur that it previously lacked. It is said that the specter of another punishing winter under the flat roof hastened the project, which began in the midst of winter in the beginning of 2007 and ended that year in April, a month when major snow can still be expected.

Considering Montmorency's record of perseverance in the face of natural forces like fire and wind, snow might just rank a distant third.

MUSKEGON COUNTY

MUSKEGON—A black-and-white photograph captures the sight of the able-bodied of Muskegon evacuating furniture, documents, and other things from its burning courthouse in 1891. Amid the fuzzy moving figures and apparent garage sale scene on the courthouse lawn is a stoic statue of a Native American chief, looking back piercingly at the camera.

Muskegon's name derives from a Native American word for marshy river. French maps called the place Masquignon or Maskigon. Its present spelling was adopted in 1840. Originally part of Ottawa County, Muskegon was organized in 1859. That same year by order of the Legislature the county seat was located in the settlement of the same name.

From the Collection of the Muskegon County Museum

For over the first decade of its existence, the county rented room above Wheeler and Huginin's Hall, a drug store on Water Street, for the court.

Some in the north wanted the seat at or near the head of White Lake. The battle boiled, along with a legal dispute over the legality of Muskegon's formation out of Ottawa's territory. One supervisor offered land plus $15,000 for the courthouse. Muskegon counteroffered land in the center of the village.

The county's first proper courthouse was completed in August 1870 for $46,183.80. George Garnsey of Chicago designed it, and Samuel Barrows of the same city built it. It featured two stories and a small bell tower. The basement jail was made of Joliet limestone. The remaining outer walls were double-pressed Milwaukee brick. County offices were on the first floor, and the courtroom on the second. The latter featured frescoes of the Goddess of Justice and the American seal by Messrs. Tevne and Alimine of Chicago. The building measured seventy by ninety-one by fifty-seven feet. At the top of the dome it was a hundred and six feet tall. In 1887 two large additions brought with them fireproof vaults that were worth their weight in gold on May 16, 1891.

The Pine Street Fire ravaged Muskegon, sweeping though seventeen city blocks and destroying 250 homes. A strong wind deposited sparks on the courthouse roof. It was only a matter of time before rubble, remnants of the walls, and the vaults were all that remained.

The city offered its council chamber for circuit court use. Voters promptly approved a $75,000 bond. The three-story Amherst sandstone structure was completed October

3, 1893, for about $100,000. Vanderlinde and Company were paid to clear the old walls and excavate the site. The general contractor for the new building was P. J. Connell and Sons.

The building measured ninety-six by one hundred twenty-seven feet. At the top of its imposing bell and clock tower it measured 165 feet tall. The building was Romanesque in design. When court first convened in the new building, the judge remarked how before the court were the same two attorneys who were appearing before the old court at the time of the fire.

The building fell victim to urban renewal. Muskegon spent $3,125,000 on the new county building it erected in 1958–59 and dedicated on May 18, 1960. It demolished the old courthouse, saving its bell for a spot on the lawn where it now rests on a pedestal. Judge Noel P. Fox, who later went from the state to the federal bench, received many of the discarded bricks after the demolition. One report claims that he intended to build a barbecue and was shocked to receive twelve truckloads of bricks on his property. Another account maintains that twelve truckloads are precisely what he ordered and that he never quite made full use of them. Many other local residents incorporated some of the courthouse's materials in their building projects.

Within sight of the bell stands a newer monument dedicated to "The Protectors" or county officers who lost their lives in the line of service. Two childlike figures clutch at the arms of a policeman and look up at him.

Magnuson and Sumner designed the new six-story modern office building along with associated architects O. J. Munson Associates. The general contractor was Herlihy Mid-Continent Company. The long ends of the building appear blue and have many windows, while the shorter ends are beige with fewer openings.

The interior of the building varies in appearance from floor to floor, due mainly to recent selective renovation of certain areas. The multiple circuit courtrooms are each appointed differently, though the problem of sight-blocking, load-bearing columns is not unique.

In 2001 the county spent $1,200,000 on a new entryway. It features an atrium that adds 1,400 square feet to the lobby. Four new elevators arrived. The second phase of renovation made major alterations to the third, fourth, and sixth floors. Additional phases will revamp other aspects of the building, including reconfiguration of courts and offices as well as heating and cooling.

The county acquired campus buildings of nearby Baker College and moved many of its offices there. The move allowed the county to convert its county building into the Michael E. Kobza Hall of Justice, which is named for a circuit judge who died in 1997.

Above his name on the beige ends of the building simple clocks tick away the minutes and the hours since an inanimate sculpture witnessing the destruction of this building's grandfather came to life and was immortalized in the black, white, and gray shades of a time-defying photograph.

NEWAYGO COUNTY

WHITE CLOUD—Newaygo County has no shortage of accounts of the origin of its name or of notable murder stories over its history. That history began with its formal organization in 1851. Earlier, it was part of Kent County.

The name is Native American in origin, but agreement ends there. Some persist in claiming that a Native American uttering bastardized English in the form of "No Way Go" or "New Way to Go" coined the name. Others look to native languages themselves to find similar sounding words that mean "land of many waters" in reference to the area's inland lakes and rivers or "slants" for the land's sloping topography. Another candidate is "Kenewaygoing"—a word that literally means "place where boy have fish bone in throat." Legend states that to dislodge the bone the boy was given dried pumpkin seed cooked to a stiff mush, which had the unintended consequence of giving him a permanent speech impediment. Finally, some assert that Newaygo was named for Naw-wa-goo, a signer of the Treaty of Saginaw of 1812.

For the early part of its history, the county seat was Newaygo, a settlement in the first-developed southern part of the county. John Brooks, a founder, was so certain that it would host the county seat that he put a block of land in trust for the purpose of serving as the site of the future county buildings. In 1852 the county spent $100 to make a twenty-by-sixteen-foot clerk's office. P. C. Spooner completed construction in May 1855 for $250. The county for a time also rented space in the Alverson Hotel. The land Brooks donated did not see plans for a proper court until 1866.

At first, prisoners were sent to Kent County. A jail was completed in the summer of 1855 for $326.04 by a Mr. Matevey. Plans called for hewn timber floors and walls,

with the latter measuring about twelve feet tall and forming a frame that was seventeen by twelve feet. There were two cells, and each had a trapdoor for entry. Voters later rejected proposals for a better facility. In 1877 the county spent $1,000 from its general fund as well as money from private subscription to build a larger frame jail and sheriff's residence.

The county office and court building was completed in mid-winter 1868. Voters at first approved $3,000 by a vote of 340 to 237 in November 1866, but the following fall another $1,000 was allocated for a second story for the courtroom. More money was needed, so the proceeds from the sale of the older county building, plus $600 advanced by select local citizens, were used.

The two-story brick building was made entirely of local materials, from the ample lumber felled nearby to the clay that was dug up and fire-born into bricks. The lime was a county product too, as was the fieldstone used in the foundation. There were arched windows on each level and a modest cornice below the roof. Landscaping, lawn care, and tree planting later added to the square.

In 1871 an observatory with small arched windows was added to the roof. In the same year, Newaygo legislators won a battle in Lansing to prevent creation of a county called Russell from portions of Kent, Montcalm, and Newaygo counties. Each of the counties had more territory than, in the minds of some, a model county should have. Presently, Newaygo enjoys more townships than most counties, as well as more miles of road, which translates into more highway funding.

At least one account surmised that the county seat would prefer splitting Newaygo along north-south lines to losing the southeastern portion of the county to a new county because the latter would probably mean losing votes that would keep the county seat in Newaygo. As population spread north and the courthouse deteriorated, Fremont and White Cloud began clamoring for a change. In 1908 White Cloud, which was once called Morgantown, Morganville, and Morgan Station for an early founder, erected a large and commodious city hall. It was more than White Cloud needed, which led some to believe that it was a not-so-subtle attempt at winning the county seat.

Sure enough, within two years White Cloud handed the keys to its city hall to Newaygo County, which converted it into a courthouse. To sweeten the deal, White Cloud offered seven years of free rent and a gift of ten years of water and electricity. The new court was brick, measuring forty by one hundred feet. It was thirty feet from the ground to the roof plate and another fifteen feet to the top of the self-supporting roof at its highest point. A portico measuring eight by twelve feet and supported by twelve-and-a-half-foot colonial pillars marked visitors' spot of ingress and egress. Above it, depending on when the photograph was taken, was lettering labeling the building as city hall or county courthouse. The old court in Newaygo was razed in 1937, and in its place stands an auditorium and city offices.

In the 1920s this court in White Cloud was the scene of dramatic proceedings stemming from the poisoning homicides of a father and son. The son, Romie "Doc" Hodell, married into the ill-reputed Dudgeon family, which lived in a desolate, rarely visited area that locals called Dudgeon's Swamp. He was found dead hanging in a barn by horse harnesses at age twenty-six on May 6, 1922. His father David had died the previous February.

Doc's death raised immediate suspicions. His feet were touching the ground and his knees were bent. Dirt was on his shoulder. Investigators determined that a blow to the back of his head near his right ear killed him. His suicide note was considered a forgery.

A vigilante mob targeted an assistant of Doc, who was taken into custody a number of times and held at length until he was exonerated. Members of the victim's family coerced two of the Dudgeons to confess that they knew the assistant was guilty. Doc's brother attached a noose to one of their necks, slung the rope over a large tree branch, tied the other end to his motorcycle, and pulled it tight. The mob grew nervous because the slightest move by anyone might cause a slip of the foot that would engage the "suicide clutch." In the end, no one was hung, and the tree that was used was cut down decades later in 1980 as a purported road hazard.

Meanwhile, investigators turned to Doc's twenty-year-old widow Meady and her mother Alice. Doc's father David was exhumed, and poison was found in his corpse as well as his son's. Prosecutors theorized that David died from the poison but that Doc did not immediately die, which caused Meady and then Alice to strike him about the head with a rolling pin. The women were tried in White Cloud, as were some male members of their clan as coconspirators. A local judge denied requests for venue changes, which led to a number of appellate proceedings. Meady was convicted and sentenced to life. Alice's jury deadlocked, and she was never tried again. At least one coconspirator enjoyed a judge's directed verdict holding that disposal of a body was not a crime under the law.

Meady maintained her innocence and developed somewhat of a following that pushed for her release. She saved her ten cents a day from her prison labor to pay for her mother's funeral in 1935. Fourteen years later she was released with savings of $400 cash and $800 in bonds. She spent the last few years of her life as a housekeeper in a Catholic rectory in Grosse Pointe.

Newaygo's new utilitarian one-story courthouse was dedicated on September 8, 1993, at a cost of $2 million. In 1983 a fire marshal declared the old courthouse unsafe because of substandard wiring. Renovations happened, but more was required. Difficulty with compliance with the Americans with Disabilities Act and a lack of space, security, and fire doors prompted the county to plan for a new courthouse. In 2002 the county unveiled an addition to the new building.

The new courthouse has gotten its share of murder trials, as has each Michigan courthouse in every historical period. Like the etymology of Newaygo, the roster of murders for the county is not lacking in colorful stories.

OAKLAND COUNTY

The zinc statue as it appeared in 2006 before inclement weather prompted its renovation and removal indoors to make way for a bronze replacement

PONTIAC—There is a land of oaks, landlocked yet dotted with lakes. The narrow trail from Detroit to Saginaw that first took root here began an exponential growth that is reflected on a smaller scale in the march of Oakland County's courthouse: from a modest windswept wooden frame to a sprawling modern complex, with a few brick and stone stops between the extremes.

Territorial governor Lewis Cass proclaimed the existence of Oakland County, Michigan's first inland county, on March 28, 1820, and declared Pontiac the county seat. Its present boundaries were set by September 20, 1822. An abundance of oak openings is the reason for the county's name, while Pontiac was the name of a prominent Ottawa chief perhaps best known for his siege of Detroit.

Oakland had fewer than sixty families when it was organized. For fifty cents a day, John Jones, an early Bloomfield settler, cleared the forest on the site of the first courthouse on the southwest corner of Saginaw and Huron Streets. Before the first courthouse was completed in 1824, court met in spartan conditions. Judge Michael E. Crofoot described the scene at the 1858 dedication of a new courthouse. "There, in July, 1820, [judges] assembled in an old log building, where the free breath of heaven wafted without interruption of those useless modern appendages—a door, floor, or chimney, and where too, assumed the grand jurors of the county, at this, the first session of a court of record in our county." At this first session, one man was licensed as an attorney and two to keep a tavern, "thus keeping up

the proper equilibrium of power which is so essential for all new counties."

The first permanent facility was not much of an improvement, according to Crofoot. "That old and dilapidated temple now tottering on its foundation, with its crumbling walls tumbling about it, its covering fluttering like the tattered garments of the old man represented as the personification of poverty, was reared (we are told), upon its present locality in 1823, where it has stood 'wasting its sweetness on the desert air' for the last thirty-five years." Six-inch wooden planks surrounded the first story, which was the jail. The second story was frame wood, and it housed the courtroom and the sheriff's quarters.

The deteriorating building was the setting of a sensational murder trial in 1846. The defendant, a handsome young doctor, was accused of methodically using arsenic to poison his beautiful wife. There was local outrage when he was acquitted, reportedly by a jury that the doctor's defense team managed to completely hoodwink.

There was a thirty-year struggle to either move the county seat to Auburn or to authorize funds for a better courthouse in Pontiac. Finally, voters in April 1856 approved funding for Pontiac, which by then was a bustling trade center with 2,000 residents. In the meantime, in 1848 Solomon Close built a long one-story wooden administrative building for $937.50. D. J. Pratt was awarded the general contract for the courthouse for $12,594. The brick building of Italianate design measured sixty by one hundred feet, eclipsing the size of the state capitol at the time. The courthouse had a cupola and, for a time, four large iron American eagles with wings spread. Shortly after its dedication, the building saw the eight-day trial of the Tulley boys for murdering their father. The building also provided space for singing schools, lectures, school exhibitions, and elections, as well as political and farmers' meetings.

By the turn of the century, a movement was afoot to raze the courthouse and replace it with a larger structure. It took about four years, and, despite a failed vote in 1902, the project passed in April 1904 by a vote of 4,757 to 3,987. For about seventeen months, the court was displaced, meeting in the basement of a Congregational church. Those premises witnessed in forty-six years about 2,000 criminal sentencings, 4,000 civil cases, and 1,200 divorces. At the dedication of this building's successor, Aaron Perry, president of the Bar, described some of these many proceedings. The court "resounded . . . to speeches that have fired the jurors with indignation, or suffused their eyes with tears—and to some that have lulled their wearied minds to involuntary slumber."

Architect Joseph E. Mills of Detroit designed and general contractor John G. Schmidt of Toledo built the 1905 courthouse, whose cornerstone was laid on August 30, 1904. Local dignitaries were invited to deliver short speeches, which were curtailed in the hot sun after Daniel L. Davis, a prominent Pontiac attorney, rambled on with no awareness of the time elapsed. He rectified matters later when he donated a large clock for the bell tower. The bell was installed in 1913. The bell survived the building, spending several years in storage until it was mounted in a place of honor on November 14, 1995, outside of the newest county courthouse.

The 1905 courthouse cost $103,142.99, plus approximately $10,000 more for furnishings, including $123.75 for cuspidors. It was a three-story building, lined with gray sandstone. The county dedicated it on November 1, 1905, followed the next day by public exercises, including a military parade. Atop the brick tower 112 feet above street level stood Lady Justice, a blindfolded figure grasping scales and a sword, symbols of the interpretation and execution of justice. W. H. Mullins in Salem, Ohio, manufactured the nine-foot statue. Stone columns measuring twenty-five feet tall flanked the two main entrances, inside which one featured a large portrait of Chief Pontiac. The tiled corridors and marble wainscoting gave the building a noticeable red motif. Court was upstairs, with offices in the basement and ground floor.

The ever-growing county felt the pangs of congestion and space limitation, even with the advent of additional administrative space in the former Masonic Temple Building, which the county acquired during the Depression. Parking became a nightmare. Commercial buildings surrounded the courthouse site. It was therefore decided to construct a large county complex on wide acreage on the outskirts of Pontiac. Over the cries of those who feared moving elsewhere would gut downtown Pontiac, plans were made and the old courthouse was eventually demolished in 1962, making room today for parking.

The county bought the first hundred acres of the new site back in 1866 from Mortimer Osman for the purpose of establishing a county poor farm. The Oakland County Service Center, as the locale is now known, stands on 620 acres, with about forty-five major facilities (2,000,000 square feet) dotting the landscape. There are about 5,600 parking spaces, of which are 1,850 by the courthouse, which come at a premium on motion day, otherwise known as Wednesday. The anchor of the Service Center is the courthouse complex, which was built in six stages beginning in 1960. With those expansions came the need for Pontiac to annex land from Waterford, as it would run afoul of state law to allow a courthouse straddling the seat's line to grow past the seat's boundary.

The Courthouse Tower measures 107,286 square feet, and it houses most of the courtrooms. Four massive numerals crown the two long sides of the building, guiding first-time visitors to 1200 North Telegraph Road. For about $3.3 million, O'Dell, Hewlett & Luckenbach Associates designed the tower, and O. W. Burke Company supervised construction. The fanfare of 1903 by far outstripped the cornerstone ceremony of June 27, 1960.

Additional offices were placed in the West Wing, which was completed in 1963 for nearly $1.6 million. The third component is the Courthouse Auditorium, which contains space for the Board of Commissioners. It was completed in 1964 and renovated in 2002. The fourth element is the Courthouse East Wing, a three-story administrative center built in 1968 for $3,010,200. The five-story West Wing Extension added 141,570 square feet in 1994 for $17 million. It was renovated in 2003, and, though it was not designed for this purpose, two new judgeships are located there, along with prosecutor offices, library services, and corporation counsel. Finally, the Courthouse North Lobby, where sheriff's deputies screen visitors, was built in 1995. Its 3,984 square feet cost $1.66 million.

The Sentinel stands guard outside of the North Lobby.

It is a shiny abstract sculpture, unveiled on May 28, 1994. It is dedicated, according to its plaque, "to the men and women of Oakland County who have served honorably in the armed forces of our county." The late Donald F. Snyder, a marine and a county resident, is the artist.

A more classical sentry stands guard at the opposite side of the building. Finding a decidedly lower perch, Lady Justice planted her feet on a new and different pedestal. Stored after the demolition of the 1905 courthouse, she again saw the light of day at another dedication on April 30, 1983. Bad weather tore off her scales and cracked her arm in 2008. Restoration followed, along with a new home inside the courthouse because the worn zinc statue would no longer stand outside exposure. A bronze replica was cast and unveiled in the same outdoor location on September 1, 2009. The stucco pedestal was also upgraded to marble matching the courthouse. The project cost about $40,000. The county now owns a mold and has accepted at least one offer to cast another statue for a private party. Each order will net the county $1,000.

Her view and her material may have changed, but there she stands, serving an equally prominent role in the continued function of Oakland County government. Squint, and surely she shall smile.

OCEANA COUNTY

HART—The former Oceana County Courthouse left a hole in the community, literally. The new courthouse was constructed around it so that the county could operate seamlessly through the transition. It was then razed and in its footprint remains a courtyard surrounded by the successor.

Unlike the footprint of the old courthouse, the current boundaries of the county fall north of and nowhere within the original lines the Legislature approved, which now fall mainly within Kent, Mecosta, and Newaygo Counties. Oceana in its current form was organized in 1855, with the seat first at Stony Creek. Earlier, it was attached to Ottawa County for judicial purposes. The board of supervisors then moved the seat to Whiskey Creek, or Roseville. The first name came from speculation about the properties of the river because an early settler sold several barrels of the spirit from there. In 1858 court convened at the Anderson house hotel. The next year court was held in the home of L. D. Eaton, which also housed county offices and hotel guest rooms.

An early court clerk on his first day of the job interrupted court, shouting, "Hold on judge! I can't get half of this talk down—you must go a little slower." The account of the incident claims that "all hands were convulsed with laughter, little becoming the dignity of a court of justice."

No commentary followed the record of a justice of the peace who colloquially wrote out a warrant on the back of a yellow envelope. Nor are there any asides connected to the story of an early jury that "absconded themselves, and went fishing" before returning at the close of evidence to convict for the unrecorded charge, which led to a sentence of ninety-nine years.

Oceana's name origin is uncertain. Some sources claim that it is due to Oceana's coastline on Lake Michigan. At least one source claims that the name derives from *The Model Commonwealth*, a novel written by James Harrington during the time of Oliver Cromwell in 1558. It was reprinted before the American Revolution and again just before Oceana was organized. It was a book about building the perfect government.

In 1864 the county decided, by a vote of 229 to 223, to move the seat to Hart, which was reportedly named for Wellington Hart, a pioneer. It was not in the center of the county geographically, but it was in the middle of active early settlement.

Pentwater, the main commercial center at the time, resisted the move and tried to gain the county seat designation. Its name is due to the narrow channel at the mouth of the lake of the same name, where the water is pent up. It went so far as to invite the board of supervisors to meet there in 1871, where they were met with a brass band, expensive cigars, and a sumptuous banquet. The efforts never proved successful, partly because Pentwater was also working against Shelby and Mears, two other contenders for the county seat. Hart quickly grew into a large settlement in its own right. A rim of high hills surrounding it delayed the arrival of the railroad until Hart offered $12,000 in inducement for a spur from Mears in 1881. Two years later Hart erected a brick hotel to counteract detractors' allegations that the seat lacked a fine hotel.

The first courthouse and county offices in Hart were in the lower floor of the residence of Lyman B. Corbin. In addition to offering the building, he paid $1,000 for Hart to receive the seat. It was on the east side of Water Street near Mechanic. It was a simple peaked-roof structure measuring sixteen by twenty-four feet with no masonry foundation and built of rough boards with batter strips to cover the cracks. Exterior steps led to the living quarters upstairs. The lower floor was one large room, and it is unclear how it functioned as both county offices and a courtroom. The Corbin building was for public use from 1864 to 1874. The county in 1870 rented the store building of a Mr. Leach for county offices.

A late-night session of the board of supervisors on December 19, 1873, approved a new court building. David Benham built it for $6,031.82 and delivered it on August 18, 1875. The county spent an additional $475 on a hot air furnace and heating system. Hart had raised a building fund of $2,500. In many ways this building was a larger version of the Corbin building.

On April 17, 1876, many arrived on the courthouse grounds in their best dress to plant centennial trees. A comparison of photographs and the current state of the grounds indicates how much the trees grew over the years.

In 1903 the grounds were improved by a monument erected by the Oceana Veterans Monument Association. Bas-relief figures of a sailor, cavalryman, and infantryman appear around the pedestal below the rifle-toting figure. The front of the pedestal reads, "to our fallen heroes" and gives the years of the Civil War. Before the monument is a plaque bearing the names of those who died in the war.

Efforts to build a larger facility met obstructions throughout the twentieth century. Finally in 1958 the county erected a flat-roofed modern facility. Orus O. Eash designed it, and Elzinga & Volkers, Inc., built it in such a way that it surrounded the old courthouse. This way, the county functioned without the need for a temporary facility during construction. All records and county property were moved into the new building, and the old building

was razed, leaving behind a courtyard in the center of the new building, which was dedicated September 27, 1958.

The courtroom receives ample natural light, which enters through a series of windows above the large horizontal wooden beams below the ceiling. The wooden furnishings are light in color, complementing the darker green carpeting and chairs for the judges, attorneys, parties, witnesses, and public. Jurors sit in wooden swivel chairs. The walls and ceiling are white, with the exception of the brick wall behind the jury box, to which portraits of past judges are affixed.

The corridors feature ample displays of county history, from war memorabilia to county records, deeds, and photographs of the old court and new court as it was being constructed. Some of the valuable items are unsecured in a show of this county's trust of the public and lucky experience so far—or perhaps both. There is also an oil painting of the old courthouse that is difficult for a visitor to miss. A large display near the front door has a partial assortment of examples of fifty types of wood indigenous to Oceana, from alder to yellow birch.

That wood may be occupying space near where ancestor wood made up the old court, whose courtyard footprint leaves behind shoes that the current facility aspires to fill.

OGEMAW COUNTY

WEST BRANCH—The ubiquity of the image of Chief Ogemaw in the county named for him suggests a deep and abiding respect and love for him as a figure. A casual walk through the Ogemaw County courthouse unmistakably reveals the great presence of his memory.

His name was Ogemaw-Ke-Ke-To, and he was born in 1794. He was elected chief of the Tittabawassee band of Ojibwa in 1815 and spoke for them at the Treaty Conferences of 1819. He also spoke before Congress in 1837 a few short years before he died in Bay City in 1840. He was a tall, handsome, and eloquent man. He was buried wearing a colonel's uniform and a medal that the president gave to him.

In 1964 the county adopted Millie Miller's impression of him as the official insignia of the county. She crafted a large wooden likeness of him, which is in the lobby of the current court. His visage appears in the circuit court seal and in watermarks on county and city stationery. His face is on the county flag, appearing on a white arrowhead on a spruce green background. An oil painting of him hangs near the main stairway along with images of the county's earlier courts. His likeness was on the ceremonial shovel used at the groundbreaking of the current court.

Ogemaw's lines were drawn in 1840, the year that its namesake died. It was attached at various times to Mackinac, Cheboygan, Midland, and Iosco Counties before it was independently organized on April 27, 1876.

West Branch, which was named for its location off the Rifle River, offered use for three years of a two-story twenty-by-forty-foot building if the county located its seat there. The county counteroffered, requiring ownership of the building and a basement or separate building with two jail cells measuring at least twelve by twenty feet. West Branch balked but reconsidered and accepted the terms when a rival location expressed a willingness to meet the county's terms.

The court was built in West Branch and occupied on July 11, 1876. West Branch became a village in 1885 and a city in 1905. Regular improvements were made to the courthouse over the coming years. On January 20, 1887, the treasurer was instructed to obtain fire insurance for $8,000, which proved fortuitous after a fire shortly thereafter on April 28 destroyed the courthouse, jail, and sheriff's residence.

The insurance company disputed its obligation, alleging that the county overestimated the actual value of what it lost. A final settlement of $5,980.56 was reached. Meanwhile, the county sought temporary facilities. It purchased a fireproof safe for records and cages for prisoners. In October it bought a building known as the old schoolhouse for a jail from M. H. French for $1,150.

In April 1888 the county decided to borrow money to rebuild on the site of the burned buildings using their foundations. A contract for two new brick buildings costing $14,999.25 was signed, and Glanfield and Sims completed the new courthouse late that year. The jail had ten cells, plus a cage in the attic for female prisoners.

The county struggled for years to properly heat the courthouse, using wood and then coal. In 1909 it was connected to city water and electricity. For a time the source of water for the buildings was a windmill pump. No action was taken, and votes for new projects were rejected in the coming decades.

A new jail for about $180,000 was completed and dedicated December 10, 1961. The old jail was used for county offices until it was demolished in 1970. Finally, as Ogemaw County approached its centennial, voters on May 7, 1973, approved a new courthouse by a vote of 1,299 to 451. Gust Construction Company of Cedar Springs submitted a winning bid of just over $2 million. Finish hardware in the amount of $21,216 was approved.

The cornerstone was laid in 1974, and the building was completed the following centennial year. Steve F. Gerganoff designed the structure. A plaque inside the building does not mention Gust. But it does credit L. G. Fenerli as the professional engineers and S. F. Sonk Associates, Inc., as the consulting engineers.

The two-story brick building is a good example of its contemporary architectural style. Columns of windows with metal bracing blend in with the brick and the lining of the flat roof. Lettering reading "Ogemaw County Building" appears on each side of the building but the rear.

A painting of the red brick courthouse and jail that the county building replaced hangs in the courtroom above the witness box, which is dead ahead of the public seating with the bench to its right and the curved jury box to its left. The wooden benches for the public match the other wood furnishings in the court, except for the parties' simple tables

and the fabric chairs. Portraits of past judges hang above the jury box, where, like behind the bench, the wall is lined with wood. The white wall behind the witness box contrasts well with the oil painting. The three walls around the public seating are cinder blocks painted white.

Unlike elsewhere in the building, the courtroom lacks images depicting Ogemaw. One hopes that the reason is that in this space deep and abiding respect is reserved for another local point of pride: the law.

ONTONAGON COUNTY

ONTONAGON—One truly must intend to go to Ontonagon, for it is not exactly on the road to anyplace. Situated in the northwest corner of the Upper Peninsula on the south shore of Lake Superior, it stands in relative isolation, a fact not lost on its 10,000 or so inhabitants.

Copper brought the first white settler, James K. Paul of Virginia, in 1843, which is the same year when the Legislature created Ontonagon County, severing it from Houghton County. He built a log cabin on the east side of the mouth of the Ontonagon River. The name is unique and is probably Ojibwa corrupted into French and corrupted again into English. Other tongue-twisting versions include Nantonagun, Nantounaganing, Nunda-Norgan, and Nindonagon. Depending on context, the original Ojibwa meant "my bowl is lost" or "hunting river." The former is based on a legend of an Ojibwa girl who dropped a bowl in the river. It is a place-name that is unique in the world to Michigan.

Daniel Cash followed Paul in 1845 and settled on the west bank of the river. Soon, a competition over the location of the courthouse arose. Cash won at first, but a special election in April 1858 moved the county seat to the public square on the east side of the river.

Ontonagon did not get a proper courthouse for some time. For a while, court was held on the second floor of the fire hall. On June 5, 1884, the County Board of Supervisors approved $12,000 for the construction of a courthouse. The old courthouse was completed on December 14, 1885, on the public square. It featured red brick, a tower, and a copper roof put together in the Romanesque style.

Though originally an east-west rivalry gripped Ontonagon County, soon a north-south division arose. The town of Ewan led an unsuccessful effort to carve a new county out of southern Ontonagon. The motive was reportedly a desire not to see its tax dollars leave local control for things like building and renovating the courthouse, which some called the "castle of corruption."

Less than a decade after its completion, the courthouse and the town of Ontonagon were engulfed in flames. The fire came on August 2, 1896. It gutted the courthouse, though some records were saved. Other than the tower atop the courthouse, which had to be removed, the fire did not succeed in destroying the courthouse. Though it leveled much of the rest of the town, only 2 of the 2,300 residents were killed. The courthouse interior was repaired, and the building remained operational.

Like elsewhere in Michigan, the natural force that

claimed Ontonogan's old courthouse was time. Wear and tear took its toll. As the surrounding blocks became more residential, space for parking cars became scarce. Room for records within the court was lacking too. Finally, the old building became impossible to heat properly.

With these considerations in mind, Ontonagon built a new courthouse on the outskirts of town in 1980. The building is modern in design and bears no resemblance to its predecessor. The old courthouse has been owned by a number of private parties who have had little luck housing any viable business inside of it. Recently it continues to stand as a half-abandoned structure on the National Register of Historic Places.

But there was a time when the forgotten courthouse was at the center of attention. On November 21, 1893, a "murder most foul"—as a local newspaper described it—happened at the hands of one Alex Enos, a twenty-four-year-old local character who ran a house of ill repute. He had been drinking that day and learned that one of his three "soiled doves" had flown the coop with a gentleman client. Enos went in a drunken rage to the railroad station at Trout Creek on the eastern edge of the county.

He corralled his woman and forcibly brought her back, cursing and firing his gun about town. Deputy George Davidson, a quiet family man standing six feet five inches tall, was summoned to deal with the trouble. As was the custom at the time, Davidson enlisted the crew of a locomotive in town at the time to back him up.

The posse reached the Enos place, where Enos was threatening his three girls with a Winchester rifle and firing into the ceiling. Noticing the posse, Enos sensed trouble. Davidson calmly approached him, put his hand on Enos's shoulder, and asked him to surrender the gun. When Enos refused, Davidson suggested that the two retire alone to a room behind the bar. There, Davidson calmed down Enos and took the rifle away from him.

But when Davidson revealed his handcuffs, Enos reacted violently, pulling out a five-shot Smith & Wesson .32 caliber pistol. Davidson saw the pistol and grabbed for Enos's hand, shouting his last words to Pat O'Brien, the railroad engineer who burst into the room, "Pat, take that revolver!"

O'Brien reached for the gun but recoiled when the first shot sailed through his left hand. The second shot hit Davidson in the abdomen, causing him to slump over. The third shot inflicted a flesh wound in O'Brien's side. The fourth shot was point-blank through the head of the stricken Davidson. Enos emptied his gun with one last wild shot that hit nobody. Enos was quickly overpowered and jailed.

The case went to trial, where Enos's attorney, C. O. Trumbull, masterfully tried the case. Some described Trumbull as the Clarence Darrow of the North. The judge refused Trumbull's request to change venue. So Trumbull turned to picking the right jury. Trumbull quickly challenged and went through the typical pool of twenty-four prospective jurors. The judge directed the sheriff to bring in another hundred candidates. Trumbull challenged these too, so another hundred were brought and finally a third hundred. The sheriff was forced to find jurors at the railroad station, enlisting traveling salesmen and others who had not already formed an opinion on the case.

Over thirty witnesses testified, and in the end Enos was convicted of manslaughter. He was a model prisoner who was released early in 1901 after seven years of confinement. In 1898, Enos sent the county clerk a painting of the courthouse as it appeared before the fire and during Enos's trial. His rendition was remarkably accurate considering that he painted it from memory. It is on display in the local historical museum, which is one of many reasons to leave the beaten path to visit Ontonagon.

OSCEOLA COUNTY

REED CITY—The footing for Osceola County's courthouse has been less than sure at times. Politically, there have been numerous efforts both successful and unsuccessful to move the county seat. Physically, there was an actual move after a relocation vote carried, a partial accidental collapse of the courthouse, and a termite problem. But through it all and to the credit of the county, service remains uninterrupted.

The Legislature in 1840 named the county Unwattin for an Ottawa chief. Three years later, the name changed to Osceola, for a Seminole chief who led his people in a war with the United States. In tribute to him and in protest of the trickery the U.S. military used to capture and kill him, several counties across the country adopted his name. The county was attached to Mecosta for judicial purposes.

In 1869 the first county elections occurred. Hersey, which was named for the first white trapper to visit the area in the 1840s, was relatively large in population. It was in the more developed southern portion of the territory, where, according to one early settler and developer, canoe met railroad.

As inducement, land and $3,500 were offered to build a court in Hersey. The final price was $8,500, which also bought a fire-resistant vault. A jail was constructed for $3,500. The county buildings were a point of pride, but soon they became the center of controversy.

As the other reaches of the county grew, residents agitated for a county seat that was more central. Reed City emerged as the strongest contender due to its size and location. It was named for James S. Reed, a founder of the set-

tlement. Earlier, it had been called Tunshla, whose meaning was not recorded, and then Todd's Slashings, in reference to the lumbered-off land of another founder.

By 1890 Hersey had only 310 residents to Reed City's 1,776 souls. The time was ripe for an election to move the county seat. Vigorous politicking and newspaper editorializing preceded the April 1891 election. Evart, another sizeable community, entered the fray. Its newspaper published damaging reports and letters inveighing against Reed City as not central enough and willing to engage in suspect plots to secure the county seat.

At last the vote happened on April 17, 1891, and Hersey held on to its courthouse by the slim margin of 1,731 to 1,721. For thirty years the matter was dropped, until the deteriorating buildings in Hersey called for repair or replacement.

It took three votes by the county supervisors, but finally they referred the matter to the people, who voted in a special election on April 4, 1927. Reed City accused Hersey along the way of being a pup that would bite the larger dogs of Reed City and Evart, convince them that they antagonized each other, and then watch them fight.

Whatever the truth of the matter, Reed City prevailed in the vote by a healthy margin of 3,163 to 2,335. Hersey lost and watched its court emptied of its records and original purpose. It would later become a bottling plant for the soft drink Vernors, an electric generator repair shop, and a vacant reminder of what was. Recently, work was being done to convert it into a public housing project.

Meanwhile, Reed City has enjoyed its status as county seat, though there was another scare in 1978 when a vote to move it to Evart failed 3,898 to 1,467. The confines of city hall welcomed the court and county offices. In 1938 a significant renovation and enlargement happened, with the aid of federal money. Roger Allen was the architect, and Fred Gietzen was the superintendent of construction. The sloping roof and small tower were leveled off to create the cube effect that was gaining popularity at the time. A good part of the brick and many of the arched windows of the original structure remained. But a new main entrance and front facade were erected.

In August 1964 a new jail and sheriff's residence costing about $200,000 were dedicated after attempts at expanding and renovating the earlier facility proved futile in the face of state inspectors' orders to condemn. The court welcomed an addition to its west side in 1960 at the price of $30,000. The east side gained a $70,000 addition in 1968, which provided needed office and vault space for the clerk and the equalization department.

Recently the court underwent an ambitious $2.1 million renovation. While construction crews dug outside, cracks formed in one section of brick. The building was quickly cleared of those who happened to still be inside during the lunch hour. At 1:00 p.m. a sixteen-by-twelve-foot section collapsed, exposing three levels of offices. The damage was repaired, along with some improvements to the interior.

In particular, the large courtroom saw its jury box shifted to the other side of the room and its bolted-down theater seating replaced with matching wooden pews. County business was disrupted but not derailed in 1999 when termite extermination was required. A local news-

paper report quoted the dedicated clerk as dreading having to again vacate her offices. She described issuing marriage licenses from the trunk of her car during the earlier construction, expressing a newfound "respect for traveling salesmen."

Meanwhile, some residents continue to talk about moving the county seat elsewhere as demographics change and as the current facility sees probate and district court, as well as the prosecutor's office, located down the street with the library in a building that used to house the county hospital. There is a running joke that the time for rotation is long overdue given that Hersey had the court for fewer decades than Reed City has had it. Others find no humor in again rocking the foundation of Osceola's coveted court.

OSCODA COUNTY

MIO—Judging by its architecture and the oversized sculpture on its lawn, the Oscoda County Courthouse of 1888 almost looks like a birdhouse. The bird of choice for Oscoda is Kirtland's warbler, a small and endangered yellow-breasted songbird that only nests in northeastern Michigan.

Oscoda's name derives from the words "ossin " and "muscoda," which together mean stony or pebbly prairie. It was organized on March 10, 1881, after being attached earlier to Mackinac, Cheboygan, Alpena, Iosco, and Alcona Counties. The county seat was temporarily at Union Corners, which was also called Indian Lake and is now a ghost town. The election in the autumn of 1881 sent the county seat to what is now Mio. Until November 21, 1883, it was called Mioe for the wife of an early settler. The records were transferred on April 15, 1882.

The early history of the county includes a humorous escape note. John Whiting was convicted of setting fire to the Au Sable jail. He broke out of his cell and found a tunnel that a convicted murderer started before being foiled. Whiting completed the tunnel and made his getaway, avoiding a sentence of six months. He left behind the following rhyming couplet. "The judge and jury have had their say / So now I think I'll have my way."

John Randall built the first courthouse at Mio and rented it for $100 a year. He supervised a company of men who in one day erected a structure measuring twelve by eighteen by ten feet. After the flagpole was fastened, the mailman proposed "three times three." So the men gave three hearty cheers for the county, its seat, and Old Glory.

Until 1888, plans for a larger courthouse slowly proceeded. Efforts to move the county seat to Luzerne and later to the north side of the Au Sable River failed. Randall offered land for $1 in 1885 for a court and jail if it were built in a year. Otherwise, the price was $100, which the county accepted in October 1885. It raised $1,000 by tax and explored getting more by bond but was delayed when it learned that by law it could not do both in one year.

Voters rejected a number of subsequent bond issues, though planning began when the county acquired a loan for $1,000. Eventually a $2,000 bond passed in July 1888 and construction commenced that same month and ended May 1889, when the county took possession and moved in. The final price was $3,794.80. The sheriff was hired to be janitor for $50 a year. George Hunter, the builder, also constructed a woodshed and an outhouse.

The building, which continues to stand, is a two-story frame structure. Rounded windows contrast its sharp architectural lines. Aluminum replaced the original white clapboard wooden siding. The same company that installed the fire hydrant in the front of the lawn connected the courthouse to water in 1891. Electricity came in 1917. Two wings containing vaults and the clerk and treasurer's offices were built in 1908 for $1,692.14.

The interior of the courthouse has a similar simple elegance. Ornamental sheeting in the courtroom, which is now stripped of much of its furniture and used for storage, is the one touch beginning to approach extravagance. A display case in the lobby presents some significant early documents, including building committee minutes from 1887 and specifications from Bay City architects Pratt & Koeppe dated May 18, 1887. Much to the chagrin of even a casual archivist, they are fastened by tacks and exposed to sunlight.

In 1994–95, a courthouse annex was renovated and opened. It dates back to World War I and was once a schoolhouse, but that function ceased in 1962 when some county services moved in. A grant under the Americans with Disabilities Act helped spur the move of the courts to the two-story brick annex. The well-appointed but mod-

est circuit courtroom is in the basement. Before the annex, court had to move to an unsuitable local community center for its business if there was an accessibility issue.

The county yet clings to its older building, with a sign continuing to call it the county courthouse. County offices still operate and keep their records there. On the lawn preens an oversize sculpture of a Kirtland's warbler behind glass and on a brick and mortar pedestal. The warbler only nests in Michigan where there are large growths of young jack pines. The first such nest was found in the western edge of the county on July 8, 1903. No other nests have ever been found more than one hundred miles away.

Growths of young jack pines typically occur in the wake of a forest fire. A plaque near the sculpture commemorates a wildlife biologist who perished before his thirtieth birthday in 1980 while trying to control a prescribed fire. The flames were meant to create nesting habitat for the warbler, but they ended up consuming 25,000 acres of the Huron National Forest. Inside the old courthouse near a stairwell, there is also a picture of a warbler.

Unlike most or perhaps all of its fellow Oscoda residents, the warbler spends its summers in the Bahamas. But one need not stretch the imagination too much to see a colony of warblers welcomed into the old courthouse, particularly now that some space in the courtroom is relatively free.

OTSEGO COUNTY

GAYLORD—The courthouse of Otsego County looks much like a Swiss chalet with its peaked roofs, stucco brick, heavy timber, and other architectural characteristics. The effect is intended by this self-described Alpine town. The downtown commercial area reflects the same style, which prevailed first as custom and now as law under a local ordinance requiring all businesses in the area to comply with the theme.

The county's boundaries were set off in 1840, and it was named Okkuddo, which probably meant "sickly" or "stomach pains." It was a three-year bug ending in 1843 with the renaming for a county in New York that in Iroquois means "clear water."

Otsego was organized as its own county on March 12, 1875. At first Otsego Lake in the more populous southern territory was the county seat. County business, including court proceedings, first occurred in the boarding house of Charles Brink. The same simple frame structure later gained additions as it became a number of different hotels and an antique shop.

Early in the county's history the northern and central populations pushed for a more convenient county seat location, which meant closer to them. The matter was put to a vote in the spring of 1876, and Otsego Lake was shocked when it lost the county seat by a vote of 172 to 140. Election officials reportedly stood by with guns ready to quell any potential disturbance as ballots were counted. The record indicates that the other side took advantage of a law requiring only thirty days of residency to vote and persuaded itinerant lumberjacks to support the removal. The centrally located Gaylord, which was originally called

Barnes, became the county seat. Its second name was for an attorney of the Jackson, Lansing & Saginaw Railroad.

But Otsego Lake would not lose quietly. It refused to turn over the county records. The sheriff led a party one night that fall that surreptitiously took whatever records it could obtain from the courthouse. Some accounts allege that other records were lost or destroyed. Indignant, county officials from the aggrieved former county seat refused to appear at meetings in Gaylord. Finally, by order of the Michigan Supreme Court they were compelled to begin coming to Gaylord on November 10, 1877. Earlier, the first circuit court session in Gaylord happened on April 16, 1876.

A proper court was not erected until 1890. It was made with brick and in the style of the time, with a cupola prominently at its top. During World War II, the cupola was an aircraft spotting post, as were several other courthouse towers throughout Michigan. The bottom floor contained the sheriff's residence and a jail. County offices were on the second floor, and the court, jury room, and judge's chambers were on the third floor.

As the northern terminus of the railroad for some time, Gaylord's population exploded. The courthouse served well, but its death knell came in the 1960s. It was at this time that Gaylord formalized its relationship with Pontresina, its sister city in Switzerland. Interest grew that decade with the arrival of members of the Swiss press corps who came to see Swiss machinery unveiled at a nearby wood-processing plant. Some credit a local ski resort with planting the seeds decades earlier for an Alpine theme.

However it emerged, Gaylord's special affinity for the

Swiss Alps is apparent. County and city leaders approved an Alpine design for the new Otsego County–City of Gaylord Building, which was dedicated on September 12, 1968, seven weeks late due to a carpenters' strike. A joint authority bonded $735,000 for the project, with the county shouldering 83.35 percent and the city the rest.

Like Otsego Lake in the county seat struggle, the old courthouse did not go down without a fight. A temporary court and county offices were placed in a school gym during construction. A probate judge refused to move, declared the effort illegal, and had the sheriff detain the chairman of the county board of supervisors in the temporary court. The matter was eventually resolved and the old court demolished.

Inside the new building is a large framed photograph of its predecessor. Like the exterior, the interior is unmistakably Alpine in its woodwork and stucco walls. Translucent green, orange, purple, and blue glass adorns several areas. Colored glass in the form of Pontresina's heraldry hangs in the city office. The courtroom has an arched ceiling and a dominant bench and jury box behind light woodwork. The judge, jurors, and attorneys enjoy cushioned black chairs, while the public must sit in plastic chairs of the same color.

Soon, the building will require a name change, for it will only house county services. The city is drawing up plans to renovate an old post office and sell or lease its interest in its current location. Next to the building is a large pavilion covering public street parking, which is at a premium on snowy days. During the warmer months it welcomes a periodic farmer's market. On the other side of the grounds is a large cannon. It is one of twenty-six from the Civil War flagship *Hartford*. It was dedicated on July 4, 1905.

Near that instrument of war is a symbol of peace: a one-ton rock. It was dedicated on May 6, 1989, as a gift from Pontresina. Its plaque reads, "Friendship, like Alpine stone, lasts forever." It is yet another slice of Switzerland in this corner of northeastern Michigan.

A photograph of the 1890 courthouse hangs within its 1968 successor.

OTTAWA COUNTY

Michigan's newest county courthouse while under construction in September 2008

GRAND HAVEN—Ottawa County welcomed its new courthouse in 1894 with a wedding on its steps. Decades later, the building's tower stubbornly resisted demolition, snapping at least two cables that attempted to pull it down and proving that a tie that binds is difficult to disturb.

The county is named for the band of Native Americans who roamed from the north bank of the Grand River to the Straits of Mackinac. The Legislature organized the county on December 29, 1837. Court was to be held in neighboring Kent County until adequate premises were available. Rev. William M. Ferry built a small wooden structure in Grand Haven on Second and Franklin Streets, where court would meet until 1857. The building also hosted church, school, and social functions. It stood until at least 1893.

Many of the county's early residents were Dutch settlers. They first considered colonizing Java and the Cape of Good Hope before choosing western Michigan. In 1840 the board of supervisors voted to move the county seat to Warren City, which only existed on paper. The court never moved, and so the county seat remained in Grand Haven.

One county history records the public shaming of the man who planned to purloin a pig. The owner heard the troubled squealing of his pig and suspected foul play. He fired his rifle at the noise, killing the pig and causing the criminal to flee. He was apprehended the next day and there was sufficient evidence of his guilt. His sentence was to parade about town with the pig on his back, holding its hind legs over his shoulders as its snout nearly dragged along the ground. The public watched, along with spectators who were passengers on newly arrived ships in port.

When he finished, the criminal fled into the bushes and never returned to Grand Haven.

In 1857 a larger two-story wooden structure and jail were built for about $2,000. During the late 1850s, county officials attempted twice to move the county seat. On both occasions the voters rejected the move, first to Eastmanville, then to Ottawa Centre. In 1864 a majority of 493 voted against removal to a wild section of Allendale. The county settled on its present borders in 1859 with the organization of Muskegon County.

In 1893 the board of supervisors approved $35,000 for a new jail and courthouse. Grand Haven as an inducement raised and offered $15,000. A countywide vote passed 3,280 to 2,388. Grand Haven voted overwhelmingly in favor, 934 to 30. The county laid the cornerstone on August 21, 1893. The new building was made of brick from nearby Spring Lake. It cost $62,660.65 to build and furnish, measuring approximately 50,000 in square feet.

Ward & Russell of Flint built the courthouse, which was dedicated on Independence Day 1894. A large crowd witnessed a wedding on the steps of the Washington Street entrance. The Victorian brownstone building would stand until the mid-1960s.

It saw little change over the years. The brass spittoons finally gave way to smoking stands in 1954. To reduce noise, carpeting covered the courtroom floors the following year. After World War II the courthouse gained two vaults, which were housed in additions on the west and southeast sides that were incongruous in appearance, likened by some to bomb shelters. The building had a wooden flagpole erected

The 1965 courthouse as it appeared in June 2005 almost four years before demolition

An interior view of Ottawa County's former courthouse

in 1934. The old mast from a sailing schooner soon rotted, and the large cement base became a flower pot until its removal in 1954.

The county erected a bronze eagle atop a twenty-ton, two-section red granite column to commemorate the local honor roll for World War I. A large wooden tripod was necessary to erect it the first time. The monument spent some time in storage during the 1960s until reassembled in 1968. The county again moved it as it made way for its newest courthouse.

The 67,000-square-foot County Building was dedicated on September 29, 1965, at a cost of $693,255. That same winter the county razed the 1894 building, which was a delicate project due to its proximity to its successor. The tower of the old courthouse stubbornly resisted demolition, snapping at least two cables connected to a crane that strained as it tugged at the tower's foundation to wrest it loose. Inclement weather temporarily aided the old building in its futile struggle.

Vander Meider & Koteles of Grand Rapids designed the modern building. It featured ample glass, porcelain panels, face brick, and steel beam columns. Inside, glass blocks and ceramic green tile adorned the surroundings. At the time of dedication, the new courtroom seated thirty-five spectators compared to the one hundred fifteen that the old courtroom could accommodate. The last criminal jury case conducted in that room was number 5,285. Osterink

Construction Company of Grand Rapids was the general contractor.

Time chipped away at this building too. Its judges split their time between it and the Fillmore Street County Complex, which is several miles away from Grand Haven in a rural part of the center of the county in West Olive. It was built in 1994. Here there are four circuit courtrooms that hear many cases, particularly juvenile ones because the juvenile detention center is nearby. Family and probate court convene here as well. Ottawa replaced the 1965 courthouse with a new courthouse completed in October 2009. The new 117,600-square-foot courthouse cost about $23 million. Its design is more retrospective, with a central tower, arched windows, and peaked roofs.

Two Grand Rapids firms designed and built the new courthouse—Fishbeck, Thompson, Carr & Huber and Owens Ames Kimball, respectively. HDR, Inc., of Chicago was a design consultant. The move began in July 2009, a few months ahead of the final finishing touches. Demolition of the 1965 courthouse began in August and took several weeks before the final wall nearest the new building tumbled to make room for parking.

The 2009 courthouse is the newest part of Ottawa County's courthouse family tree. It is in part heir to the building that greeted its community with a wedding so large it had to happen outside and that bade the people farewell in a tug-of-war that twice ended with a broken bind.

PRESQUE ISLE COUNTY

ROGERS CITY—"Almost an island" may be the literal translation of Presque Isle, but the name may as well be synonymous with struggle. Standing in relative isolation on the shore of Lake Huron in the northeastern tip of the Lower Peninsula, conflicts with the elements and between political factions have marked much of its history.

Settlement began peacefully enough in the 1860s when Francis Crawford came with his family to start a quarry. The stone proved too flaky for building, so he turned to logging. Eventually, Presque Isle would be home to a massive limestone quarry, convincing city leaders in 1962 to dub Rogers City, the county seat, "Limestone City." Presently, the city calls itself "The Nautical City."

William E. Rogers is the namesake. He was a distinguished graduate of West Point, a veteran of the Civil War and on assignment with the U.S. Corps of Engineers to do a survey when he came to the area in early 1868. Included in his party was Albert Molitor, a man who would later become the local despot.

The two men formed a company and began laying out a town and bringing in people, particularly German and Polish immigrants. Everyone depended exclusively on the company for employment and for provisions. After a particularly harsh 1870–71 winter, Rogers tired of the venture and returned to New York. The settlement nearly starved and welcomed the first ship in late April with shouting and cheering.

Molitor quickly consolidated control of the company and the region. He reportedly was an illegitimate son of King William I of Württemberg and nearly found death and intrigue in Europe before escaping to America and fighting for the Union. Now he had his chance to claim a throne for himself.

Because everyone depended on him for work and on his well-stocked store for survival, the will of Molitor was the law of the land. He could demand fourteen-hour days from his workers, and he charged exorbitant prices for his goods. Wives and daughters of the town that he fancied he could have any night of his choosing.

Without the capital of Rogers, Molitor had to bleed the county for finances. The first record of the Board of Supervisors meeting is from 1871. A rivalry between Rogers City and Crawfords Quarry developed, for both wanted the county seat. The latter built an octagon-shaped courthouse for $1,000 in 1874, and $50 was spent on an upright wood-burning stove.

Rogers City had a courthouse too, and competing elections were held in each in 1875. Local lore has it that during this time of bitter fighting no sooner was a courthouse built in one spot than it was burnt under mysterious circumstances.

Rogers City won when Molitor lobbied the Legislature to award it the county seat on the basis that the county had not been properly formed originally. Previously, the county was part of Mackinac, then Cheboygan, and finally Alpena Counties. An order instructing Crawfords Quarry to turn over the wooden stove and the county records was issued. The county treasurer escaped with them to the woods, and they were never located.

Meanwhile, Molitor was passing bonds to finance his business. He obtained $8,000 for a schoolhouse that turned out to be a one-story frame building, which probably only cost $500. Money was scarce and workers were paid in credit at Molitor's store. There was no railroad, and boats were rare. It was commonly known that one had to deal with Molitor to prosper.

In 1874 a group of 200 to 300 men surrounded Molitor's store and sent in a committee that demanded that he produce the county books. He refused, telling the committee to head to a "warmer climate." He was seized and taken outside, where he glared with flashing eyes and an erect head past the guns and pitchforks of the mobs. When one man flashed a rope and said Molitor would hang unless he turned over the books, Molitor uttered a loud laugh, threw open his collar and dared the mob to do it, which it did not. All day there was a standoff, and Molitor ate his dinner with an unspoiled appetite at a table in the middle of the road. The mob dispersed at nightfall.

But Molitor's days were numbered. A smaller group of men carried out the deed on August 23, 1875. He was wounded in a quasi drive-by shooting when the men shot him through the window of his store, killing a young clerk and mortally wounding Molitor. He escaped to Detroit on a steamship and died on September 18.

Nearly sixteen years later in 1891, one of the culprits made a full confession. He apparently suffered a series of losses and his conscience told him that the Lord would forgive him and inflict no more harm if he told the story. He and those he implicated were tried in Alpena in 1893 because no impartial jury could be found in Presque Isle. Five men, including the confessor, were convicted and sentenced to life in prison. Governor Hazen S. Pingree pardoned four of the men a few years later. A. T. Bliss, a subsequent governor, pardoned the confessor in 1901.

Around the same time, the town of Onaway in the eastern edge of the county had become the largest at over 3,000. A push for it to become the new county seat emerged. Merritt Chandler, a prominent local citizen, built a large gray stone building in 1909 with a tower and a green roof and donated it as a courthouse.

The drive failed, along with an attempt to carve out a new county for Onaway called Forest County, which fell nine votes short in Lansing in 1911. But a compromise was reached. Terms of court would alternate between the courthouses in Rogers City and Onaway, an arrangement that existed until the mid-1940s. The renovated Onaway courthouse is now the local library and historical museum.

The 1909 courthouse in Onaway

Rogers City has built around its historic courthouse, lining the original wood with a brick exterior, as well as building a large annex that was completed in 1988. William C. Fuller & Associates from Harbor Springs was the architect, and the constructor was Louie's Construction Services of Onaway.

As the battle with Onaway raged, Presque Isle faced a new struggle with natural forces. One of Michigan's worst forest fires destroyed 2.5 million acres, taking many farms, mills, homes, and lives, in October 1908. A drought in the summer and fall dried out the ample vegetation that grew from a warm and moist spring season. Gale force winds fueled the five-mile-wide fire, which did not stop until it hit Lake Huron.

But through it all, Presque Isle has managed to carve out in its own way a prosperous existence. Its setting is downright pleasant and betrays no inkling of the many struggles endured in its endeavor to find and live the good life.

ROSCOMMON COUNTY

ROSCOMMON—Depending wherefrom one looks, the Roscommon County Courthouse presents many faces. The bulk of the exterior is a light-colored brick. But the front entrance is a dark and shiny polished stone. Elsewhere the front of the building is lined with variously sized and shaded masonry work that appears to be sandstone.

Roscommon County was first set off as Mikenauk County in 1840. Three years later state representative Charles O'Malley was instrumental in changing the name to Roscommon, for his native county in Ireland. One source claims that Ros means "wooded promontory or pleasant place," and Coman was a sixth-century Irish saint.

The county was organized in 1875. On April 15 at Hall Farm in Houghton Lake Heights, which until 1956 was just called The Heights, 152 male residents cast their votes for county leadership. The farm was on the southwest shore of the lake named for Douglas Houghton, Michigan's pioneer geologist. The lake has also been called Muskegon and Red Lake.

The men met in the one spot that could accommodate them and, for a time, a court. The board of supervisors first met at the Hall Farm on June 10, 1875. Roscommon Station was designated the county seat, but a recently erected small log building on the Hall Farm was the first courthouse.

Before the arrival of that courthouse, Roscommon was attached to Midland for judicial purposes. William Stocking walked sixty-five miles over two and a half days to defend himself against a murder charge. He allegedly shot a drunk French fur trapper in the leg after the trapper pushed him aside and began paddling away in Stocking's canoe. The Frenchman died of gangrene. When Stocking

was acquitted because he was defending his property, the celebrating lumbermen hoisted the small man on their shoulders, carried him to the closest saloon, handed him a fiddle, and the party commenced. The next day he began his long walk home.

Soon the fight was on for the county seat, primarily between the smaller and more organized Roscommon and the larger and more dispersed Houghton Lake. Prudenville and St. Helen also entered the fray. Some pressed for Prudenville because it was near a rail line from the notorious vice town of Meredith, while others argued for Roscommon because a railroad connected it to Bay City, where the judges were. Apart from Roscommon, each town lacked either a railroad, post office, or central location.

Roscommon won a special election on February 28, 1878. An early letter describes how lumbermen who could not speak English were registered to vote as Joe Pocket. "If we had too many Joe Pockets we gave them a middle name." The vote had its irregularities and does not seem properly recorded anywhere. The Legislature put the issue to bed on May 8, 1879, when it designated Roscommon the permanent county seat, at least until the county again rejected a move on April 3, 1961, by a vote of 1,780 to 1,694. Harry L. Parker, a Roscommon Township supervisor, received a contract to move records and county property from the court on the Hall Farm to the new court in Roscommon.

George O. Robinson, a lawyer and businessman from Detroit with interests in Roscommon, donated land for a courthouse. Prominent citizens, especially attorneys, moved from Houghton Lake to Roscommon, which incorporated as a village on January 4, 1882.

The court was built in 1879 on a hill on the site of the present courthouse. A June election in the same year approved $1,000 at 10 percent interest. The total cost of the building was $1,500. A sketch of it and its jail neighbor appears in the lobby of the current court. The old two-story court was wooden and painted white with a dark roof and trim down its corners and around its many windows. Fifteen dollars was approved for the cost of its dedication. The first order of business in the new building on September 1, 1879, was correcting a serious oversight: construction of a bathroom. The county also approved the purchase of six spittoons.

In 1913 the county erected a Civil War memorial outside the court. The stone tablet is topped with a small shape of a cannon. It remained when the old court was razed and its hill flattened. Before then, Roscommon gained the distinction of electing Michigan's first female sheriff. Jane Johnston reportedly ran because her husband was limited by law from seeking a third term. She was quoted in a newspaper article saying that she would sign necessary papers "but my husband will be the real sheriff." Quite the opposite was true for Alice M. Marsh, who was elected in the same election without opposition. She was, according to one source, a "corking good deputy treasurer for ten years" and better than any man for the job.

Pyramid Construction Company erected the new courthouse in 1964. Ralph S. Gerganoff designed the one-story flat-roofed building. It cost $520,000, half of which a federal land grant defrayed. At the laying of the cornerstone, a flight attendant for an Irish airline, who was from Ireland's Roscommon County and had friends in Michigan's Roscommon, attended and participated. She placed an Irish penny in the mortar.

Like the exterior, the interior of the courtroom pro-

jects a number of different looks. The wall behind the bench is lined by the same wood that makes up the furnishing but not the seating. It is decorative and attractive. The other three walls are functional cinder blocks painted white.

An addition was constructed in 1975, bringing the total square footage of the courthouse to 29,466 feet, including 3,906 square feet in the basement. The county obtained additional space in an annex located in part of a former school building next door.

The county recently began exploring options for a facility that will provide about 46,000 square feet. An architectural firm did a study in December 2004. The county may expand the current site, potentially closing off two streets that run by it. Or it may build a facility elsewhere, which might prompt another look at the county seat question. Preliminary estimates project a price tag of $18–26 million, depending on which option the county selects.

Come what may, the county courthouse stands ready to present yet another face to visitors and employees alike.

SAGINAW COUNTY

SAGINAW—Colorful characters abound in the history of the courts of Saginaw County. From the accused and convicted to the judge and juror, these individuals enliven the story of the courthouses of Saginaw.

Saginaw County's name means "Land of the Sauk" in Ojibwa. The Sauk were a warlike tribe that met its demise in 1520 after an Ojibwa incursion into their territory. As part of Michigan, Saginaw was first attached to Oakland County and then organized in its own right on March 2, 1831. Saginaw City, known just as Saginaw by the post office and in present times, was designated the county seat. One account claims that one commissioner's love of whiskey convinced him to conspire with a crooked commissioner's love of gain to select land near where a landowner would bribe them with other plots.

Court first met in a schoolhouse. Later, the county leased the Saginaw City Bank for $50 a year. Voters approved $10,000 in bonds in 1837, and the contract for building a courthouse was sold at auction for $9,510 to Asa Hill, who reportedly died of malaria before construction ended. Building materials allegedly sat unused and nearly wasted away. The failure of a local wildcat bank contributed to the delay. Eventually the county found labor to finish some of the work, but the grand jury room would have to serve as the courtroom for fifteen years because it took that long to complete the second story. The 1843 white clapboard building was Greek Revivalist in design, featuring four Ionic columns.

A contemporary described the building with a critical eye. "There is nothing architecturally beautiful about it, yet the records which it contains are very complete, and the county officials genial, affable gentlemen. Such men and records lend to the county offices an importance which the building under any other circumstances never possesses."

Another account writes of an elderly man convicted of grand larceny and protesting to the judge at his sentencing. He said, "But Judge, look at that damned jury. To think that such a miserable looking set of desperadoes should find me guilty, is more than I can stand; but go ahead, Judge; don't let me interrupt you."

Another criminal made a daring escape after a failed attempt. He was drying his moccasins when his captors found him, so he fled barefoot while carrying his footwear and cut his foot severely on the ice. Unable to go to jail and taken to a hotel to convalesce, he arranged for his wife, brother, and sister to visit. He posed as his sister and leaned heavily on his brother when he left. The wife, meanwhile, pleaded for more time with the accused, which was reluctantly granted. Three hours later, the sheriff discovered the man missing, who reportedly made his way to Wisconsin, where his wife later joined him and "they lived there respectably for many years."

There was also the case of the unaware, over-assuming judge. He presided over a case that he considered small, too long to try and not terribly difficult to decide. He tried subtly revealing his inclination and, then, during deliberations when he learned there was but one holdout among the jurors, he intimated that he might excuse the lone holdout. Just then a small country man wedged between two city dwellers stepped forward a bit and said, "No, judge, don't do that, I'm the only man on your side." In the modern era, a different judge is remembered for telling habitual vagrants that they could have thirty minutes or thirty days—thirty minutes to leave town or thirty days in jail.

Noted local architect Frederick W. Hollister designed the High Victorian red brick courthouse that was built in 1884–85. Dawson & Anderson of Toledo built the structure at a cost of $92,712. The building measured 152 by 130 by 160 feet. It had a large central tower and a series of fourteen zinc statues above each gabled entrance. John Siddons & Co. of Rochester, New York, built the statues. The 55-by-47-foot courtroom had black walnut trim and a heavy brass rail. A large chandelier with a double row of gas burners dominated the center of the ceiling, with smaller counterparts in each corner.

North and south wings were added in 1926–27, doubling the size of the building. The additions were painted to match the original courthouse. A black-and-white pho-

tograph of the old courthouse appears in the courtroom of the old building's modern successor, which is called the Saginaw County Governmental Center. In 1971, the board of commissioners approved the $11 million facility. It has a horizontal look, with large windows set apart by narrow bone-colored piers. On January 23, 1972, the county held a public auction, selling off what it could of the old building, which was then razed on September 15, 1972. The statues were sent to Saginaw Valley College. The clock and works from the tower were saved.

Twenty years later, on August 30, 1992, the county unveiled a new clock tower in front of the governmental center. Behind glass, visitors can see the clockworks. Above, the bell and hammer are on view. Its chime, like the memory of the colorful characters described above, echoes across the green grass of the land of the Sauk.

SANILAC
COUNTY

SANDUSKY—A number of symbols on the county flag tell part of the story of Sanilac County. Approved in 1984, the design features a golden background with blue figures depicting the Port Sanilac lighthouse, wheat, a cow, a hunter, a fish, and a boater. A figurine in the form of a Native American bowman signifies Michigan's only petroglyphs, which are in the northwest part of the county on Cass River.

Governor Lewis Cass named the county for a Wyandotte chief. The land at first encompassed what would become Tuscola and Huron Counties and was attached first to Oakland and then to St. Clair Counties. Sanilac's organization came at the hands of the Legislature in 1848, which designated Lexington as the county seat until 1853. That settlement at various times was also called Greenbush and Monrovia. A relation by marriage to Ethan Allen named it in honor of the revolutionary battle where Allen fought.

The county courthouse and offices had various locations about town until 1857. A building was erected in the west part of the village according to the specifications of George S. Lester for $2,750. The poor young county required a subscription of $1,268 from residents to assist in paying for construction. In 1860 an additional $1,000 was approved for a larger structure in Lexington. The carpet for the courtroom cost $30.

Several rounds of voting and legal proceedings between 1870 and 1879 marked the county seat competition. Sandusky, Carsonville, Elk's Corner, and Forestville all vied for the designation. In the end Sandusky prevailed in April 1877 by a vote of 1,314 to 1,201. But the seat would not move

for nearly three years. Some viewed the move as premature given the lack of roads leading to Sandusky as well as the general dearth of development there. Voters by a margin of 655 approved $20,000 in bonds for building construction.

The county completed the fine Victorian building in 1879, and by January 1880 the task of moving the seat was complete. County leaders ordered thirty-six spittoons but no furniture at first. Acoustical problems led to the purchase of carpeting and drapes. Those who defeated earlier proposals to buy shades espoused the virtues of sunlight.

In late 1881 W. J. Philips was discovered dead with a slit throat and a fractured skull. He was from Iowa and came to the area to purchase cattle. He was last seen on a Thanksgiving Day train from Port Huron. Suspicion turned to a Mr. Dixon, who behaved strangely and was seen with large sums of money, perhaps the cattle money of Philips. Authorities took Dixon into custody, searched him, and made the mistake of allowing him to ingest the poison that he called medicine. He died two days later, perhaps taking with him the truth of the Philips murder.

A devastating fire struck the courthouse on January 17, 1915. It began in the furnace room in the northeast wing and gutted the building from the basement to the roof. Faulty wiring was blamed. The fire extinguished itself by about 3:30 a.m., leaving behind only fire-scorched walls. Two days later the vaults were opened, and the county records appeared intact.

Voters in the spring of 1915 approved a bond for $80,000. The county would spend the same amount in 1984

to build a barrier-free entrance. The cornerstone was laid in the summer, and the building was dedicated in April 1916.

The three-story red brick building stands atop a lighter-colored foundation, which matches the two imposing columns of its front facade. A monument commemorating World War I faces in the same direction. Near it a period machine gun rests on the lawn. A large gazebo occupies another corner of the square. As one walks around the old building, its twin wing, a modern addition, appears. It bears some resemblance to its older sibling, though it is more utilitarian in appearance.

County offices take up much of the complex, particularly on the second floor of the historic building. The third floor houses the circuit courtroom, a dignified space with ample wooden furniture and trim. A blue carpet provides a subdued contrast, along with the white walls. Unlike most courthouses, the jury box has an unusual three-row configuration. Long flat wooden benches welcome the public. Large windows transmit plenty of natural light.

Like the gold and blue county flag, the red brick courthouse is a symbol in its own way too, telling the story of the county named for venerable Chief Sanilac.

SCHOOLCRAFT COUNTY

MANISTIQUE—Were it not for a typo, the county seat of Schoolcraft County would be Monistique. Founders intended to name the city after the Monistique River, whose name is from Onamanitikong, a native word for vermilion.

But the state Legislature misspelled it and wrote "Manistique" and it stuck, even for the previously named river. The act passed in 1871, when Schoolcraft was carved out of Marquette County. Later, Alger County would be carved out of Schoolcraft, leaving the southern territory bordering Lake Michigan.

Father Baraga started a mission in Schoolcraft in August 1833. But civilization first really came with Charles T. Harvey, who built a dam on the Manistique River. He was an engineer and conceived the Soo Locks in Sault Ste. Marie. In honor of his wife, whose maiden name was Eps, the settlement was called Epsport before it became Manistique.

Onota was the first county seat, building a courthouse in 1873. Four short years later a large fire devastated the village, which never rebounded. Onota held jealously onto the seat for two more years, but it was finally moved to Manistique on June 15, 1879.

In its early history, Schoolcraft County depended on Chippewa and then on Marquette for county governance. The county population in 1880 was 1,575. The first courthouse, a two-story wooden structure with a three-story tower, served the county from 1885 until 1901, when the second courthouse was completed.

It was an ornate square stone structure with a tower capped by a large statue of an eagle. Like many of its sister structures elsewhere in Michigan, a fire in the night claimed this building. It happened on March 9, 1974. Over 200 people came to watch the spectacular destruction. Vivid photographs of the building and its tower engulfed in flames are on display in the new courthouse. The contents of the 1901 cornerstone were retrieved on March 20, and some items from it are also on display.

All was well on September 18, 1976, when Schoolcraft County during America's bicentennial unveiled its modern and new courthouse designed by G. Arntzen & Co. It is 42,129 square feet and cost $2,173,549.73. But a couple of disputes threatened to derail construction.

First, the city and the county argued over who should collect the $4,300 building permit fee. The more dramatic struggle pitted labor activists against Omega Construction Company, Inc., the constructors, and local law enforcement. The protestors objected to the use of nonunion labor.

Crowds of protestors obstructed access to the construction site. A truck tire and a radiator were punctured. A pellet shot reportedly struck another vehicle's windshield. Omega's construction trailer was overturned. Eventually, Circuit Judge William F. Hood granted Omega's request for an injunction, which, coupled with the arrival of thirty state troopers to assist the overwhelmed local police force, ensured the completion of the new courthouse.

Inside of the new building is a large bronze mural by Jack E. Anderson. It was hung in August 1977. It proudly states that Schoolcraft has the highest percentage of state and federal land of any county in Michigan, due in large part to Seney National Wildlife Refuge and Hiawatha National Forest. It also depicts the old wooden courthouse and the new courthouse in bas-relief.

The county is named for Henry Rowe Schoolcraft,

noted explorer and ethnologist. Originally a geologist, he accompanied territorial governor Lewis Cass on an expedition to the Upper Great Lakes in 1820. Schoolcraft soon became an expert on Native Americans, which led to his appointment as Indian agent for the tribes of Lake Superior. He married a woman who was part Ojibwa and, along with him, understood and appreciated Native American culture.

The government, in need of reliable data on Native Americans, encouraged Schoolcraft, and in 1836 he was promoted as superintendent of Indian Affairs for Michigan. He negotiated several treaties, including the treaty of March 28, 1836, which enabled America to gain title to the northern third of Michigan's Lower Peninsula and the eastern half of the Upper Peninsula.

Part of that territory bears his name now, and the government had no problem whatsoever spelling it properly.

SHIAWASSEE COUNTY

CORUNNA—Shiawassee County, or at least the architect of its courthouse, has a penchant for Corinthian columns, the most ornate of the ones then available. Apart from the four massive pillars dominating the front entrance, there are smaller counterparts in the tower, on the doors themselves, in plasterwork, and in the design of the interior of the courtroom.

Shiawassee's name refers to sparkling water or to a river, either one that is straight ahead or one that twists about, depending on what sources one consults. It originally contained parts of neighboring counties, and its seat on paper was Byron, though no courts were ever built there. When Shiawassee's present borders were set, Byron, which was once in the center, was now in the southeastern corner of the territory. An act of the Legislature on February 26, 1836, removed the seat from Byron, and by July 1 what would become Corunna was the seat. An early settler reportedly named the town for Corunna, Spain, from which he returned with sheep that he took all the way to Cincinnati.

After the county was organized on March 13, 1837, court did not meet for several months until December 4 at the office of the county clerk in the schoolhouse in Shiawassee Exchange. In October 1838, court moved to the house of Lucius W. Beach at Shiawasseetown, then in November to Owosso in rooms above the store of Gould, Fish and Company.

The following year the county contracted with Stephen Hawkins to build a county office building for $382.50. The wooden building measured twenty by thirty-six feet and proved too small for both offices and the court. Later that year Shiawassee rented for $30 a year another structure in Corunna for court. Around this time Alexander McArthur,

an agent for Corunna, wrote to the county commissioners that in Corunna his house would serve as a tavern with ample accommodations and supplies while court was in session and that stables "accommodating upward of fifty horses will be prepared, and an abundance of provender is already provided."

In 1850 a committee formed to explore building a two-story brick courthouse measuring forty by sixty feet and costing about $4,500. The contract went to George O. Bachman, who completed the structure along with a small tower. Historical accounts state that the sheriff took over the building on January 6, 1854, but it was probably in public use for at least two years before then. The old court was moved off the public square. The owners sold it to a Baptist community that made it a church. South of the new courthouse the county in the mid-1860s erected a fireproof county office building.

Before the courthouse met the wrecking ball in April 1903, it met the perhaps more destructive instrument of negative national attention from the press. Corunna is the setting of Michigan's last public lynching. William Sullivan was accused of killing a farmer in Durand on New Year's Day 1893, with an axe and raping and shooting his wife, who survived and reportedly identified Sullivan as the assailant. He was found drunk in Detroit on May 21 and spirited away to Durand and then Corunna in avoidance of some angry mobs.

Over two thousand people surrounded the jail, with a masked group of twenty confronting the sheriff, dragging Sullivan out, and stringing him up a few feet east of the jail. At least one account asserts that Sullivan slit his own throat when he heard the mob howling for his neck. He

reportedly broke a whiskey bottle from newspaper reporters interviewing him and intent on loosening his tongue.

Others maintained that the sheriff was derelict for giving the mob only token resistance before they murdered Sullivan, who awaited justice in a court of law. The state undertook an investigation, but no one was ever charged, and voters later returned the sheriff to office by a vote of two to one. One estimate contends that over twenty-two thousand people came to glimpse the casket of the man who sparked such blood lust. An enterprising hardware salesman cut up a long piece of rope and sold the pieces as souvenirs. The tree on which Sullivan was hung later died after people stripped it of its bark for mementos.

The manner in which justice under law gave way to lawlessness in 1893 stands in stark opposition to the center of justice Shiawassee erected beginning with the laying of its courthouse cornerstone on May 4, 1904. Judge Hugh McCurdy spoke at the event, hoping that the courthouse would be more than a building and a testament to human ingenuity, but that it may "become in fact as well as in name the temple of justice." Voters approved $75,000 for the new courthouse, which ultimately cost closer to $140,000.

George Rickman and Sons of Kalamazoo built it, and Claire Allen of Jackson designed it. Allen also drew plans for courthouses in Van Buren and Hillsdale Counties, as well as for Shiawassee's twin in Gratiot County. Shiawassee's architectural style is Beaux-Arts Classical, which Americanizes several elements of the French Renaissance design. It measures one hundred sixteen by eighty-six feet, with Berea sandstone exterior walls. The baroque cupola has three levels with a tiled dome atop its hipped roof.

The tower once had a flagpole at its crest, but lightning struck and shattered it in the 1920s, and it was not replaced. Earlier in the same decade, an acrobat in a traveling circus made use of the pole for quite a show. The line running through the pulley at the top of the pole snapped, and no one dared to crawl up and try to run a new one through it. Thinking it was good publicity, the acrobat climbed up the pole and accomplished his task before a large crowd.

Below the tower on the inside is a large rotunda that dominates the interior lobby area. It is ringed with an elegant metalwork railing that is similar to the stairway leading up to the second floor. Near the landing of the steps is a large mural depicting figures representing free speech and free press with the unpunctuated inscription "when tongue and pen alike are free safe from all foes dwells liberty."

The oak-paneled courtroom features elaborate stenciling and murals. Above it is a dome illuminated by stained glass and featuring paintings of twelve winged female figures holding each sign of the zodiac.

In 1990 an altogether different female figure made her mark on Shiawassee's history of law and order: an armed bride working undercover. She was part of an elaborate plan by law enforcement to apprehend several criminals who were invited to a staged wedding. As is the custom for such folk, they were asked to check their weapons at the reception. Undercover police held on to their weapons and waited for their cue to make their arrests, which was when the band played the 1960s hit "I Fought the Law."

On this occasion and most others in Shiawassee, the law won, as the song croons. The many Corinthian columns of its courthouse stand tall, straight, and steadfast in their support of the ideal that justice under law must prevail, whatever the mob or any criminal defendant might prefer.

ST. CLAIR COUNTY

PORT HURON—If, as some philosophers believe, one can never step into the same river twice, one wonders if it is possible to hear the same bell ring more than once. In Port Huron, there is a spot where these abstract questions are in plain view.

St. Clair County was established during territorial times in 1821. Some sources claim that the name is for General Arthur St. Clair, the first governor of the Northwest Territory. Others say that the name derives from the lake and the river that French explorer La Salle named. He chose, as was usual practice at the time, the name of the saint whose day it was when La Salle passed on August 12, which is the day of St. Clair. English maps first gave "St. Clare" as the place's name, but by 1755 it was appearing with its present spelling.

The village of St. Clair was the first county seat, which was called Palmer for a while but never officially registered with the postal service. Court was first held at the home of James Fulton, who also built by his house the first jail, which he used additionally as a root house. In 1827–28, the first two-story courthouse was built with logs covered with clapboard. The county paid Charles Phillips and Daniel Stewart $350 for the building, with the Legislature contributing $150. The second story was not finished and a stairway not installed until 1830. The jail was on the lower floor. In 1839 a small addition on the south end was finished, and the entire upper floor was converted into a large courtroom.

An early case contested the ownership of two similarly aged and marked calves. One answered to Ruby and the other to Rosa. But only one calf was before the court, and it had to be decided to whom it belonged. A colorful attor-

ney quipped that a judge could easily recognize the difference between the names "but it would be otherwise with a calf educated in the country." It is unknown if this attorney won the case, but it was recorded that "even Judge Green let himself smile."

The old courthouse was destroyed by fire in 1855. A brick replacement cost $1,500, which citizen contributors paid for mostly under the leadership of Harmon Chamberlin. The brick building was dedicated in 1859.

The southern end of the county wanted the seat closer to them. The first proposal to move the seat came in 1825, and the struggle ebbed and flowed for nearly fifty years. Port Huron, which was once called Desmond, was the chief rival. The courthouse fire revived the dispute, which led to an 1861 vote to move, which was frustrated by an injunction and the Michigan Supreme Court.

In 1865, the county board approved removal if Port Huron would finance the buildings. Port Huron obliged, and the vote carried 1,978 to 405. Again, the Michigan Supreme Court overturned the vote, based this time upon the wording of the ballot.

Port Huron opted for an end run around the opposition. In October 1870, the board overwhelmingly and the voters narrowly (2,584 to 2,467) approved a move to a third location: Smith's Creek. Authorities never took any concrete action to effectuate the move. Instead, the very same month the board voted for removal to Port Huron. Months later, in a special election, the voters approved, 2,958 to 2,426. Port Huron offered use of rooms in the third ward school building for county offices and the court.

St. Clair filed suit to stop the move, and an injunction

was entered. A probate judge, meanwhile, moved records to Port Huron. Other records did not move so easily. Rumors of armed confrontation swirled. But cooler heads prevailed; as one account describes, the competing factions "agreed to stack their guns and await the decision of the court." Eminent lawyers from the state argued the case, and in October 1871 the "unhappy controversy" ended when the Michigan Supreme Court upheld the move. For Port Huron, the third time was a charm, and the seat remains there.

The school that was offered burned down, but the papers were saved. The many county offices were strewn about town as Port Huron's plans to build a city hall were aired, and the county was promised space in the building. The cornerstone was laid on October 30, 1872, on land where the McMorran Auditorium now stands. The building was completed in February 1873, at a cost of $31,440. Officially, it was called the County Courthouse, but locals always called it City Hall. It was designed in the grand tradition of many other Michigan courthouses—brick, with steep lines and a clock tower.

In 1896, two wings nearly doubling the building's space were added. A fire on President's Day 1949 badly damaged the building, which was nearly unoccupied due to the holiday. Janitors were heating floor wax in the usual manner when their bucket exploded and the blaze took its course. Most of the third floor was destroyed, and the building was a shadow of its former self, as it lost its prominent clock tower. The bell, which fell three stories during the fire, escaped relatively unscathed. Scars of the fire included water-soaked walls, chipped paint, and sagging floors. Now the three-story additions stood above the two-story center of the building.

Before long, the wounded building was razed, and the county completed work on a modern-inspired building near the banks of the water. There were obstacles along the way, as bond and tax proposals were rejected in 1949, causing the city and county to create a building authority. The 75,700-square-foot building required 8,000 cubic yards of concrete, 450 tons of reinforced steel, and 325,000 bricks. The bricks appear in the rear of the building, and the front and sides are reinforced concrete faced with limestone. The cornerstone was laid on June 18, 1953. Wyeth and Harman, Inc., designed it. Construction contracts went to Collins

and Catlin Co. of Port Huron and A. J. Etkin Construction Co. of Detroit. The $2.3 million building was first dedicated as the County-City Building. In 1978, the city left for its new building across the street. For a time, the County Building had a large space between its name, after the removal of the word City.

Expansion and renovation were approved in 1980, and the project cost upward of $5 million. New matching wings on both sides jutted up above the building, and a third floor was added. The additions were dedicated in October 1982. The interior of the building boasts a few interesting murals, including an inventive design in one hallway depicting a freighter going by in the river, as if the viewer can see through the wall. Near the entrance, carpets obscure part of a mosaic that is an early view of Lake Huron flowing into the St. Clair River.

Because the new wings blocked out the sound of the 1890 bell from Baltimore's McShane Bell Foundry, the bell needed a new perch. The bell was rededicated on December 4, 2002, inside of a replica of the 1873 clock tower, which is on the front lawn with the building as its backdrop.

From the right spot and on a warm day, one can see the resurrected clock tower, the historian's symbol of continuity and permanence, and the flow of the river, the philosopher's example of constant change. As the bell stands mounted and still while the current of the river flows, history and philosophy clash. Does one ever step into the same courthouse?

ST. JOSEPH COUNTY

CENTREVILLE—While a number of Michigan counties had their records held ransom by warring sides in the context of county seat disputes, St. Joseph stands alone as the victim of a criminal record heist for ransom. The county paid, had its damaged records unearthed from the ground for return, and filed suit in federal court against the middle men in Chicago who handled the transaction.

St. Joseph County is named for a river that French explorer La Salle is said to have named. Organized on November 4, 1829, the county's first temporary seat was located in White Pigeon. The first court of record was at Asahel Savery's tavern but later moved to the more desirable White Pigeon Academy.

According to an account of an early divorce case, the court concluded that "David should have Aurora as an 'Amulet' no longer to charm away sorrow, and bade her resume her maiden name and single blessedness."

The seat moved for about a year to what is now Lockport Village, but popular uproar persuaded the governor to declare on November 22, 1831, pursuant to statutory authority, that the seat would be the centrally located and aptly named Centreville. Generous land donations sweetened the deal. The court first convened in a leased room in the only frame house in town, which was also a harness shop, on the corner of Main and Clark Streets.

That building was erected in 1832, the same year that the county authorized construction of a jail. Completed in July 1833, the jail welcomed quite a character as its first temporary resident. The drunk man was, according to the parlance of one source, more than "half seas over" when authorities took him into custody. He promptly found a pile of wood shavings on the floor and "was soon snoring like a contented pig." The jailer left the cell unlocked and found the man missing the next day. At nightfall, the man returned and offered twenty-five cents to sleep there again.

In February 1841, the county resolved to build a wooden courthouse, which was completed in the autumn of 1842 at a cost of about $7,000. Judge Connor furnished plans and a list of needed materials. John Bryan erected the two-story Greek Revival building, a white clapboard structure with a peaked roof and a small tower just above and behind a portico standing atop four round columns. In 1860, the county constructed separate fireproof offices for $3,200.

On the night of June 28, 1872, unknown bandits stole the county records, consisting of twenty-two volumes each of deeds and mortgages, three index books, and about one hundred deeds and mortgages not yet recorded. The county received a ransom letter from Chicago that demanded $5,000 in exchange for return of the records. The board of supervisors authorized $3,000 but privately told the sheriff to act at his discretion to reclaim the records at any cost.

For $3,500 a deal was struck, and the buried records were unearthed in badly damaged condition and returned to St. Joseph. A law firm in Chicago accepted the money, transferred the records for the culprits, and soon found itself defending a suit by the county in federal court in Grand Rapids. The county prevailed at the trial level but ultimately lost on appeal when the U.S. Supreme Court ordered a new trial. Local histories do not record the existence or the outcome of a second trial.

The courthouse was razed in 1899 to make room for a new red brick and sandstone one. Sydney J. Osgood of Grand Rapids designed the Romanesque Revival building, which was completed at a cost of $33,000. Centreville pur-

chased the clock for the seventy-five-foot tower for $850. It boasts four faces with diameters of five and a half feet. The building was dedicated on August 1, 1900, and a column of local citizens paraded the clock on their shoulders as it reportedly kept accurate time throughout the march. In 1956, the eight-day mechanical clock was made electric for $960.

The interior boasts intricate woodwork, grand staircases, marble floors, wall murals, and frosted glass doors. The building narrowly averted the wrecking ball in the 1970s, when its successor was in the planning stages. Determined citizens rallied to preserve the building while an adjacent new courts building was completed by Johnson-Klein, Inc., the general contractor, in 1975 for $1.3 million, with the help of Claude M. Wade, the consulting engineer. Kammeraad Stroop Van Der Leek, Inc., designed the modern counterpart, which bears little resemblance to the older courthouse, perhaps because the two were not originally meant to stand concurrently.

Inside, the 1900 courthouse has changed. For security reasons, court is now held in the new St. Joseph County Courts Building. From 1976 to 1995, the third floor of the old building was closed by order of the fire chief. Pigeons came to nest there instead. It was renovated in the 1990s, and the building was rededicated on August 1, 1997. Governor John Engler was the guest speaker. About $3.8 million in

grants and delinquent tax funds paid for, among other things, installation of an elevator, new utilities, window replacements, a fire alarm system, new steel structural support, and fresh murals modeled after the original ones in the courtroom. Clark Construction Co. of Lansing did the renovation work according to the plan of architects Wigen, Tinckell, Meyer & Associates, Inc., of Saginaw.

The expansive old courtroom with its vaulted ceiling and rows of wooden seats is now the meeting room for the county commissioners. An old spittoon remains. Outside of the old courtroom, the county displays a newer relic: a computer that it bought for the clerk in 1984 for $4,371. It was retired in 1998.

That tired, obsolete computer occupies a place along a line that stretches back to the earth-worn volumes of records held for ransom about a century earlier for an amount nearly equal in absolute dollars to that machine's purchase price. The county likely values those records much more, adjusted of course for inflation and for the fact that they are irreplaceable.

TUSCOLA COUNTY

CARO—If local lore is accurate, there was a time that all of Tuscola County's records could fit along with two men in a canoe. It happened in 1866, after voters approved the move of the county seat from Vassar to Centreville, which later changed its name to Caro.

Tuscola County was separated from Saginaw and organized on March 2, 1850. The seat was located for the time being at Vassar, in the southwest corner of the county. The legislative act provided that Vassar would have that distinction until 1860, when a permanent location would be chosen locally.

Tuscola's name origin is uncertain. Some claim that it derives from "Tusco," which means "warrior," while others point to "Tusci," which means "level land." Taken together, "warrior prairie" may be the intended meaning.

When 1860 rolled around, a long list of places, some of which became ghost towns, vied for the county seat: Almer, Centreville, Heartts, Ketchum Plat, Moonshine, Vassar, Wahjamega, Watertown, and Watrousville. The battle broiled for six years, with plenty of back and forth before voters in April 1866 chose Centreville 962 to 719.

Centreville was located just about dead center in the county and was settled for the purpose of campaigning for the county seat. It changed its name for a time to Tuscola Center to avoid confusion with the Centreville in St. Joseph County. Finally at the suggestion of an early settler who shortened the name of Cairo, Egypt, the seat was renamed Caro in 1869. It incorporated as a village in 1871.

Peter D. Bush donated land in Caro on which to build a courthouse. He helped acquire a temporary facility: a wood-framed former Universalist church relocated from Almer Township in 1866.

Months went by, and the records from Vassar fifteen miles down the Cass River were not forthcoming. So Bush went with his friend, Indian Dave, in a canoe in the dark early morning hours and secured the records, which were deposited in the former church on the corner of State and Sherman Streets.

In 1873 the county constructed a two-story brick court designed by Porter and Watkins. Atop its tower was a flagpole. The building cost about $15,000, with village taxpayers in Caro covering $3,000 to smooth its arrival.

During the 1880s the father of late billionaire J. Paul Getty was an attorney who practiced in Caro and likely made the courthouse his professional stomping grounds before his son was born.

This courthouse met the wrecking ball with the erection of Tuscola's present art deco courthouse of 1932. During construction the McNair block housed a temporary facility. William H. Kuni of Detroit designed the building, like its younger twin in Alpena. But the two were built of different materials and have evolved differently over the years. Cecil M. Kelly of Flint and formerly of Caro erected the building in 1932. He used Indiana limestone atop a Minnesota granite foundation. The cornerstone was laid May 27, 1932, and the building was dedicated on January 24, 1933.

The building's dimensions are one hundred twenty by seventy-five by forty feet. The main facade of the building, which is capped by a round clock, is balanced by two recessed wings flanking it. Rows of windows are recessed in

five vertical bays under rounded arches. Slim piers separate the windows from the wings. The structure cost $180,000, which voters paid by a special tax they approved seven years earlier. They enabled the county to create quite a landmark, judging by the historical marker dedicated on May 22, 1984.

Inside, the building has changed somewhat over the decades. The lobby retains its vaulted ceiling with colorful

This stained glass is the prized centerpiece of the Tuscola County Courthouse.

painted tile and moldings, as well as wainscoted marble. An elevator was added in space that was once a maintenance closet and part of the treasurer's office. The courtroom shrank by about half to make room for office space, a law library, and, now, district court. The county has an annex building kitty-corner to the courthouse.

The most striking interior feature of the Tuscola County Courthouse is the unique twelve-by-eighteen-foot stained glass window behind the steps to the circuit courtroom on the second floor. Detroit Stained Glass Works made the work of art, which purports to depict General Lewis Cass meeting with Native Americans on the banks of the Cass River to sign a treaty. The window's caption is vulnerable to two historical quibbles. First, the river was the Saginaw River. Second, there was a meeting, but it was probably not for the purpose of signing a treaty.

Whatever the body of water and whatever the aim of the gathering, the window commemorates an important event on a nearby river. The same such kind of event brought to Caro from Vassar via canoe the spoils of its county seat battle of 1860–66.

VAN BUREN COUNTY

PAW PAW—A bas-relief likeness of Martin Van Buren looks out from above an entrance to the courthouse in the county named for him. He gazes across the street to the park where four posts mark the contours of his building's predecessor, which was vacated and moved onto Main Street.

Van Buren, as secretary of state for President Andrew Jackson, was one of the men honored with a so-called Cabinet County in Michigan. His county was first set off, named, and attached to Cass County during Michigan's territorial times. When Michigan became a state, Van Buren County was organized on March 18, 1837.

On May 27 of the same year, the board of supervisors first met in Lafayette. By 1867 its name would change to Paw Paw for the abundant fruit of the same name along the Paw Paw River. Lawrence, which is nine miles west, wanted the county seat and had some claim to it on paper during territorial times. But court was never held and no county buildings ever erected there. An 1840 act of the Legislature settled all doubt and selected Lafayette, though the controversy would run for decades as the county seat question periodically flared hot.

The county paid $3 for use of a schoolhouse in Lafayette for the court. In January 1841 it approved $50 for another year of use of the private building of Joshua Bangs for county offices. In April 1842 it awarded a contract of $2,410 to Reuben E. Churchill and Stafford Godfrey to complete woodwork and $494 to Henry W. Rhodes to do masonry work for the courthouse.

Van Buren expected work to take about eighteen months, but it took about three years, with court probably

first convening in the new building for its June 1845 term. The white frame two-story building with a peaked roof would serve its function for fifty-five years. After the county vacated it, it was moved about two blocks to a commercial location and converted into a feed store. It later became the village hall, a role it continues to fill. Four posts mark the corners where the courthouse once stood on land that is now a public park. Atop the posts are copper ornaments that are also on the current courthouse.

In 1875 the county spent $1,000 and citizens in and around Paw Paw contributed another $2,850 to erect a fireproof brick building for county records. This building is now a museum that displays the contents of the 1901 cor-

The 1840s courthouse was moved two blocks from the courthouse lawn to its present location, where it serves as a village hall.

nerstone of the current courthouse. Seventy-two items, including a forty-five-star flag, a tiny Bible, walnuts, and buckwheat or corn (local historians disagree, and efforts to germinate the seeds have been unsuccessful), presumably for absorbing moisture, were found inside the stone.

Before the stone could be laid, the county had to settle funding for construction, as well as the persistent county seat question. It is believed that for many years a majority of voters would have favored a move from Paw Paw, but suitors could never muster the requisite two-thirds vote of the county supervisors. That changed in 1900 when Paw Paw's supervisor reportedly threw his support behind a vote so that the public could once and for all settle the question.

Now Paw Paw's main competitor was South Haven. A spirited—some say bitter—campaign followed. First South Haven offered $50,000 in bonds to help pay for construction. Paw Paw countered with a matching offer. Perhaps mindful of the two towns' generosity, voters in April 1900 rejected by a large majority a bond proposal of $60,000. At the same time, they narrowly voted down a move of the seat from Paw Paw by a tally of 4,438 to 4,082. A special election in July approved a county loan of $35,000. It was time to build.

Thousands gathered in Paw Paw on September 1, 1900, for the laying of the cornerstone, many of whom took advantage of special rail rates. Hon. Frank T. Lodge of Detroit was the featured orator, who said the following.

We lay here today something besides a mere material block of senseless stone. We also commend to erect an unseen but nonetheless substantial temple of human character, which is more stable than the strongest ramparts the cunning workmanship of man can build. In the unseen structure every man and woman of this county must fill his own place.

Claire Allen of Jackson designed the courthouse in the classical revival style. George Rickman & Sons of Kalamazoo submitted the low bid for construction. The total cost, including the courthouse, jail, land, and furnishings, was about $120,000. The courthouse was occupied in February 1903.

The first case in the new building was *William Culver v. South Haven & Eastern Railroad Company,* a "cause celebre in the state." He eventually recovered $25,000 for losing his legs underneath a freight car. Another memorable trial was the Tabor murder. A reporter for the *Detroit Free Press* somehow surreptitiously placed himself near the outside of the jury room window to scoop the verdict. It is believed

that he used a set of fire escape stairs and made his way around the exterior of the building on an eighteen-inch ledge. Inside the building at another point in its history observers recall the anguish and compassion in the eyes of a judge who happened in the corridor upon the abandoned rag doll of a child at the center of a custody battle.

The beige stone exterior and red Spanish tile roof support the building's most prominent feature: a large clock tower. Open double archways appear gossamer from the street level, where one can take in the view of the clock and the small green copper dome at its crest. Inside the lower level of the tower visitors are encouraged to sign a brick. Along the way one can see that scrap stone chiseled away from material used for beam supports was used in lieu of and to save bricks. Another consideration must have been the great effort expended to lift such stone with ropes and pulleys, and the risk and energy required to safely lower any remaining stone.

White paint obscured and absorbed the signatures in the upper level of the tower, many of which were left by those who faithfully and continuously served as plane spotters during World War II. The white paint came for illumination purposes with the installation of the Oradell Rupert memorial clock in 1986.

In 1974 an annex attached to the rear of the building opened up 34,000 square feet of new space. Several county functions later moved across the street to a newer administration building that originally was an office building designed with architectural cues similar to the courthouse. The interior of the historic building is substantially original, from the now decorative fireplaces to the safe that cannot be moved from the former treasurer's and now prosecutor's office because the walls were built around it.

Four murals adorn the courthouse interior. The most

noted is the semicircular 1908 painting by Louis Van Ness, which is prominently positioned along the main stairway to the second-floor courtroom. It depicts a bare-chested Athena resting near the head of Medusa and holding a long spear.

The interior of the nearby courtroom is also eye-catching. The wood finish of the bench, barriers, and theater-style seating is consistent and dark. High curved ceilings make room for electric chandeliers that replaced fluorescent lights and were designed from a photograph to mirror the original gas chandeliers, which were removed and taken away without a trace. To avoid the need for scaffolding, cranks lower them down to the floor in the event that bulbs need replacing. Behind the bench, like in some other Michigan courtrooms, a book and a sword symbolize the interpretation and the execution of justice, respectively. The only incongruous elements are the modern gray-and-black cushioned juror chairs, where aesthetics and period design appear to have given way to contemporary comfort.

But the eyes of Van Buren's stone likeness remain unchanged and unblinking. He looks in the direction of the Civil War cannons on the lawn: across the street and back in time to the footprint of the earlier courthouse and forward to his second centennial, when the light of day will greet the new time capsule placed in the spot of the first one.

WASHTENAW COUNTY

ANN ARBOR—In an arbor in a far-off land stands a court whose contours its predecessor shaped while making way for parking, a perennial problem in this now-congested county seat.

Washtenaw's name derives from Washtenong, the native name for the Grand River. Apart from grand, some believe that the word means "land beyond." The territorial government drew the county boundaries in 1822. The county was organized on November 20, 1826, and originally attached to Wayne County. Years passed before it erected its first courthouse.

Instead, court convened first at the home of Erastus Priest in January 1827, when the county population was about 1,500. In the same year, John Allen donated land for a courthouse, fulfilling a condition for Ann Arbor to become the county seat. Ann Arbor's name derives from the common first name of two early settlers' wives and from the abundant groves or arbors of oaks that welcomed them.

In 1834 John Bryant erected the first courthouse, which was to last forty-four years. A lithograph depicts the Greek Revival two-story wooden frame structure, which was painted white with rows of windows and a darker peaked roof. Above the entrance stood a small hexagonal cupola. The courtroom was on the second floor, while the first housed county offices. Money by subscription paid for a fence, trees, and the leveling of surrounding ground.

For years the county was dissatisfied with the building, but the cost of new construction deterred any action. It welcomed delegates from all over in Michigan in September 1836 to discuss an offer from Congress to resolve the boundary dispute with Ohio and bring Michigan into the Union.

A historical marker notes that this "Convention of Assent" rejected the proposal but later accepted the congressional plan at the "Frostbitten Convention" on the bitterly cold December 14. Michigan entered the Union on January 26, 1837.

In the same year Ann Arbor welcomed the University of Michigan, which would grow into a massive center of education and research that is synonymous with the city's name. Settlement grew with the paths of two major roadways that ran through Ann Arbor to Chicago—the Territorial and the Chicago Roads.

In 1876 Ann Arbor offered $20,000 if the county would spend $40,000 on a building. Later the city increased the windfall to $25,000 on the condition that it received a council room in the new structure. Voters in the spring of 1877 approved a $40,000 loan.

The county laid the cornerstone on October 25, 1877. G. W. Bunting of Indianapolis was the architect. McCormick & Sweeney of Columbus, Indiana, was the general contractor. The building cost $83,000 and measured 80 by 127 by 54 feet, with a tower rising 152 feet from the basement. The building featured brick walls nearly three feet thick and trimmed with stone. The basement walls were stone. The roof was slate and ironwork made up the cornices and stairs. A total of 1,165,000 bricks made by Joseph Andet of Ann Arbor were used, of which 65,000 had to be pressed brick of uniform color and quality. The county paid $4.25 for every thousand bricks.

Each corner of the building had a small tower. Between each pair of towers stood a figure of justice. Luther Thomas donated money to install a Seth Thomas eight-day clock.

It had a six-and-a-half-foot illuminated French plate dial that was three-eighths of an inch thick and featured a two thousand-pound bell. The bell from the old court went to the Third Ward school.

In the 1950s the county faced a dilemma. It wanted a new courthouse, but it feared that the terms of Allen's gift of land prohibited it from keeping the land or profiting from its sale if it moved the courthouse. The situation meant that a costly temporary facility might be required while the empty old court was razed and replaced.

But Ralph S. Gerganoff, the architect, found a solution. He designed an L-shaped building that hugged the old courthouse, within a foot at some points. The cornerstone for the new building was placed in 1954. The building was completed a year later, at which point many of the contents of the old building were simply handed from window to

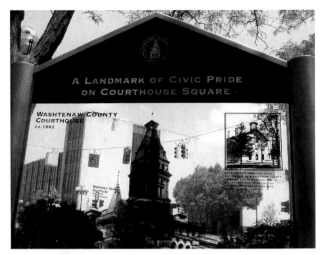

The courthouses of Washtenaw County appear in tandem, thanks to this inventive work of public art.

window. The old building was razed and its footprint paved over into a parking lot, which is now a valued commodity in downtown Ann Arbor.

The interior features a variety of courtrooms, some of which are twins with high ceilings and distinctive stone facades behind the judge's bench. The exterior of the building depicts a number of figures in bas-relief near lettering giving the name of the courthouse. Smaller lettering invites those seeking service to visit the county's Web site. Another sign of the county's technological prowess emerged in 2005, when jurors began receiving payment for their service electronically through cards they could redeem at an automated teller machine inside the courthouse. The measure was expected to save Washtenaw the cost of processing and mailing checks, which jurors would not receive for weeks.

Plaques and signs about history connected to the building dot its locale. Across the street folded over a short concrete wall is a metallic reproduction of a flyer encouraging everyone to attend the 1877 cornerstone ceremony. A procession, speakers, and railroad "half fare" are advertised. Next to it stands a large piece of glass depicting Washtenaw's first two courthouses. One may look through it to see all three courthouses in time-bending juxtaposition, at least during the few moments in the day when the traffic clears as motorists search for parking near the intersection of Main and Huron streets.

WAYNE COUNTY

DETROIT—Michigan's oldest and most populous county lays important claim to Michigan's past, present, and future trajectory. One might rightly consider it, now and then, Michigan's capital county. Inexorably, it had, has, and will have an important hand in the development of Michigan.

Detroit has always been the seat of government and commerce for the surrounding area. The name derives from the French word for strait, as Antoine de la Mothe, Sieur de Cadillac landed in July 1701 along the river connecting Lakes Erie and St. Clair. There were no courts during French rule, for the commandant decided virtually all cases, and his will was final. For a time, the village priest decided some cases, too.

A tambour, or drummer, in Cadillac's company was tried in 1705 for criminally assaulting a twelve-year-old girl. His sentence was death, and his executioner reportedly escaped his own death sentence by agreeing to personally impose the drummer's punishment. From 1734 to 1760, local notary Robert Navarre took control and acted as judge. No record of Detroit's judicial affairs was ever found in Montreal, suggesting to historians that such matters were handled locally.

The British took over in 1760, holding on to Navarre and basically imposing military rule. Mayor Henry Gladwin tried a Native American woman accused of killing an English trader with the help of a Native American man who escaped. She was convicted and publicly hanged in 1763. Four years later, the British established the office of justice of the peace and with its tenure began the public record of Detroit, though no records resembled anything like a court proceeding. By 1789 the Court of Common Pleas, which later became the Court of King's Bench, took root with

the appointment and arrival of Judge William Dammer Powell. Britain acted several years in contravention of the Treaty of Paris, which placed Detroit under American control. The British vacated Detroit after they surrendered the Northwest Territories to General "Mad Anthony" Wayne on July 11, 1796.

Wayne County was named for him on August 15, 1796, by proclamation of Winthrop Sargent, acting governor of the Northwest Territories. An earlier attempt to organize the territory came in October 1778, when the Virginia Legislature proclaimed Illinois County, acting first to establish a county west of the Allegheny Mountains. In June 1792, the governor of Upper Canada included Michigan in his proclamation of Kent County, which stretched to Hudson Bay.

These earlier proclamations never took root on the ground and were ignored. Sargent's proclamation technically lacked the force of law. He was only empowered to act in the absence of the governor. Governor St. Clair was in fact present in the territory at the time of the proclamation. St. Clair preferred to wait for direction from the president. Despite St. Clair's displeasure with the proclamation, he accepted it and appointed officers, and everyone went about their business.

At its inception, the territory of Wayne County included all of Michigan and large parts of northern Ohio, Indiana, Illinois, and Wisconsin. The borders of the county fluctuated with some regularity until the present boundaries were set on November 20, 1826, encompassing 626 square miles.

The line of territorial courts first began with attachment to courts located in the Indiana Territory. The distance of the court from Detroit and the difficulty of travel made it virtually impossible for residents to gain access to public justice. Only later were local courts established. Sessions were held in the Old Council House and in the Old Capitol Building. Detroit was the territorial capital and, after statehood in 1837, the state capital until 1847.

Detroit's City Hall housed the court from 1836 to 1844. Thereafter, the county for one year rented the Williams Building on the corner of Jefferson and Bates. Then the county built a two-story county building with frontage on Congress (eighty feet) and Griswold (thirty-two feet). The courtroom, which was used until 1871, was on the second floor. It was described as not "commodious, elegant, nor even comfortable." This courthouse was first occupied on June 9, 1845. The contractors were Messrs. Jackson and Perry, and the superintendents of construction were Messrs. Hunt and Farrer. The building was patched up and held together until completion of Detroit's city hall. In the summer of 1859, nearby excavation damaged one of the walls. A newspaper reporting the cave-in wrote that the "county offices are altogether too small and are dark, dingy places, more suitable for cattle stalls than public offices." Construction of a neighboring building blocked out sunlight for the register of deeds, so he moved his office and records across the street.

When Detroit opened its fine city hall in 1871, Wayne County began renting a large courtroom on the third floor for $12,000 a year. The county and the city could not agree on plans to expand, so the county contemplated its own space. It selected half of the block bounded by Randolph, Congress, Brush, and Fort Streets, only to find later that the whole block was needed. The land alone cost $550,000 to acquire in 1895. Ground was broken in September 1896. Officials laid the cornerstone on October 20, 1897, when the foundation, which itself cost $636,000 along with bare walls and the roof, was ready. All told, at least $1.6 million was spent on the extravagant building.

Architect John Scott & Co. designed the English Baroque edifice. Controversy swirled as officials considered what kind of stone to use, with northern quarries near Lake Superior hoping for Portage entry red sandstone. Contemporary aesthetic sensibilities preferred white, which meant eastern granite for the lower story and Berea sandstone for the rest of the exterior. Inside, there are at least seven varieties of foreign marble and nine domestic. The columns are all scagliola, or imitation marble. A minimum of five kinds of woods finished the interior, with mahogany predominating. The judges initially rotated every three months through the six differently designed courtrooms, no doubt desiring to experience the beauty of each well-appointed room.

A hipped roof crowns the four-tiered colonnaded tower. Relief figures are visible elsewhere, including a scene in the pediment of the portico of General Wayne conferring with Native Americans. Sculpture ornaments more than a few spots. Private donors in 1904 paid for the two twenty-foot copper-plated figures representing Progress and Victory, and they are pulled by quadrigae, or four-horse chariots. The artist was John Massey Rhind of New York. They were recently removed for restoration, which raised some eyebrows when the $668,000 cost to the public was announced. In a similar vein, $30,000 in monthly rent for the tower's scaffolding, which sat idle for several months as no work was done, drew criticism.

At its unveiling, however, the building garnered unrestrained praise. Mayor William C. Maybury likened buildings to people. "What is true of individuals is true of buildings, and the real adornment of this Building is the fact that it becomes a place of justice and equity." Indeed, the courthouse saw its share of notable cases—from the charges of lewd and lascivious conduct hurled at Mae West to the murder trial of Dr. Ossian Sweet. The former resulted in a dismissal, despite, at that time, West's shocking appearance in court wearing red shoes and a red dress. The latter concerned the self-defense claim of a prominent African American doctor whose newly bought home in a predominantly white neighborhood drew an unruly mob. Clarence Darrow defended Sweet, and Judge Frank Murphy instructed the jury that "a man's house is his castle," and, regardless of race, he has the right to defend it and those inside it if he has good reason. Sweet was acquitted.

Court is no longer held in the Old Wayne County Building. It was restored in 1987 and is currently owned and

managed by a private entity that rented the building to the county. The county executive, commissioners, and other offices occupied the bulk of the space. Recently the county did not renew the lease, opting to relocate to its newly purchased and nearby art deco Guardian Building. The fate of the 1897 building is uncertain.

Two buildings house the Wayne Circuit Court, which in 1997 was consolidated by legislative act with the Detroit Recorder's Court. The civil division is at the Coleman A. Young Municipal Center whereas the criminal division is at the Frank Murphy Hall of Justice.

The Coleman Center was completed in 1955 for $26 million pursuant to a joint city-county building authority established in 1948. Bryant & Detwiler Co. built it according to the design of architects and engineers Harley, Ellington & Day, Inc. Its 737,000 square feet is divided between the thirteen-story tower for city departments and the nineteen-story Courts Tower. There is no basement between the two buildings because a decades-old eighteen-foot-diameter sewer line is located below the ground-level link.

The complex stands at the corner of Jefferson and Woodward, overlooking two symbols of Detroit: The *Spirit of Detroit* sculpture by Marshall M. Fredericks and the *Joe Louis Fist* sculpture by Robert Graham. In a typical day, about 2,500 employees work in the complex and 8,000 members of the public visit. The twenty-four elevators make about a million stops every twenty-four days. Korean War steel shortages forced the authority to abandon building the easterly portion of the complex. But caissons were placed in anticipation of 208,000 square feet of potential expansion.

Several blocks away near Greektown stands the Frank Murphy Hall of Justice. Only four floors were occupied when it was dedicated on December 19, 1969, in the wake of a snowstorm, which lowered public turnout. Many of Murphy's associates and former employees were in attendance. A secretary from his mayoral days recalled how at City Hall he sincerely treated everyone like family and had them stay late every Christmas Eve to gather around a tree and open gifts.

The twelve-story building cost about $14.5 million. Eberle M. Smith Associates Inc. conceived of the modern design, and Darin & Armstrong Inc. constructed it. The hum and rattle of escalators reverberates as passengers are whisked to the busy courtrooms on floors two and three. The lobby features a portrait of Murphy and a plaque commemorating the Sweet trial as a Michigan legal milestone.

A statue outside the building pays further tribute to Murphy. Labor union funds paid for the artwork, which on its stone pedestal describes Murphy as a "humanitarian-statesman" and "advocate of justice." Sculptor Carl Mills fashioned *Hand of God*—a disembodied hand supporting a sure-footed nude figure looking skyward.

The allegory of the sculptor applies equally to the history of Wayne County. In it there is an unseen hand, cradling Michigan's civilization as it ascends, firmly looking beyond itself.

One of the many courtrooms inside of the Coleman A. Young Municipal Center

WEXFORD COUNTY

CADILLAC—The Battle of Sherman had little to do with the Civil War or the general by that name, though the town was named for him. The battle instead had everything to do with where Wexford County would have its county seat and build its courthouse. The political maneuvering and eventual physical confrontation gave rise to a local mythology that is part and parcel of the story of its courthouse.

The county was first platted in 1840 and named Kantawaubet. In 1843 it was renamed for land in the southeastern portion of Ireland. It was relatively unsettled until the Legislature organized it on May 30, 1869, attaching neighboring Missaukee County to it. Sherman, a town on the western edge of the county, was named the county seat.

County offices first were located in the respective homes of the officers. Circuit court was first held at the log hotel of Sylvester Clark. In January 1870 the board of supervisors approved a $5,000 budget for county buildings. They hired architect William Holdsworth Sr. of Traverse City and builder J. H. Wheeler. The Grand Rapids & Indiana Railroad donated land for the project.

That summer, the frame of the building was erected. It was completed in 1872 along with a jail. The court was a two-story frame wood building with a pitched roof and a small tower. The same year, Clam Lake first tried to get the county seat but the supervisors voted it down. Clam Lake would grow into the city of Cadillac, which is named for Detroit's founder, Antoine de la Mothe, Sieur de Cadillac. Clam Lake faced a greater margin of defeat in 1873 because the Sherman faction swelled its number of votes by per-

suading the Legislature to add Cleon Township of neighboring Manistee County to Wexford.

Wexford reportedly traded drinks in saloons for signatures on local petitions that the Legislature required before it would reassign Cleon. Fictitious names supposedly made their way onto the list of signatories too. Sherman did have the argument that Cleon was a mere six to eight miles from Fremont, whereas the county seat in Manistee was twenty-five miles away through a difficult swamp. Cleon remained part of Wexford until 1881. Clam Lake learned a valuable lesson about manipulating townships and the Legislature to gain board of supervisor votes.

Manton, which was named for an early settler, joined the fray and began agitating for a move along with Clam Lake. Both towns quickly outstripped the population of Sherman. When Clam Lake was poised to become the city of Cadillac, it stood ready to gain three votes on the board of supervisors.

To counteract that change, Sherman moved to admit new townships sympathetic to its cause. A gag rule limiting debate at a contentious meeting was employed. Soon the three-way contest between Sherman, Manton, and Cadillac led to divide-and-conquer strategies and uneasy alliances and suspicions.

Manton won the requisite two-thirds majority of supervisor votes to move the county seat, but the popular vote in April 1879 rejected the proposal 971 to 290. But soon there was yet another vote. Cadillac was ready to support the vote, figuring that wrestling the seat away from Sherman would mean eventual victory for Cadillac. Sherman supported the proposal too, figuring that Manton might lose the popular vote again and, even if the vote prevailed, preferring a move to Manton over Cadillac. The public spoke in 1881 and resoundingly approved the move to Manton 1,109 to 146.

Now Cadillac moved to send the seat down the final leg of its march from Sherman. Cadillac pressed for new townships to swell its votes on the board. Its representative persuaded the Legislature to assign Cleon back to Manistee and thus reduced Sherman's votes on the board.

The board met on Valentine's Day 1882, and anything but love and romance was in the air. The new township representatives were seated, and questions about their membership were referred to a committee. The nineteenth resolution in Wexford's history to move the county seat passed 12 to 6, just barely meeting the two-thirds requirement. In April the popular vote endorsed the removal 1,363 to 636.

Manton had not even finished erecting county buildings. The courthouse was a shell of a building measuring twenty-two by forty feet and hastily put together. It was roughly partitioned for county offices, but there was no courtroom just yet. For a time, records were kept in various locations around Manton, including once in a barn where a wagon was used as a desk.

Not wanting to defend against injunction proceedings, Cadillac sent a train the very next morning after the election to claim the county property in Manton. The unusual train consisted of a locomotive, caboose, boxcar, and flatcar. It pulled within one hundred feet of the courthouse, and the sheriff and about twenty men loaded up most of the records within half an hour.

When they attempted to remove the safes, they met opposition from some folk in Manton. Here the details are

difficult, if not impossible, to know. Whatever the nature of the meeting in Manton, the Cadillac delegation returned with everything but the safes to a festive atmosphere.

Some empty flatcars were added to the train, and "First Volunteer Regiment, Cadillac Militia," as one account described them, made its way to Manton. They were armed with rifles, clubs, poles, crowbars, and even a broom. For entertainment they had one barrel of whiskey, an untold number of bottles, and the Mark Comedy Company Band. There again was a confrontation of unknown nature and severity, and the safes were brought to Cadillac.

Local lore speaks of a casualty buried with an axe, the instrument of death, lodged in the corpse. There is also talk of Manton women spreading lard and butter on the rails to try to foil the men of Cadillac. It seems that rifles were only fired in celebration.

In the aftermath, Wexford went for many years without a permanent court facility. For a few days county business was transacted from the train that brought the records. Then the county occupied the second floor of the Holbrook & May's Building. In 1884 it signed a five-year lease for the second floor of the Cornwall & La Bar Building. After this lease, the county used the brick building on Mason Street that a lumber company built. In 1890 the county moved its offices and court to the second floor of the Masonic building, where it remained until the 1913 court was completed.

Cadillac donated land for the courthouse on a hill overlooking Clam Lake. There was a $25,000 building fund plus a $50,000 bond, which carried with an eight-hundred-vote majority, that paid for most of the construction. A jail was built at the same time, and it was used until 1960, after which time its successor on Carmel Street took over in 1963.

The courthouse was dedicated on October 17, 1913, and Governor Ferris was present to speak. The court looks much like that of Montcalm County, with the notable exception of the red Spanish tile dome atop Wexford's. Edwyn A. Bowd of Lansing was the architect, and T. F. Banhagel of the same city was the general contractor.

The court's best face is its front facade, which features four imposing columns below a large portico. One must stand back many paces to see the dome. The exterior is mainly brick, with significant areas of stone trimming the top of the building and making up the foundational walls near the ground.

The interior boasts an attractive lobby with intricate tile floors. The courtroom on the second floor was reduced in size, with a shorter paneled ceiling installed. The court-

house underwent some extensive renovations in the early 1990s. On July 17, 2002, Wexford broke ground on a $4.4 million addition to the courthouse. Its exterior is mainly matching brick and modern in design with a flat roof. It connects to just one side of the historic courthouse, leaving the rest in about its original state.

It stands on its hill, a prize for some and a bitter reminder for others. Visitors unaware of the Battle of Sherman would find no clue of it by the mere appearance of the building. But for those with special knowledge, it is a symbol full of deep and perhaps contradictory meaning.

THE MICHIGAN SUPREME COURT

LANSING—It is altogether fitting and proper that the journey should end at the Michigan Hall of Justice, where Michigan's court of last resort is anchored. The Michigan Supreme Court is the lodestar in the firmament containing the other courts described herein. It binds all these courts together jurisprudentially as it guides them with its final, binding pronouncements interpreting Michigan law.

The Hall of Justice traces its lineage back to the private home of James May, a prominent resident of Detroit. The Territorial Court, as it was then known, came into being on July 24, 1805. Lacking official chambers, the court met at various houses—first May's—and taverns, in exchange for a fee. One source claims that the court met "sometimes on a woodpile." The court's hours were irregular, and its often late-night sessions could be jovial, with free-flowing alcohol and supper service competing with the flowery oratory of lawyers for the attention of the judicial panel. Some cases were decided without the presence of clients or counsel.

Beginning in 1828, more formality was introduced, and the court began meeting in proper locations such as the newly built Capitol and the Council House in Detroit. The court, however, grew nomadic with the implementation of the 1835 Constitution, which required circuit riding. Different locations were required in different years, though Detroit and Lansing were invariably on the list, with more sporadic appearances of Ann Arbor, Kalamazoo, Pontiac, and Adrian. Apart from the various locales, sites within each city varied, with no fewer than five locations in Detroit alone.

Finally, the Legislature decided in 1873 to locate all sessions of the court in Lansing, the new capital that was constructed between 1872 and 1878. Beginning in January 1879, the court met on the third floor of the Capitol, an elegant edifice made primarily of Amherst sandstone, limestone, and about nineteen million bricks. The Old Supreme Court Chambers, as it is now known, is a room measuring thirty by fifty-four square feet, with a twenty-foot ceiling and elaborate finish, including Michigan pine and walnut. Until January 1970, it was the permanent site of the court. In its ninety years there, sixty different justices decided about 38,000 cases and heard almost 10,000 oral arguments. The court still uses the Chambers every October to hear the first cases of its new term. Otherwise, the room now houses

The Old Supreme Court Chambers in the Capitol still welcomes the court every October to hear the first cases of the new term.

the Senate Appropriations Committee. Upon leaving the Capitol, Chief Justice Thomas Brennan distinguished the chambers of the court from the court itself: "This courtroom is old at 90 years; the Supreme Court is young at 133." He arrived at the latter figure by counting the years from Michigan's statehood.

For thirty-two years, the itinerant court found itself in "temporary" quarters on the second floor of the G. Mennen Williams Law Building, where it shared space with the attorney general, the current exclusive tenant of the Williams Building. The modest maple-paneled courtroom featured a green marble facade behind where the justices sat. About eighty spectators could fit in the room, where twenty-six different justices sat, considered 63,000 matters that were filed, and issued eighty-three volumes of the court's written opinions. After the court's final public business in the Williams Building, the justices' exit was symbolic. Rather than leaving through a separate side door, they departed through the main public doorway, and the courtroom at that moment was retired.

On October 12, 1999, a groundbreaking ceremony for the Hall of Justice finally happened on the west end of the mall, which is anchored in the middle by the Capitol and

on the east by legislative offices. The judicial branch would occupy space on a field that was once a residential neighborhood. Because Michigan was among the last states in the Union to construct a separate building for its judicial branch, it had the time and opportunity to build a facility that made the wait worthwhile.

Albert Kahn Associates designed the horseshoe-shaped monolith, and Christman Company built it with 2,930 tons of steel, 16,000 cubic yards of concrete, and 14,000 pieces of limestone. It cost about $88 million. The six-story building, which is 280,000 square feet, has ten elevators, 1,200 interior doors, 224 windows, and a sixteen-foot skylight dome above the courtroom of the Supreme Court on the top floor. It is said that the angle of the sunlight through the windows beneath the dome is particularly unforgiving to lawyers at the podium in April. The furnishings, mahogany bench, and other interior designs are contemporary interpretations of the Old Supreme Court Chambers. Some small touches connect the two courtrooms. Most notably, the wooden board listing cases on call from the Chambers was moved to the new courtroom. The building's horseshoe design has the advantage of natural points for additional wings, should the need for expansion arise. About 300 people work in the building.

The Hall of Justice also has space and a courtroom for the Michigan Court of Appeals, Michigan's intermediate appellate court since 1964. Its judges, who are elected in four separate districts, hear cases throughout the state in randomly assigned three-judge panels. In addition to Lansing, the Michigan Court of Appeals maintains courtrooms in a state building in downtown Grand Rapids and in the New Center of Detroit at Cadillac Place, the former world headquarters of General Motors. For northern case calls, this court arranges for space at various county courthouses,

often in Petoskey, Marquette, and Escanaba. Similarly, while each justice of the Supreme Court has offices in the Hall of Justice, several maintain separate chambers in Detroit or Traverse City.

On the ground level, the innovative Learning Center welcomes visitors to its 3,800-square-foot exhibit space. It was conceived as a resource for schoolchildren and adults to learn about Michigan's legal system, from its history to its continued impact on people and society. Its doors opened to the public on November 1, 2002.

The Hall of Justice was dedicated on October 8, 2002. Chief Justice Maura Corrigan lauded former Chief Justice Dorothy Comstock Riley for the building's curved appearance, as if to embrace the other branches of government: "It stands independently, yet in relation to the Capitol. To me it seems to be arms outstretched, both shielding and embracing. This building is a bulwark, protecting, through faithful adherence to our constitution and laws, the democratic process that goes on across the way at our Legislature." Rather than cut a ribbon, the many judges present all ceremoniously and simultaneously dropped their gavels.

A rotunda inside the building quotes the Michigan Constitution. "All political power is inherent in the people. Government is instituted for their equal benefit, security and protection." Outside, the inscriptions do not quote. Rather, they declare without elaboration four powerful ideals: Freedom, Equality, Truth, and Justice.

Explicitly etched on the exterior or not, every hall of justice in Michigan was built to stand for these ideals. One hopes that, on account of the good people behind each of Michigan's courthouses, these ideals prevail in every instance and not just at the stage of last resort.

SELECTED BIBLIOGRAPHY

This selected bibliography lists the primary historical references that underlie the author's account. He also relied upon a multitude of periodical clippings, county directories, building dedication pamphlets, and other various documents, many of which are housed at the various courthouses, libraries, and historical societies he visited and many of which bore no date or name of author or publication. Certain copies are on file with the author. Where appropriate, the author's text recorded oral history and his own observations. The general references are listed first, followed by material grouped alphabetically by county.

GENERAL

Barfknecht, Gary W. *Murder, Michigan.* Davison, MI: Friede Publications, 1983.

Cole, Maurice F. *Michigan Courthouses Old and New.* Royal Oak, MI, 1974.

Eckert, Kathryn Bishop. *Buildings of Michigan.* New York: Oxford University Press, 1993.

Harmon, Charles E. *A Matter of Right: A History of the Michigan Court of Appeals.* Lansing, MI: Michigan History Magazine and Michigan Court of Appeals, 2002.

Historical Michigan Courthouses. Historical Activities Committee of the National Society of Colonial Dames of America in the State of Michigan, 1966.

History of the Lake Huron Shore. Chicago: H. R. Page & Co., 1883.

History of the Upper Peninsula of Michigan. Chicago: Western Historical Company, 1883.

King, Jonathan, Ernest O. Moore, and Robert E. Johnson. *The Michigan Courthouse Study.* Edited by Sally A. Guregian. Ann Arbor: Architectural Research Laboratory, University of Michigan, 1981.

Michigan County Histories: A Bibliography. Lansing, MI: Michigan Department of Education, States Library Services, 1978.

One Court of Justice. Michigan Supreme Court Administrator.

Powers, Perry F. *A History of Northern Michigan and Its People.* Chicago: Lewis Pub. Co., 1912.

Quaife, Milo M. *Condensed Historical Sketches for Each of Michigan's Counties.* Detroit: J. L. Hudson Co., 1940.

Romig, Walter. *Michigan Place Names.* Detroit: Wayne State University Press, 1986.

The Traverse Region. Chicago: H. R. Page & Co., 1884.

ALCONA

Gauthier, Doris A. *Harrisville—The Formative Years, 1853 to 1920.* 1999.

Glimpses of Huron Shore in Early Days and the Story of Harrisville. Compiled by Mae E. Stannard and Beatrice Plumb Hunzicher. Harrisville, MI: Alcona Historical Society, 1997.

ALGER

Alger County: A Centennial History, 1885–1985. Edited by Charles A. Symon. Munising, MI: Alger County Historical Society, 1986.

ALLEGAN

Thomas, Henry F. *A Twentieth Century History of Allegan County, Michigan.* Chicago: Lewis Pub. Co., 1907.

ALPENA

Boulton, William. *Complete History of Alpena County, Michigan.* Mt. Pleasant, MI: Central Michigan University Press, 1964.

Haltiner, Robert E., and Ana Teber. *The Town That Wouldn't Die.* Traverse City, MI: Village Press, 1986.

Knowing the Thunder Bay Region. Compiled by Writers' Program of the Work Projects Administration in the State of Michigan, 1941.

Law, John Wesley, and Delores Law. *Home Was Alpena.* Alpena, MI: Village Press, 1975.

Oliver, David D. *Centennial History of Alpena County, Michigan.* Alpena, MI: Argus Print House, 1903.

ANTRIM

McDuffie, Mary Kay. The Court House. Bellaire, MI: Bellaire Area Historical Society, 1974.

ARENAC

Chamberlain, H. A. *History of Arenac County.* 1912.

BARAGA

Lambert, Bernard J., ed. *Baraga County Historical Book.* Baraga County, MI: Baraga County Historical Society, 1973.

Through the Years: Houghton, Keweenaw, Baraga and Ontonagon Counties. Marceline, MO: Heritage House, 1999.

BARRY

Barry County, Michigan History. Hastings, MI: Selections from the Hastings Banner, 1985.

Burpee, Harold D. *Fresh Out of the Attic—Tid-Bits of Barry County History.* Hastings, MI, 1964.

BAY

Gansser, Augustus H. *History of Bay County.* Chicago: Richmond & Arnold, 1905.

History of Tuscola and Bay Counties. Chicago: H. R. Page & Co., 1883.

BENZIE

Case, Leonard. *Benzie County, A Bicentennial Reader,* 1976.

Historic Structures in the Benzonia-Beulah Area. Beulah, MI: Bicentennial Committee of the Libraries of Benzonia and Beulah, Michigan, 1976.

BERRIEN

Carney, James T., ed. *Berrien Bicentennial.* Berrien County Bicentennial Commission, 1976.

Coolidge, Orville W. *A Twentieth Century History of Berrien County, Michigan.* Chicago: Lewis Pub. Co., 1906.

History of Berrien and Van Buren Counties. Philadelphia: D. W. Ensign Co., 1880.

BRANCH

Collin, Henry P. *A Twentieth Century History and Biographical Record of Branch County.* New York: Lewis Pub. Co., 1906.

History of Branch County. Coldwater, MI: Branch County Historical Society, 1979.

History of Branch County. Philadelphia: Everts & Abbot, 1879.

CALHOUN

Carver, Richard. *A History of Marshall.* Virginia Beach, VA: Donning Co. Publishers, 1993.

Gardner, Washington. *History of Calhoun County.* Chicago: Lewis Pub. Co., 1913.

CASS

Glover, L. H. *A Twentieth Century History of Cass County, Michigan.* New York: Lewis Pub. Co., 1906.

Historical Reflections of Cass County. Cass County Historical Commission, 1981 (Stanley R. Hamper, consultant).

Mathews, Alfred. *History of Cass County.* Chicago: Waterman, Watkins & Co., 1882.

CHARLEVOIX

Byron, M. Christine, and Thomas R. Wilson. *Vintage Views of the Charlevoix-Petoskey Region.* Ann Arbor: University of Michigan Press, 2005.

CHEBOYGAN

Robinson, George. *History of Cheboygan and Mackinac Counties.* Detroit: Union Job Print Co., 1873.

Ware, W. H. *Centennial History of Cheboygan County and Village.* Cheboygan, MI: Northern Tribune Print., 1876.

CHIPPEWA

Color the History of the Sault. Sault Ste. Marie, MI: Chippewa County Historical Society, 2004.

Newton, Stanley. *The Story of Sault Ste. Marie and Chippewa County.* Sault Ste. Marie, MI: Sault News Print Co., 1923.

CLARE

Meek, Forrest B. *Michigan's Timber Battleground—A History of Clare County: 1674–1900.* Harrison, MI: Meek, Clare County Bicentennial Historical Committee, 1976.

Sellers, T. M. *Spikehorn: The Life Story of John E. Meyer.* Harrison, MI: Spikehorn Creek Camp, 1994.

CLINTON

The History of Clinton County, Michigan. St. Johns, MI: Clinton County Historical Society, 1980.

History of Shiawassee and Clinton Counties, Michigan. Philadelphia: D. W. Ensign & Co., 1880.

CRAWFORD

The First Hundred Years: An Introduction to the History of the Grayling Area. Mt. Pleasant, MI: Enterprise Printers, 1972.

Grayling and Crawford County History and Miscellanea. Collected and compiled by Mrs. Harry Sanders and Mrs. Roy Wedge, 1970.

DELTA

Jacques, Thomas Edward. *A History of the Garden Peninsula.* Iron Mountain, MI: Mid-Peninsula Library Cooperative, 1979.

Our Heritage: Garden Peninsula, Delta County, Michigan, 1840–1980. Garden Peninsula Historical Society, 1982.

DICKINSON

The Dickinson County Courthouse and Jail. Compiled by William J. Cummings, 1988.

Dickinson County, Michigan: From Earliest Times through the Twenties. Compiled by William J. Cummings. Iron Mountain, MI: Dickinson County Board of Commissioners, 1991.

EATON

The Courthouses of Eaton. Charlotte, MI: Eaton County Historical Commission, 1978.

Durant, Samuel W. *History of Ingham and Eaton Counties.* Philadelphia: D. W. Ensign, 1880.

SELECTED BIBLIOGRAPHY

EMMET

Byron, M. Christine, and Thomas R. Wilson. *Vintage Views of the Charlevoix-Petoskey Region.* Ann Arbor: University of Michigan Press, 2005.

GENESEE

Ellis, Franklin. *History of Genesee County.* Philadelphia: Everts & Abbot, 1879.

Portrait and Biographical Record of Genesee, Lapeer, and Tuscola Counties, Michigan. Chicago: Chapman Bros., 1892.

Smith, William V., ed. *An Account of Flint and Genesee County from Their Organization.* Dayton, OH: National Historical Association, 1924.

Wood, Edwin Orin. *History of Genesee County, Michigan.* Indianapolis: Federal Pub. Co., 1916.

GLADWIN

Gladwin County First Settler Centennial 1861–1961. Compiled by Bernice Walker Ritchie. Gladwin County Centennial Committee, 1961.

Gladwin History Then & Now. Compiled by Bernie Walker Ritchie Fries. Gladwin, MI: Gladwin County Record, 1990.

GOGEBIC

Cox, Bruce K. *Gogebic County Homicides, 1885–1920.* Wakefield, MI: B. K. Cox, 1993.

History of Gogebic County. Compiled by Victor Lemmer. Ironwood, MI: Victor F. Lemmer, 1956.

GRAND TRAVERSE

Grand Traverse and Leelanau Counties. Edited and compiled by Elvin L. Sprague and Mrs. George N. Smith. Indianapolis: B. F. Bowen, 1903.

Wakefield, Lawrence. *All Our Yesterdays: A Narrative History of Traverse City and the Region.* Traverse City, MI: Village Press, 1977.

GRATIOT

Portrait and Biographical Album of Gratiot County. Chicago: Chapman Bros., 1884.

Tucker, Willard D. *Gratiot County, Michigan.* Saginaw, MI: Press of Seemann & Peters, 1913.

HILLSDALE

Hillsdale Area Centennial. Hillsdale, MI: Centennial Book Committee, 1969.

150 Years in the Hills and Dales. Harold Cater and Kathleen Dawley, eds. Hillsdale County Historical Society and Bicentennial Commission, 1976.

HOUGHTON

Robinson, Orrin W. *Early Days of the Lake Superior Copper Country.* Houghton, MI: D. L. Robinson, 1938.

Taylor, Richard E. *Houghton County: 1870–1920.* Charleston, SC: Arcadia Pub., 2006.

Through the Years: Houghton, Keweenaw, Baraga, and Ontonagon Counties. Marceline, MO: Heritage House, 1999.

HURON

Huron County, Michigan. Huron County Historical Society. Charleston, SC: Arcadia Pub., 2001.

Portrait and Biographical Album of Huron County. Chicago: Chapman Bros., 1884.

Taylor Scott, James. *The Settlement of Huron County.* Toronto: Ryerson Press, 1966.

INGHAM

Caesar, Ford Stevens. *Bicentennial History of Ingham County, Michigan.* 1976.

Cowles, Albert E. *Past and Present of the City of Lansing and Ingham County, Michigan.* Lansing, MI: Michigan Historical Publishing Association, 1905.

Durant, Samuel W. *History of Ingham and Eaton Counties.* Philadelphia: D. W. Ensign, 1880.

IONIA

Branch, Elam E. *History of Ionia County.* Indianapolis: B. F. Bowen & Co., 1916.

Dillenback, Jackson D. *History and Directory of Ionia County, Michigan.* Grand Rapids, MI: J. D. Dillenback, 1872.

Portrait and Biographical Album of Ionia and Montcalm Counties. Chicago: Chapman Bros., 1891.

Schenck, John S. *History of Ionia and Montcalm Counties.* 1881.

Smith, Yvonne P., ed. *Ionia, Michigan Centennial: 1873–1973.*

IOSCO

History of Iosco County, Michigan. East Tawas, MI: Ionia County Historical Society, 1981.

Thornton, Neil. *Law and Order North of Saginaw Bay.* Tawas City, MI: Printer's Devil Press, 1988.

IRON

Bernhardt, Marcia A. *The Jewel of Iron County.* Caspian, MI: Education Committee, Iron County Museum, 1976.

Hill, Jack. *A History of Iron County, Michigan.* Iron Mountain, MI: Reporter Publishing Co. 1955.

ISABELLA

Fancher, Isaac A. *Past and Present of Isabella County, Michigan.* Indianapolis: B. F. Bowen & Co., 1911.

Portrait and Biographical Album of Isabella County, Michigan. Chicago: Chapman Bros., 1884.

JACKSON

DeLand, Charles V. *History of Jackson County, Michigan.* Logansport, IN: B. F. Bowen, 1903.

Deming, Brian. *Jackson: An Illustrated History.* Woodland Hills, CA: Windsor Publications, 1984.

History of Jackson County, Michigan. Chicago: Inter-State Publishing Co., 1881.

KALAMAZOO

Dunbar, Willis F. *Kalamazoo and How It Grew.* Kalamazoo: Western Michigan University, 1959.

Fisher, David, and Frank Little, eds. *Compendium History and Biography of Kalamazoo County.* Chicago: A. W. Bowen & Co., 1906.

History of Kalamazoo County. Philadelphia: Everts & Abbott, 1880.

Houghton, Lynn Smith, and Paula Hall O'Connor. *Kalamazoo Lost & Found.* Kalamazoo: Kalamazoo Historic Preservation Committee, 2001.

KALKASKA

Kalkaska County, 1871–1971. Kalkaska, MI: Centennial Book Committee, 1971.

McCann, Lyle. *Early Days and Early Ways.* 1972.

Trippleton, Dawn, ed. *Big Trout Black Gold, The History of Kalkaska County.* Kalkaska, MI: Kalkaska Genealogical Society, 2002.

KENT

Fisher, Ernest B., ed. *Grand Rapids and Kent County, Michigan.* Chicago: Robert O. Law Co., 1918.

History of Kent County, Michigan. Chicago: C. C. Chapman & Co., 1881.

Lydens, Z. Z., ed. *The Story of Grand Rapids.* Grand Rapids: Kregel Publications, 1966.

KEWEENAW

Frimodig, David M. *Keweenaw Character: The Foundation of Michigan's Copper Country.* Lake Linden, MI: John H. Foster Press, 1990.

Monette, Clarence J. *The History of Eagle River, Michigan.* Lake Linden, MI: W. H. Curtin, 1978.

Through the Years: Houghton, Keweenaw, Baraga, and Ontonagon Counties. Marceline, MO: Heritage House, 1999.

LAKE

Carper, Kathy, ed. *Pictorial History of Lake County, Michigan.* 1998.

Lake County: A Collection of Historical Writings. Lake County Historical Society, 1994.

LAPEER

History of Lapeer County, Michigan. Chicago: H. R. Page & Co., 1884.

Portrait and Biographical Record of Genesee, Lapeer, and Tuscola Counties, Michigan. Chicago: Chapman Bros., 1892.

LEELANAU

Grand Traverse and Leelanau Counties. Edited and compiled by Elvin L. Sprague and Mrs. George N. Smith. Indianapolis: B. F. Bowen, 1903.

Littell, Edmund M. *100 Years in Leelanau.* Leland, MI: The Print Shop, 1965.

LENAWEE

Knapp, John I., and R. I. Bonner. *Illustrated History and Biographical Record of Lenawee County.* Adrian, MI: Times Printing Co., 1903.

Lindquist, Charles N. *Lenawee County: A Harvest of Pride and Promise.* Chatsworth, CA: Windsor Publications, 1990.

Whitney, William A. *History and Biographical Record of Lenawee County.*

LIVINGSTON

Crittenden, A. Riley. *A History of the Township and Village of Howell.* Howell, MI: Livingston Tidings Print, 1911.

History of Livingston County. Philadelphia: Everts & Abbott, 1880.

LUCE

A Brief History of the Tahquamenon Valley. Newberry, MI: Luce County Historical Society, 1976.

The History of Luce County. Researched by Hilja Pekkarinen and compiled by Minnie Ida Mattson. Newberry, MI: Luce County Historical Society, 1981.

Luce County History. Luce County Historical Society 1985.

Taylor, Charles Sprague. *Tahquamenon Country: A Look at Its Past.* Ann Arbor, MI: Historical Society of Michigan, 1991.

MACKINAC

Michilimackinac. St. Ignace, MI: Michilimackinac Historical Society, 1958.

Robinson, George. *History of Cheboygan and Mackinac Counties.* Detroit: Union Job Print Co., 1873.

MACOMB

Eldredge, Robert F. *Past and Present of Macomb County.* Chicago: S. J. Clarke Pub. Co., 1905.

History of Macomb County, Michigan. Chicago: Leeson & Co., 1882.

MANISTEE

History of Manistee, Mason, and Oceana Counties, Michigan. Chicago: H. R. Page & Co., 1882.

McRae, Shannon. *Manistee County.* Charleston, SC: Arcadia Pub., 2006.

SELECTED BIBLIOGRAPHY

MARQUETTE

Beard's Directory and History of Marquette County. Detroit: Hadger & Bryce, Steam Book and Job Printers, 1873.

Biographical Record of Houghton, Baraga, and Marquette Counties, Michigan. Chicago: Biographical Pub. Co., 1903.

Marquette City and County Directory. Detroit: R. L. Polk & Co., 1899.

MASON

Historic Mason County. Ludington, MI: Mason County Historical Society, 1980.

History of Manistee, Mason, and Oceana Counties, Michigan. Chicago: H. R. Page & Co., 1882.

MECOSTA

Big Rapids, Michigan—The Water Power City. Big Rapids, MI: Seely & Lowrey, 1906.

Portrait and Biographical Album of Mecosta County, Michigan. Chicago: Chapman Bros., 1883.

MENOMINEE

Ingalls, E. S. *Centennial History of Menominee County.* Menominee, MI: Herald Power Presses, 1876.

MIDLAND

Portrait and Biographical History of Midland County. Chicago: Chapman Bros., 1884.

Yates, Dorothy Langdon. *Salt of the Earth: A History of Midland County, Michigan.* Midland, MI: Midland County Historical Society, 1987.

MISSAUKEE

Missaukee County Family Histories. Lake City, MI: Missaukee County Historical Society, 1983.

MONROE

Bulkley, John McClelland. *History of Monroe County.* Chicago: Lewis Pub. Co., 1913.

Wing, Talcott E., ed. *History of Monroe County.* New York: Munsell & Co., 1890.

MONTCALM

Dasef, John W. *History of Montcalm County.* Indianapolis: B. F. Bowen, 1916.

Portrait and Biographical Album of Ionia and Montcalm Counties. Chicago: Chapman Bros., 1891.

Schenck, John S. *History of Ionia and Montcalm Counties.* Philadelphia: D. W. Ensign & Co., 1881.

MONTMORENCY

Jacobson, Carol S. *Life in the Forest: The History of Montmorency County, Michigan.* Atlanta, MI: Montmorency County Historical Society, 1981.

Johnson, Charles F. *Montmorency County: Where the Old Settlements Were Located.* Grand Rapids, MI: C. F. Johnson, 1994.

MUSKEGON

Eyler, Jonathan. *Muskegon County: Harbor of Promise.* Northridge, CA: Windsor Publications, 1986.

History of Muskegon County, Michigan. Chicago: H. R. Page, 1882.

Portrait and Biographical Record of Muskegon and Ottawa Counties, Michigan. Chicago: Biographical Pub. Co., 1893.

NEWAYGO

First Hundred Years, 1973–1973—White Cloud Area. White Cloud, MI: White Cloud Area Centennial Historical Book Committee, 1973.

First Hundred Years—Newaygo, Michigan. Newaygo, MI: Newaygo Centennial Committee, 1953.

Portrait and Biographical Album of Newaygo County, Michigan. Chicago: Chapman Bros., 1884.

Thompson, Robert I. *Newaygo White Pine Heritage.* Newaygo, MI: Newaygo City Bicentennial Committee, 1976.

OAKLAND

Hayman, Arthur A., ed. *Oakland County Book of History.* 1970.

Seeley, Thaddeus D. *History of Oakland County.* Chicago: Lewis Pub. Co., 1912.

OCEANA

History of Manistee, Mason, and Oceana Counties, Michigan. Chicago: H. R. Page & Co., 1882.

Oceana County History. Hart, MI: Oceana County Historical Society, 1992.

OGEMAW

West Branch Area: First One Hundred Years. West Branch, MI: West Branch Area Centennial Committee, 1975.

ONTONAGON

Jamison, James K. *This Ontonagon Country: The Story of an American Frontier.* Ontonagon, MI: Ontonagon Herald Co., 1948.

Johanson, B. H. *This Land, the Ontonagon.* Iron Mountain, MI: Ralph W. Secord Press of the Mid-Peninsula Library Cooperative, 1984.

Through the Years: Houghton, Keweenaw, Baraga, and Ontonagon Counties. Marceline, MO: Heritage House, 1999.

OSCEOLA

Pictorial History of Osceola County. James Crees, ed. 1998.
White, Marjorie Brown. *Reed City Centennial: One Hundred Going on Two Hundred.* Reed City, MI: Chamber of Commerce, 1975.

OSCODA

Oscoda County, 1881. Mio, MI: Au Sable River Valley Historical Society, 1979.
Times to Remember: Memories and Stories of Early Au Sable and Oscoda. Mio, MI: Au Sable River Valley Historical Society, 1974.

OTSEGO

History of Otsego. Compiled by Dorothy Dalrymple. 1975.
Otsego County, Michigan. Paducah, KY: Turner Pub. Co., 2002.
A Step Back in Time. Vols. I–III. Gaylord, MI: Otsego County Historical Society, 1999, 2001, 2004.

OTTAWA

Boeskool, Jack, ed. *Reflections of Ottawa County, 1837–1987.* Grand Haven, MI: Ottawa County Sesquicentennial Committee, 1987.
Grysen, Angelina. *The Sheriff: Ottawa County Law and Order.* Lansing, MI: W. Curtis Co., 1999.
Historical and Business Compendium of Ottawa County, Michigan. Grand Haven, MI: Potts & Conger, 1892.
Lillie, Leo C. *Historic Grand Haven and Ottawa County.* Grand Haven, MI, 1931.
Portrait and Biographical Record of Muskegon and Ottawa Counties, Michigan. Chicago: Biographical Pub. Co., 1893.
Rasmussen, Diane, and Mary Ann Willoughby. *Bicentennial Heritage Book.* Grand Haven, MI: Ottawa County Bicentennial Committee, 1976.

PRESQUE ISLE

Rogers City: Its First Hundred Years. Rogers City, MI: Rogers City Centennial Committee, 1971.

ROSCOMMON

Carman, Beulah. *Capsules of Time—A Saga of Houghton Lake.* Houghton Lake, MI: Bankov Printing, 1987.
Carman, Beulah. *Looking Back.* Houghton Lake, MI, 1979.

SAGINAW

Ederer, Roselynn. *Forever Young at Heart.* Saginaw, MI: Thomastown Pub. Co., 2003.
Gross, Stuart D. *May It Please the Court: A History of the First 150 Years of the Law Profession in Saginaw County.* Saginaw, MI: Dornbos Press, 1987.

History of Saginaw County. Chicago: Chapman & Co., 1881.
Mills, James Cooke. *History of Saginaw County.* Saginaw, MI: Seeman & Peters, 1918.

SANILAC

DuMond, Neva. *Thumb Diggings.* Lexington, MI, 1962.
Portrait and Biographical Album of Sanilac County. Chicago: Chapman Bros., 1884.
Trumble, Hazel Arnold, ed. *Sanilac County History.* 1984.

SCHOOLCRAFT

Manistique Centennial Book. Manistique, MI: Manistique Centennial, Inc., 1960.

SHIAWASSEE

Cumming, John. *The Lynching at Corunna.* Mt. Pleasant, MI: Private Press of John Cumming, 1980.
Daboll, Sherman B. *Past and Present Shiawassee County.* Durand, MI: S. J. Clarke Pub. Co., 1906.
Echoes of Yesteryear. Corunna, MI: Shiawassee County Historical Society, 1996.
History of Shiawassee and Clinton Counties, Michigan. Philadelphia: D. W. Ensign & Co., 1880.

ST. CLAIR

Endlich, Helen. *A Story of Port Huron* (1981).
History of St. Clair. Chicago: A. T. Andreas & Co., 1883.
Jenks, William Lee. *St. Clair County, Michigan: Its History and Its People.* Chicago, Lewis Publishing Co., 1912.

ST. JOSEPH

Cutler, H. G., ed. *History of St. Joseph County.* Chicago: Lewis Pub. Co., 1911.
History of St. Joseph County. Philadelphia: L. H. Everts & Co., 1877.

TUSCOLA

History of Tuscola and Bay Counties. Chicago: H. R. Page & Co., 1883.
Portrait and Biographical Record of Genesee, Lapeer, and Tuscola Counties, Michigan. Chicago: Chapman Bros., 1892.

VAN BUREN

History of Berrien and Van Buren Counties. Philadelphia: D. W. Ensign Co., 1880.
Paw Paw Centennial, 1859–1959. Paw Paw, MI: Paw Paw Centennial Assoc. Inc., 1959.
Rowland, O. W. *A History of Van Buren County, Michigan.* Chicago: Lewis Pub. Co., 1912.

WASHTENAW

Art Work of Washtenaw County. Chicago: W. H. Parish Publishing Co., 1893.

Beakes, Samuel W. *Past and Present of Washtenaw County.* Chicago: S. J. Clarke Pub. Co., 1906.

Bordin, Ruth. *Washtenaw County, An Illustrated History.* Northridge, CA: Windsor Publications, 1988.

History of Washtenaw County. Chicago: Charles C. Chapman & Co., 1881.

Stephenson, O. W. *Ann Arbor: The First Hundred Years.* Ann Arbor, MI: Ann Arbor Chamber of Commerce, 1927.

WAYNE

Burton, Clarence M., and M. Agnes Burton, eds. *History of Wayne County.* Chicago: S. J. Clarke Pub. Co., 1930.

Farbman, Suzy, and James P. Gallagher. *The Renaissance of the Wayne County Building.* Detroit: Smith, Hinchman & Grylls Associates, 1989.

Mowitz, Robert J., and Deil S. Wright. *Profile of a Metropolis.* Detroit: Wayne State University Press, 1962.

WEXFORD

Wheeler, John H. *History of Wexford County, Michigan.* Logansport, IN: B. F. Bowen, 1903.

THE MICHIGAN SUPREME COURT

Noto, Scott A. *A Brief History of the Michigan Supreme Court.* Lansing, MI: Michigan Supreme Court Historical Society, 2001.

LIST OF COUNTY COURTHOUSES

Alcona County
106 Fifth Street
Harrisville, MI 48740-0308

Alger County
101 Court Street
Munising, MI 49862

Allegan County
113 Chestnut Street
Allegan, MI 49010

Alpena County
720 West Chisholm Street, Ste. No. 2
Alpena, MI 49707

Antrim County
203 E. Cayuga
Bellaire, MI 49615

Arenac County
120 North Grove Street
Standish, MI 48658

Baraga County
16 North Third Street
L'Anse, MI 49946

Barry County
220 West State Street
Hastings, MI 49058

Bay County
515 Center Avenue
Bay City, MI 48708

Benzie County
448 Court Place
Beulah, MI 49617

Berrien County
811 Port Street
St. Joseph, MI 49085

Branch County
31 Division Street
Coldwater, MI 49036

Calhoun County
315 West Green Street
Marshall, MI 49068

Cass County
120 North Broadway
Cassopolis, MI 49031-1398

Charlevoix County
203 Antrim Street
Charlevoix, MI 49720

Cheboygan County
870 South Main Street
Cheboygan, MI 49721

Chippewa County
319 Court Street
Sault Ste. Marie, MI 49783

Clare County
225 West Main Street
Harrison, MI 48625

Clinton County
100 East State Street, Suite 2600
St. Johns, MI 48879

Crawford County
200 West Michigan Avenue
Grayling, MI 49738

Delta County
310 Ludington Street
Escanaba, MI 49829

Dickinson County
705 South Stephenson Avenue
Iron Mountain, MI 49801

Eaton County
1045 Independence Boulevard
Charlotte, MI 48813

Emmet County
200 Division Street, Ste. 130
Petoskey, MI 49770

Genesee County
900 S. Saginaw Street
Flint, MI 48502

Gladwin County
401 West Cedar Avenue
Gladwin, MI 48624-2088

Gogebic County
200 North Moore Street
Bessemer, MI 49911

Grand Traverse County
400 Boardman Avenue
Traverse City, MI 49684

Gratiot County
214 East Center Street
Ithaca, MI 48847

Hillsdale County
29 North Howell Street
Hillsdale, MI 49242

Houghton County
401 E. Houghton Avenue
Houghton, MI 49931

Huron County
250 E. Huron Ave
Bad Axe, MI 48413

Ingham County
315 S. Jefferson
Mason, MI 48854

Ionia County
100 Main Street
Ionia, MI 48846

Iosco County
422 Lake Street
Tawas City, MI 48764

Iron County
2 South Sixth Street
Crystal Falls, MI 49920

Isabella County
200 North Main Street
Mt. Pleasant, MI 48858

Jackson County
312 S. Jackson Street
Jackson, MI 49201

Kalamazoo County
201 W. Kalamazoo Avenue
Kalamazoo, MI 49007

Kalkaska County
605 North Birch Street
Kalkaska, MI 49646

Kent County
300 Monroe N.W.
Grand Rapids, MI 49503

Keweenaw County
5095 4th Street
Eagle River, MI 49950

Lake County
800 Tenth Street
Baldwin, MI 49304

Lapeer County
255 Clay Street
Lapeer, MI 48446

Leelanau County
301 East Cedar Street
Leland, MI 49654

Lenawee County
425 North Main Street
Adrian, MI 49221

Livingston County
200 East Grand River
Howell, MI 48843

Luce County
407 W. Harrie St.
Newberry, MI 49868

Mackinac County
100 North Marley Street
St. Ignace, MI 49781

Macomb County
40 North Main Street
Mt. Clemens, MI 48043

Manistee County
415 Third Street (Government Center)
Manistee, MI 49660

Marquette County
Baraga Avenue
Marquette, MI 49855

Mason County
304 East Ludington Avenue
Ludington, MI 49431

Mecosta County
400 Elm Street
Big Rapids, MI 49307

Menominee County
839 Tenth Avenue
Menominee, MI 49858

Midland County
220 West Ellsworth Street
Midland, MI 48640

Missaukee County
111 S. Canal St.
Lake City, MI 49651

Monroe County
106 East First Street
Monroe, MI 48161

Montcalm County
211 W. Main Street
Stanton, MI 48888

Montmorency County
12265 M 32
Atlanta, MI 49709

Muskegon County
990 Terrace
Muskegon, MI 49442

Newaygo County
1087 Newell Street
White Cloud, MI 49349

Oakland County
1200 North Telegraph Road
Pontiac, MI 48341

Oceana County
100 State Street
Hart, MI 49420

Ogemaw County
806 West Houghton Avenue
West Branch, MI 48661

Ontonagon County
725 Greenland Road
Ontonagon, MI 49953

Osceola County
301 West Upton Ave.
Reed City, MI 49677

Oscoda County
311 Morenci
Mio, MI 48647

Otsego County
225 West Main Street
Gaylord, MI 49735

Ottawa County
414 Washington, Room 301
Grand Haven, MI 49417

Presque Isle County
151 East Huron Avenue
Rogers City, MI 49779

Roscommon County
500 Lake Street
Roscommon, MI 48653

Saginaw County
111 South Michigan Avenue
Saginaw, MI 48602

Sanilac County
60 West Sanilac Avenue, Room 203
Sandusky, MI 48471

Schoolcraft County
300 Walnut Street, Room 164
Manistique, MI 49854

Shiawassee County
208 N. Shiawassee Street
Corunna, MI 48817

St. Clair County
201 McMorran Boulevard, Room 1100
Port Huron, MI 48060

St. Joseph County
125 West Main Street
Centreville, MI 49032

Tuscola County
440 North State Street
Caro, MI 48723

Van Buren County
212 Paw Paw Street
Paw Paw, MI 49079

Washtenaw County
200 North Main Street, Suite 120
Ann Arbor, MI 48107

Wayne County
201 City-County Building
Detroit, MI 48226

Wexford County
437 East Division Street
Cadillac, MI 49601

LIST OF COUNTY
WEB SITES

Alcona: www.alconacountymi.com/
Alger: www.algercounty.com/
Allegan: www.allegancounty.org/
Alpena: www.alpenacounty.org/
Antrim: www.antrimcounty.org/
Arenac: www.arenaccountygov.com/
Baraga: www.baragacounty.org/
Barry: www.barrycounty.org/
Bay: www.baycounty-mi.gov/
Benzie: www.benzieco.net
Berrien: www.berriencounty.org/
Branch: www.co.branch.mi.us/
Calhoun: www.calhouncountymi.org/
Cass: www.casscountymi.org/
Charlevoix: www.charlevoixcounty.org/
Cheboygan: www.cheboygancounty.net/
Chippewa: www.chippewacounty.net
Clare: www.clareco.net/
Clinton: www.clinton-county.org/
Crawford: www.crawfordco.org/
Delta: www.deltacountymi.org/
Dickinson: www.dickinsoncountymi.gov/
Eaton: www.eatoncounty.org/
Emmet: www.emmetcounty.org/
Genesee: www.co.genesee.mi.us/
Gladwin: www.gladwinco.com
Gogebic: www.gocebic.org
Grand Traverse: www.grandtraverse.org/
Gratiot: www.co.gratiot.mi.us/
Hillsdale: www.co.hillsdale.mi.us/
Houghton: www.houghtoncounty.net
Huron: www.co.huron.mi.us/
Ingham: www.ingham.org/
Ionia: www.ioniacounty.org
Iosco: http://iosco.m33access.com/
Iron: www.iron.org/
Isabella: www.isabellacounty.org
Jackson: www.co.jackson.mi.us/
Kalamazoo: www.kalcounty.com
Kalkaska: www.kalkaskacounty.net
Kent: www.accesskent.com
Keweenaw: www.infomi.com/county/keweenaw/

Lake: www.lakecountymichigan.com
Lapeer: www.lapeercountyweb.org/
Leelanau: www.leelanaucounty.com/
Lenawee: www.lenawee.mi.us/
Livingston: www.co.livingston.mi.us/
Luce: www.informi.com/county/luce/
Mackinac: www.mackinaccounty.net
Macomb: www.macombcountymi.gov
Manistee: www.manisteecountymi.gov
Marquette: www.co.marquette.mi.us/
Mason: www.masoncounty.net
Mecosta: www.co.mecosta.mi.us/
Menominee: www.menomineecounty.com
Midland: www.co.midland.mi.us/
Missaukee: www.missaukee.org
Monroe: www.co.monroe.mi.us/
Montcalm: www.montcalm.org
Montmorency: www.infomi.com/county/montmorency/
Muskegon: http://co.muskegon.mi.us/
Newaygo: www.countyofnewaygo.com
Oakland: www.oakgov.com
Oceana: www.oceana.mi.us/
Ogemaw: www.ogemawcountymi.gov
Ontonagon: www.infomi.com/county/ontonagon/
Osceola: www.osceola-county.org
Oscoda: www.oscodacountymi.com
Otsego: www.otsegocountymi.gov/
Ottawa: www.co.ottawa.mi.us/
Presque Isle: www.presqueislecounty.org
Roscommon: www.roscommoncounty.net
Saginaw: www.saginawcounty.com
Sanilac: www.sanilaccounty.net
Schoolcraft: www.schoolcraftcounty.net
Shiawassee: www.shiawassee.net/home.html
St. Clair: www.stclaircounty.org
St. Joseph: www.stjosephcountymi.org
Tuscola: www.tuscolacounty.org
Van Buren: www.vbco.org/
Washtenaw: www.ewashtenaw.org
Wayne: www.waynecounty.com
Wexford: www.wexfordcounty.org

Design and composition by Mary H. Sexton

Text font, Minion, was designed for Adobe by Robert Slimbach. Based on classical old style types from the late Renaissance period, Minion was created with current technology in mind.
   —Courtesy Fonts.com